Organizational Culture and Performance

Organizational Culture and Performance

The Practice of Sustaining Higher Performance in Business Merger & Acquisition

Henrietta Mbamalu Okoro

HAMILTON BOOKS
AN IMPRINT OF
ROWMAN & LITTLEFIELD
Lanham • Boulder • New York • London

Published by Hamilton Books
An imprint of The Rowman & Littlefield Publishing Group, Inc.
4501 Forbes Boulevard, Suite 200, Lanham, Maryland 20706
www.rowman.com

86-90 Paul Street, London EC2A 4NE, United Kingdom

British Library Cataloguing in Publication Information Available

Library of Congress Cataloging-in-Publication Data

Names: Okoro, Henrietta, 1968– author.
Title: Organizational culture and performance : the practice of sustaining higher performance in business merger & acquisition / Henrietta Okoro.
Description: Lanham : Hamilton Books, [2023] | Includes bibliographical references and index. |
Summary: "The scope of the book is multi-disciplinary in business curricula and research discourse. It provides a valuable business curricula resource in courses such as organizational behavior, leadership decision-making, knowledge management, business information systems, business management, marketing, social sciences, and other business-related courses"—Provided by publisher.
Identifiers: LCCN 2022039729 (print) | LCCN 2022039730 (ebook) | ISBN 9780761873280 (paperback ; alk. paper) | ISBN 9780761873297 (epub)
Subjects: LCSH: Corporate culture. | Corporate reorganizations. | Organizational behavior. | Consolidation and merger of coporations.
Classification: LCC HD58.7 .O555 2022 (print) | LCC HD58.7 (ebook) | DDC 658–dc23/eng/20220825
LC record available at https://lccn.loc.gov/2022039729
LC ebook record available at https://lccn.loc.gov/2022039730

∞™ The paper used in this publication meets the minimum requirements of American National Standard for Information Sciences—Permanence of Paper for Printed Library Materials, ANSI/NISO Z39.48-1992.

To our Almighty God
To my late parents,
Chief Sylvester Igwe Mbamalu and Lolo Matilda Nnuezue Mbamalu

and

To my husband and four children
Sir Cyriacus Okoro
Sylvester, Michael, Stacy, and Mayme

"I think as a company, if you can get those two things right—having a clear direction on what you are trying to do and bringing in great people who can execute on the stuff—then you can do pretty well."

– Mark Zuckerberg, CEO, Facebook

"Determine what behaviors and beliefs you value as a company and have everyone live true to them. These behaviors and beliefs should be essential to your core that you don't even think of it as culture."

– Brittany Forsyth, VP of Human Relations, Shopify

"Corporate culture is the only sustainable competitive advantage completely within the entrepreneur's control."

– David Cummings, Co-Founder, Pardot

"Everyone on the team plays an equal role. My role is to create the wave, and everyone on our team keeps the wave going."

– William Wang, Founder, Vizio

"Performance more often comes down to a cultural challenge, rather than simply a technical one."

– Lara Hogan, Senior Engineering Manager of Performance, Etsy

"It's important for us to create a culture of innovation that values and rewards risk."

– Barbara Landes, CFO, PBS

"Our secret weapon for building the best culture is open and honest feedback."

– Gina Lau, Team Operations, HelloSign

Contents

List of Illustrations

LIST OF TABLES

LIST OF FIGURES

Objectives of the Textbook

This book captures the critical elements of managing organizational culture and performance in merger organizations. The book is an excellent resource for researchers, administrators, top-level executives, and managers who are considering or facing the prospect of a merger. The objectives of writing this textbook are to:

- Outline the need for managing organizational culture traits and performance in merged organizations.
- Explore the leadership theory behind merger, acquisition, and organization culture
- Explain the concepts, metrics, and techniques that form the backbone of merger activities.
- Provide clear examples and illustrations that tie merger concepts with real-world scenarios.
- Understand the relationship between organizational culture traits and organizational performance.
- Understand the historical perspective of organizational culture and its variables
- Analyzes the global bank mergers and their acquisition trends
- Procedures to follow when managing distressed banks and mergers
- Guidelines to follow when addressing merger and acquisition integration challenges
- Provide best practices in the recent merger trends
- Discussion of the ways to achieve merger and acquisition success
- Understand quantitative research, literature review, data collection, data analysis, results, and interpretations

Intended Readership/Users

This multi-disciplinary book covers facets of organizational culture traits, behaviors, mergers and acquisitions, and integration challenges and success factors. The book will be a valuable resource for curricula in business courses, such as organizational behavior, leadership decision-making, knowledge management, business information systems, business ethics, business intelligence, information governance, economics, banking, marketing, and other business-related courses. The book further provides an excellent resource for business sectors that grasp market globalization, organizational leaders, higher institutions, scholars, professionals, researchers, and project managers, in various industries and other corporate sectors with the synergy intent of merger and acquisition to sustain market diversification, increase in customer base, improved performance, and business synergy expansion. The book also serves as an excellent resource for student researchers, emphasizing the quantitative research method.

Foreword

The rapid growth in mergers and acquisitions of companies in the United States and globally, numerous research conducted under the auspices of industry and research institutions render it a difficult task to learn and interpret facts generated daily.

The book *Organizational Culture & Performance: The Practice of Sustaining Higher Performance in Business Merger & Acquisition*, written by Dr. Henrietta Okoro, explains mergers and acquisitions in a manner that is easy to understand. This book captures the critical elements of managing organizational culture and performance in merged organizations. The book is an excellent resource for researchers, administrators, top-level executives, and managers who are considering or facing the prospect of a merger. The book covers key areas with real-life examples applicable to organizational mergers and acquisitions.

The book's readers will find thorough documentation of the literature review, and the book covers in detail the background and historical perspectives of organizational culture challenges. Furthermore, the book explains mergers, the background of mergers and acquisitions, why mergers take place, different types of mergers, the advantages and disadvantages of mergers, and theories behind mergers.

The contribution of Dr. Henrietta Okoro is to present the content in an easy-to-read and understandable manner. The book provides an in-depth understanding of various topics such as:

- Background of organizational culture challenge
- Review of the literature
- Methodology
- Results
- Discussion
- Conclusions and recommendations

The book forms a valuable addition to the existing body of knowledge. Throughout the book, Dr. Henrietta Okoro draws from compelling examples of the merged organizations. She demonstrates the relationship between organizational culture and performance and how it can enhance employee retention, job satisfaction, and higher organizational performance.

This book is specially intended for university students, researchers, and practitioners interested to learn about the organizational culture and performance dealing with mergers and acquisitions.

Raj K. Singh, Ph.D.
Professor of Practice in Management
School Business
University of California, Riverside
California 92521

Preface

Recent merger waves in most organizations fail to increase organizational performance and sustain competitive advantage. Several U.S. organizational mergers were unable to maintain market competition and retain employees. Most consolidated and merged banks in developing countries are in distress and have failed to increase organizational performance. Currently, organizational leaders face challenges regarding integrating two or more merged cultures to maintain employee commitment, job satisfaction, and employee retention. Based on the author's rich academic and managerial experience, this book gives a unified treatment of the strategic and tactical aspects of organizational culture and performance in pre-and post-merger phases. The book integrates a quantitative correlational and regression study with collected data in Nigeria's sample merged bank in Abuja, Federal Capital Territory (FCT). The study findings show that a measure of the combination of cultural traits (mission, involvement, consistency, and adaptability) had a significant relationship with each of the organizational performance measures (employee commitment, job satisfaction, and employee retention). The findings revealed that a lack of cultural integration during a merger and acquisition was related to merger failure and decreased organizational performance. Merger failures were linked to inadequate employee commitment, reduced job satisfaction, and increased employee turnover, indicating lower organizational performance. Hence, the study implication shows that cultural differences may hinder organizational performance, which expands the research domain to include a merged bank in a developing country.

This book is the product of the research in Organizational Culture and Performance. It is imperative to provide solutions to the failed mergers and strategies for sustaining higher performance in partnership mergers and acquisitions. In this book, Dr. Henrietta Okoro integrates organizational culture traits with insights from research to provide readers with distinctive strategies to improve and sustain employee retention, job satisfaction, and higher organizational performance. The first chapter of the book provides the background of cultural challenges. The author focused on the perspective of organizational culture traits during the merger in companies, its advantages, and the theories behind the Mergers. Readers will gain insights into the cultural traits that increase learning and team building through these examples.

In the second chapter, Dr. Henrietta Okoro described the historical perspective of mergers and acquisitions in organizations, the diversity climate, and four categories for assessing organizational effectiveness: Clan culture, Adhocracy Culture, Market Culture, and Hierarchy Culture, as well as the current trends in mergers and acquisitions worldwide. The study explored the employees' cognitive aspects, growth mindset, commitment, and intellectual humility in fostering learning in organizations to sustain higher performance. Emphases were made on distressed banks, global bank mergers, acquisitions trends, and implications for sustainability.

In the third chapter, the author explained the supporting theories, such as the transformational leadership and equity theories, and their implications in the merger environment. The fourth chapter focused on data analysis, findings, and results. Emphasis was made on the importance of validity and reliability in research using internal and external factors. The fifth chapter discusses integrating organizations amongst the complexity of the modern IT environment for enterprise architects. The steps of unifying entities to help create a joint facility are based on the corporate strategy. Unifying entities lay the foundation for all future actions and help to speed up the realization of synergies between the acquired and acquiring companies in a merger and acquisition deal.

Chapter five explained the business architecture during pre-merger and post-merger, its challenges, perspectives on successful mergers and acquisitions, post-merger integration checklist, change management for improved effectiveness, merger bibliography best practices, top-level executives' perspectives, significant reasons why mergers fail, and ways to mitigate the challenges. The chapter further highlighted information governance on mergers, future of digital transformation to organizational culture, real-world perspectives of organizational culture and mergers, and building the organization of the future.

The final chapter, six, focused on the conclusion and recommendations. The study findings were interpreted to explain each hypothesis tested. The study's limitations and implications for Organizational Leadership and Scholars were highlighted. Recommendations were provided to leaders in various industries and future research prospects. The study's learnings include job satisfaction, employee commitment, thinking beyond financial gain in mergers and acquisitions, failure as a learning tool, and the cultural traits necessary to sustain creativity and higher organizational performance. Throughout the book, Henrietta Okoro draws from compelling examples of the merged organizations and research in the social sciences to demonstrate the relationship between organizational culture and performance and how it can enhance employee retention, job satisfaction, and higher organizational performance. The author, with extensive experience in academics and professional environment for over 24 years, offered a summary and discussions at the end of the chapters, providing a "real-world" perspective to empirical and theoretical insights on mergers and acquisitions.

—Dr. Henrietta M. Okoro
DM/IST, MBA, BSc., CSTE, CDPSE

Acknowledgments

Thanks to Professor Raj Singh, my mentor, and my husband, Sir Cyriacus Okoro, who, without their contributions and support, this book would not have been written.

Abbreviations

AI	Artificial Intelligence
ANOVA	Analysis of variance is an analysis tool used in statistics that splits an observed aggregate variability found inside a data set into two parts.
BHU	Baltimore Hebrew University
BHI	Baltimore Hebrew Institute
BEA Systems, Inc.	is a defense, security, and aerospace company that specialized in enterprise infrastructure software products and was acquired by Oracle Corporation on April 29, 2008.
BRCD	Brocade Communications Systems, a network equipment maker
BNM	Bank Negara Malaysia
BMW	Bayerische Motoren Werke AG, commonly referred to as BMW is a German multinational corporate manufacturer of luxury vehicles.
BRICS	BRICS is an acronym for Brazil, Russia, India, China, and South Africa. Goldman Sachs economist Jim O'Neill coined the term BRIC (without South Africa) in 2001, claiming that by 2050 the four BRIC economies would come to dominate the global economy 2050. South Africa was added to the list in 2010.
CBN	Central Bank of Nigeria
CC	Control of Corruption
CEO	Chief Executive Officer
CG	Corporate Governance
CLM	Contract Lifecycle Management
CPD	Continuous Process Development
CVF	Competing Values Framework

DF	Degrees of freedom
DG	Data Governance
DOCP	The Denison Organizational Culture and Performance (DOCP) survey instrument was used to collect data on the independent culture variables that comprise the cultural traits of (a) mission, (b) consistency, (c) involvement, and (d) adaptability (Denison & Neale, 1998).
DNA	is also the deoxyribonucleic acid, the hereditary material in humans and almost all other organisms.
3D	is a three-dimensional form, of an image or a picture produced in it.
EDS	Electronic Data Systems
FCT	Federal Capital Territory
FDI	Foreign Direct Investment
FDRY	Foundry Networks, an Ethernet technology company
FDIIN	Foreign Direct Investment Inflows (FDIIN)
FDIOUT	Foreign Direct Investment Outflows
GDP	Gross Domestic Product
GE	Government Effectiveness
GTE	General Telephone Electric
G7	The Group of Seven (G7) is an inter-governmental political forum consisting of Canada, France, Germany, Italy, Japan, the United Kingdom, and the United States. Its members are the world's largest IMF advanced economies and the wealthiest liberal democracies.
G20	G20 is the Group of Twenty of an intergovernmental forum comprising 19 countries and the European Union (EU). It focuses on addressing major issues related to the global economy, such as international financial stability, climate change mitigation, and sustainable development.
HEI	Higher Education Institutions
HPQ	Hewlett-Packard
IMF	International Monetary Fund
IBM	International Business Machines, a leading US computer manufacturer
IPO	Initial Public Offer
IMAA	Institute of Mergers, Acquisitions, and Alliances
IT	Information Technology

LDP	Label Distribution Protocol that automatically generates and exchanges labels between routers. Each router locally generates labels for its prefixes and will then advertise the label values to its neighbors.
LEC	Local Exchange Carriers
M&A	Mergers and acquisitions
OCI	Organizational Culture Inventory
PS	Political Stability
RBC	Royal Bank of Canada
RL	Rule of Law
RQ	Regulatory Quality
SAP	is one of the world's leading producers of software for the management of business processes, developing solutions that facilitate effective data processing and information flow.
SBC	School of Broadcasting and Communication
3G	is a mobile communications standard that allows mobile phones, computers, and other portable electronic devices to access the internet wirelessly.
TQM	Total Quality Management
TU	Towson University
VA	Voice Accountability

Chapter 1

Introduction

The book focuses on studying the relationship between organizational culture and performance in a merged Nigerian bank. As corporate culture and merger relationships draw attention to global businesses, the need for strategies to manage cultures within a merged environment is increasing (Rodriguez, 2008).[1] The Riegle–Neal Act of 1994 contributed to the dynamic change in the U.S. banking industry due to removing barriers to interstate banking (Becher & Campbell, 2005).[2] The Central Bank of Nigeria (CBN) mandated the Nigerian banking industry to perform bank consolidation and mergers to meet the minimum required share capital (Aburime & Uche, 2008)[3]. Despite the monetary authorities' efforts to regulate the banking industry through mandatory consolidation and mergers, most Nigerian banks are still in distress (Ezeoha, 2005, 2007; Toby, 2006).[4,5] The study used quantitative correlational and regression research within the theoretical field of organizational culture, transformational leadership, and equity theory. The study was designed to determine if the corporate culture is related to organizational performance within a merged bank in Abuja, Nigeria's federal capital territory. Chapter 1 of the study provides a broad overview highlighting the background of the research problem, the purpose and significance of the study to leadership, the research questions and hypotheses that the study sought to answer, the theoretical framework within which the study investigated the three research questions and hypotheses, the definitions of key terms used in the study, the basic assumptions made, and the anticipated limitations and delimitations of the study.

1.2 BACKGROUND OF ORGANIZATIONAL CULTURE

Advancements in technological innovations and business globalization have contributed to merger increases in different industries such as banking, auto, telecommunication, accounting, professional, and operating companies

(Badrtalei & Bates, 2007; Reiskin, 2006; Sidener & Kinsman, 2008). Despite all the investment in recent mergers, most mergers still face challenges of maintaining high performance (Atkinson, 2005; Garver, 2006; Terranova, 2007). Some of the consequences of merger failure relate to high employee turnover, decreased job satisfaction, and low performance (Badrtalei & Bates, 2007).

Organizational culture is one of the vital aspects of merger management (Badrtalei & Bates, 2007). When two different cultures collide, the effects can be disruptive; they can weaken morale and cause low productivity. Most mergers fail to produce positive results and meet target expectations (Badrtalei & Bates; Pooley, 2005). Many organizations are still undergoing mergers and acquisitions (M&A) when over 56% of unions fail (Atkinson, 2005; Dyer, Kale, & Singh, 2004; Pultz, 2005). For an organization to have a successful merger with another organization, the merger participants need to understand the objective of the merged company, its cultural values, and its management of human resources (Tanure & Gonzalez-Duarte, 2007). Leaders of a merging organization should not impose existing cultures on the employees; instead, cultural integration might help to facilitate the change process.

Organizational culture has many definitions that spring from earlier anthropological and sociological works. In 1958, anthropologist Williams defined culture as symbols of shared dimensions that require clarification (Reigle, 2001). The characters can be company logos or signs of identity. Laudon and Laudon (2006) define organizational culture as the assumptions about what products and services to make, how and where to make the products, and who the target customers are. The anthropologist Taylor 1871 divided the concept of culture into various attributes such as morals, laws, customs, behaviors, and knowledge (Reigle, 2001). Organizational culture also relates to cognitive components, such as values, beliefs, and assumptions (Schein, 1992).

The present study focused on an organizational culture defined by Schein (1992), which comprises a group's shared pattern, assumptions, values, and norms. These corporate activities involve the cultural environment that leads employees to complete tasks, maintain customer satisfaction, and solve internal and external problems. The different ways that people in a group solve problems affect the organizational norms and standards of operation more critically in a merger environment. Schein's (1992) definition of culture involves the way people conduct business, behave, and adapt to change.

The current study also measured how business is conducted according to its organizational mission. The study was designed to study behavior by focusing on the teams' involvement, employee retention, and job satisfaction. Adaptation to change was based upon consistency and the maintenance of core values. Reflecting on the importance of the research to social and theoretical concerns, the study's results helped explain why mergers occur, the advantages of mergers, and the theories behind mergers.

1.3 WHAT IS A MERGER?

A merger is a business strategy to combine or integrate with another company and operate as a single legal entity. Both companies agreeing to the merger are usually equal in size and scale of practices. There are different types of mergers that the enterprises could adopt, depending on their goals and strategies. Consequently, mergers are different from an acquisition. Mergers happen when two or more companies combine to form a new entity, whereas an acquisition is the takeover of a company by another company.

1.4 WHY MERGERS TAKE PLACE

Most organizations merge with other companies to increase their size (Lambrecht & Myers, 2007; Lausberg & Stahl, 2009). The motives for mergers might include synergy, agency, and hubris (Berkovitch, Elazar, & Narayanan, 1993). The reason synergy helps different organizations to cooperate and work together towards a common purpose. The concept of synergy supports the idea that teamwork is more effective than individual efforts. Most organizations with synergy motives tend to go into the merger. Differentiating the three reasons, the synergy motive suggests that organizations achieve economic gain from mergers. Agency motives indicate the enhancement of management welfare. The hubris hypothesis relates to managers' mistakes without synergy gains (Berkovitch et al., 1993).

Merger and acquisition could be an exhilarating tool for expanding a company, but before pursuing a deal, it is necessary to determine the reasons behind the transaction. Such as what outcome to achieve from M&A that the company could not realize otherwise?

Hence, there are a variety of reasons to acquire, and although each company's situation might be different, the most deals fall under one of these common categories:

Topline growth—as a source of response to a declining market or a drop in market share.

Follow customers—to retain existing customer base to achieve greater product breadth or deeper market reach.

Leverage technologies—to acquire the fastest and most-effective way to add powerful technologies, the company is lacking.

Consolidation—to purchase a direct competitor to provide economies of scale and cost reduction but may not change the company's overall strategic position.

Stabilize financials—leverage the company financial statements and incorporate a higher-margin business.

Expand customer base—to acquire a company to buy a customer portfolio, or to accelerate the expansion into new markets

Expand talent—to acquire more attractive talents and skills because of the people it brings with it, such as technology innovators, an exceptional sales team, or seasoned executives

Defensive positioning—to acquire a company to prevent a competitor from owning it so that you can protect your current and future market position.

Mergers and acquisitions are the business transaction where the control and ownership rights of organizations and business divisions are acquired by a target company or merged with the target company. There are eight types of Mergers and Acquisitions which include: (1) product extension, (2) horizontal, (3) vertical, (4) conglomerate, (5) Market extension, (6) Concentric, (7) Reverse Takeover, and (8) Acqui-hire

Ten Reasons Why Organizations Merge

Organizations merge due to several reasons. Below are some of the reasons an organization could undergo a merger and acquisition.

To gain access to a larger market and customer base.

To reduce competition and achieve economies of scale.

To secure more resources and increase the scale of operations.

To benefit their shareholders.

To enter new markets and diversify their offering of products and services, consequently increasing profits.

To help companies acquire assets that would take time to develop internally.

To lower the tax liability, a company generating substantial taxable income may look to merge with a company with significant tax loss carried forward.

To eliminate competition among companies, thus reducing the advertising price of the products.

To help reduce prices to benefit customers and ultimately increase sales.

To help in restructuring, planning, and utilization of financial resources.

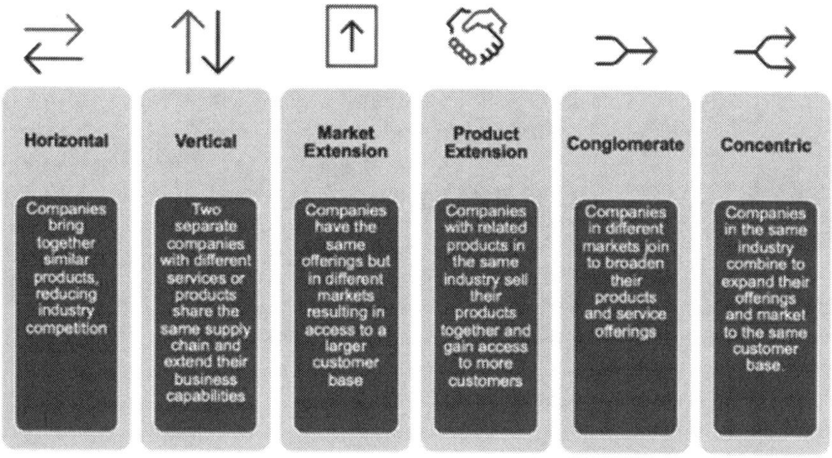

Figure 1.1. Types of Mergers & Acquisitions
Source: LeanIX

1.5 TYPES OF MERGERS

Product Extension Merger

The product extension merger happens between companies operating in the same market. The merger outcome focuses on adding a new product to the existing product line of one company. As a result of the merger, companies can access a more extensive customer base and increase their market share. A product-extension merger and acquisition occur when two businesses that create related products in the same industry merge to sell their products together and expand access to more customers to increase profits. An example is when Broadcom, a Bluetooth manufacturing company, incorporated and acquired Mobilink Telecom Inc., a chip and mobile design supplier. The merger outcome showed an alliance between the two products that support each other.

Horizontal Merger

A horizontal merger is a consolidation of companies selling similar products or services. A horizontal merger improves economies of scale and reduces competition. Horizontal mergers integrate similar products and reduce competitors in an industry. An example of a horizontal M&A would be the integration of Facebook and Instagram. The social media platforms are not the same, but merging ensures that they will not develop into direct competitors.

Vertical Merger

A vertical merger happens when companies operating in the same industry but at different levels in the supply chain merge. Such mergers happen to increase supply chain control, efficiency, and synergies. Vertical M&As arise to boost profits, efficiency, and product offerings. When two separate companies with different products or services share the same mission and extend their business capabilities. Vertical M&As do not require a company to acquire its competition. An example is a merger between AT&T and Time Warner in 2018. AT&T, one of the world's largest communications companies, merged with Time Warner to integrate wireless services to boost consumer performance and more choice.

Conglomerate Merger

A Conglomerate merger is an alliance of companies operating in unrelated activities. The integration takes place only if the coalition increases the shareholders' wealth. A conglomerate merger and acquisition is the merger between two businesses in totally unrelated markets. This type of merger creates an opportunity to decrease costs while increasing efficiency. The conglomerate merger does not affect competition because the two merging businesses are in different industries. Instead, the merger lowers the likelihood of more competition in the future. For example, is when Amazon acquired Whole Foods in 2017.

Market Extension Merger

Organizations operating in distinct markets, but selling the same products, combine to access a bigger market and more significant customer base. A market-extension M&A occurs when two businesses that produce the same effects in distinct needs join together. This type of merger and acquisition helps both companies access a more extensive customer base. An example of a market extension merger is RBC Centura Banks Inc., a wholly owned subsidiary of Royal Bank of Canada (RBC), that acquired Atlanta-based Eagle Bancshares Inc. for about $153 million. RBC Centura, based in Rocky Mount, is a $12 billion financial services company. The merger of RBC Centura and Eagle Bancshares, Inc., headquartered in Atlanta, Georgia, and is the holding company for Tucker Federal Bank. The Tucker Federal Bank is one of the leading banks in the Atlanta region. This merger helped RBC Centura grow its businesses in North America and expand its customer base.

Concentric Merger

A concentric merger and acquisition occur when two companies in the same industry combine to provide a broader range of products and services. These organizations share a similar mission, technology, distribution, and marketing channels. An example is a merger between Kraft and Heinz. Kraft is a producer of lunch meats and condiments

Heinz is a producer of sauces and frozen foods. The merger between Kraft and Heinz helped to integrate the sell their products rather than competing.

Reverse Takeover

A reverse takeover is a form of merger and acquisition where a private company acquires a public company to use the transaction to go public and avoid the costly initial public offer (IPO) process. Depending on how the merger deal is structured, a reverse takeover could involve the public company acquiring the private company or vice versa. However, a reverse takeover aims for the private company to take control of the newly merged company and for the new business to be publicly listed. An example of the reverse takeover is the acquisition of US Airways by America West in 2015.

Acqui-Hire

The acqui-hire merger occurs when the biggest companies in the world with more excellent talent and intellectual property capital assets acquire another company as a proven way for companies to ensure that the acquiring company is winning the talent race in their industry. The Acquire-hire acquisition is the most seen in the technology sector. A shortage of programmers means that the big tech companies will strive to get the most value-added talent, including buying over other smaller companies. An example of the acquire-hire merger is Facebook's acquisition of Drop.io in 2010, bringing Drop.io Chief Executive Officer (CEO) Sam Lessin onto the Facebook top-level executives.

1.6 ADVANTAGES OF MERGERS

Implementing mergers might result in economic gain, co-branding, and an increase in firms' size (Appelbaum, Lefrancois, Tonna, & Shapiro, 2007; Mitleton-Kelly, 2006). Some possible advantages of mergers and acquisitions include attaining economies of scale, integrating resources, maintaining competitive advantage, market diversification, and reducing inefficiencies (Appelbaum, Lefrancois, et al., 2007). Other reasons for acquiring growth through mergers and acquisitions might include gaining proprietary rights to products and services, increasing the customer base, increasing shares, and penetrating more business locations towards market globalization (Rosen, 2006; Streeter, 2006).

The Sixteen Advantages of Merger and Acquisition

1. Increases market share—when organizations merge, the new company gains a larger market share and a competitive advantage.
2. Avoids replication—is the merging of organizations that produce similar products helps to avoid duplication and eliminate competition. The merger also results in reduced prices for the customers.
3. Decreases the cost of operations—organizations could attain economies of scale, such as bulk buying raw materials, resulting in cost reductions. The investments in assets are spread out over a larger output, which leads to higher returns from economies of scale.
4. Expands business into new geographic areas—corporate merger helps businesses to expand in some geographical regions.
5. Prevents closure of an unprofitable business—organizational mergers help save a company from going out of business and save many jobs for employees.
6. Job opportunities—organizational mergers that embrace expansion help to create job opportunities.
7. Economies of Scale—strengthening of merger and acquisition activity creates economies of scale. Some of the benefits of the new vision company include increasing access to capital, lower costs due to higher volume, and better bargaining power with vendors and distributors.
8. Economies of Scope—mergers and acquisitions create economies of scope that are not possible through natural growth. An example is the Facebook acquisition of Instagram and WhatsApp applications to have more business and customer base scope. Economies of scope allow companies to tap into the demand of a much larger client base.
9. Synergies in Mergers and Acquisitions—the synergies process is usually described as 'one plus one equal three.' This means that synergies value multiplies and comes from two companies working together in tandem to make a more powerful impact in the business arena. An example of synergies in mergers is the Disney acquisition of Lucasfilm. Lucasfilm was already a massive cash generator through the Star Wars franchise. Still, Disney could add theme park rides, toys, and merchandise to the customer, offering to their already established business focal points.
10. Benefits in Opportunistic Value Generation—the merger and acquisition deal could happen through opportunistic value generation when a

company is not actively pursuing an acquisition. The symbol of these acquisitions is that the purchase price is less than the fair market value of the target company's net assets. Some of these companies might be in financial hardship, but a deal could be made to keep the company buoyant. At the same time, the buyer benefits from adding immediate value as a direct consequence of the transaction.

11. Increased Market Share—among the main benefits of mergers and acquisitions is increased market share. An example is where a retail bank is interested in reaching a particular geographical footprint. The bank could adopt a merger as a critical factor in achieving market share. These benefits of increased market share result in a high level of industry consolidation in retail banking. Another example is the Spanish retail bank Santander, acquiring smaller banks to allow them to become one of the largest retail banks in the world.
12. Higher Levels of Competition—in theory, the larger a company, the more significant its performance. The bigger a company, the more competitive it becomes. Thus, companies entering mergers help the company attain a higher level of competition and sustain the benefits of economies of scale. An example is the upstart companies entering the plant-based meat market and offering a range of vegetable-based 'meats.
13. Access to Talent—they have the best talents increasing the competitive advantage of companies. The recruitment industry emphasizes acquiring the best skills in the job market. Entering a merger helps eliminate the most significant talent shortages and will invariably be a variant of 'people that can code' such as in the tech industry. In the fourth industrial revolution, the demand for huge programmers contributed to increased merger deals while searching for the best talents. An example is the Silicon Valley tech industry having access to the best talent and could acquire any smaller firm to explore their best skills.
14. Risk Diversification—risk diversification is provided across various categories in industries within one portfolio. This helps to even out some assets if they perform poorly in other portfolios. Generating more revenue streams helps to spread risk across those weaker revenue flows rather than having it focus on just one channel. Therefore, when one revenue stream drops, an alternative revenue stream will pick up while diversifying the acquiring company's risk.
15. Quicker Strategy Implementation—mergers and Acquisitions help make a long-term strategy become a mid-term strategy. Upon closing the merger and acquisition, a company could merge its business to grow faster and increase its client base, distribution, and brand value. This also goes for fields like new product development and research

and development, where a natural strategy could rarely match the speed provided by merger and acquisition.

16. Tax Benefits and Shelter—mergers and acquisitions can, at times, bring tax benefits and shelter if the target company is in a strategic industry or a country with a favorable tax rule. An example is a United States pharmaceutical company exploring smaller Irish companies with plans to move their headquarters to Ireland to benefit from its lower tax base. This relates to the "tax inversion" deal. An example of the tax inversion merger is the Pfizer and Allergan 2016 merger with over $160 billion but was subsequently prevented by US government intervention.

1.7 DISADVANTAGES OF MERGERS

A merger is an agreement between two or more organizations to form one company to gain more market share or enter new market areas and maximize profits. Mergers also help companies to restructure their business units according to market changes. Consequently, a merger helps companies sustain market changes and increase customer base, but the merger also has some associated challenges. Some of the disadvantages of a merger include

The Nine Disadvantages of Merger and Acquisition

1. Products or services price increase—a merger could result in reduced competition and a larger market share. Consequently, the new company could gain a monopoly and increase the prices of its products or services.
2. Unemployment—the organizational merger may opt to eliminate the underperforming assets of the other company, thus causing employees to lose their jobs.
3. Gaps in Communication—the merged companies may have different organizational cultures; hence the merger could cause a communication gap and affect the performance of the employees.
4. Difficult in Synergies—an organizational merger could prevent economies of scale that aren't accessible to synergies among the merged companies.
5. Conducted for the Wrong Reasons—companies should not undertake mergers thing. It is simple. The process of merger and acquisition is complex and rarely easy.
6. Distract from the Daily Management of a Business—despite that mergers and acquisitions add value for a business, the central value creation that gets on in any business should be its day-to-day operations. The

process of the merger could distract the daily operation. For example, pulling managers away from the company's operations for merger meetings and collaborations could significantly distract them from their daily tasks. This could be a hindrance to the merger's purpose. Therefore, a good merger plan needs to be implemented before any deal to ensure that the correct time is allocated for each manager's participation in the process.

7. Value Distraction—the mismanagement at some part of the merger and acquisition process destroys the value of the business. When managers do not monitor the activities, the mismanagement could cause more harm to both the acquired and acquiring company. Without the proper care at the pre-merger and post-merger stages of the deals, such as origination, negotiations, due diligence, deal closing, or integration, the value can be destroyed without good planning and execution.
8. Inaccurate Valuations—as merger and acquisition transactions are complex with some unique considerations, the valuation methods could be inaccurate. An example is Amazon's acquisition of Whole Foods, which was seen as a deal that would generate significant value for both companies in many quarters. Amazon is a high-end distribution chain for its grocery fulfillment efforts, with Whole Foods access to the world's most potent e-commerce engine. Still, the merger deal did not roar a success, with higher expectations.
9. Diligence is a Complex and Time-Consuming Task—the merger and acquisition due diligence is a complex and time-consuming task. The most successful deals were those where the M&A lifecycle management platform was mainly used to eliminate time. An example of the M&A management platform is DealRoom's experience to help maximize the pros and minimize the cons.

The Best Contract Lifecycle Management (CLM) Software (2022)

- DocuSign CLM
- SAP Ariba Contracts
- Conga Contracts
- LinkSquares
- Evisort
- Icertis Contract Management Software
- Contract Logix
- SirionLabs CLM
- Ironclad CLM
- CobbleStone Contract Insight

- Agiloft Contract Management Suite

1.8 THEORIES BEHIND MERGERS

Merger and acquisition theories revolve around value increasing, value reducing, and neutral values (Weston, Mitchell, & Mulherin, 2004). Value-increasing theories include transaction cost efficiency (Hunt, 2007), synergy (Cigola & Modesti, 2008), and disciplinary (Jackson, 2007; MacDonald, 2005). Value-reducing theories include agency costs (Katz & Shelanski, 2007; Paliwal, 2007) and management entrenchment (Zhao & Chen, 2008). Value neutral theory centers on the hubris hypothesis (Kiymaz & Baker, 2008; Moeller, Schlingemann, & Stulz, 2005). The use of the discipline concept allows merger organizations to change management with poor performance records into new administration to improve the performance of the new firm. The management entrenchment concept is considered a management-specific investment to increase managers' value rather than shareholders' value. Leaders need to apply culture integration to merger strategies in different companies to leverage business expectations towards higher performance during and after a merger. In line with the study's objective, the focus was on identifying the relationship between culture on performance in a merged banking company.

1.9 PROBLEM STATEMENT

The general problem is that failed mergers and acquisitions have been shown to cause low organizational performance relating to a reduction in shareholders' value, a high rate of employee turnover, and a decrease in customer base (Atkinson, 2005; Chew & Sharma, 2005; Epstein, 2004). Prior studies showed that over 56% of mergers and acquisitions fail and do not increase organizational performance (Atkinson, 2005; Dyer et al., 2004; Pultz, 2005). A high rate of employee turnover results in a loss of talented employees and prevents knowledge sharing during the merger process. In the 1990s, the U.S. banking industry's decrease in financial performance resulted in 30% overlapping expenses due to inadequate cultural integration among the merged banks. The specific problem is that organizational leaders face challenges integrating two or more merged cultures to maintain employee commitment, job satisfaction, and employee retention (Afzal, Butt, Rehman, & Safwan, 2009; Mancheno-Smoak, Endres, Potak, & Athanasaw, 2009; Morellec & Zhdanov, 2005; Rothman, 2008). About 75% of the mergers fail because of a lack of cultural integration (Effects of Organizational Culture,

2002). Understanding the significant relationship between the combination of cultural traits and performance variables in a merged bank could yield helpful information for developing strategic plans for merger success. The study results contributed to the body of knowledge needed to address the low-performance problems in a merged bank by analyzing the relationship between organizational cultures and performance. Corporate cultures include the following traits: mission, consistency, involvement, and adaptability. The arrangement involves employee commitment, job satisfaction, and employee retention. A quantitative correlational and regression research methodology was used to survey all bank employees in a merged bank in Abuja, Nigeria, to achieve the purpose.

1.10 PURPOSE STATEMENT

The quantitative correlational and regression study examined the relationship between organizational culture and performance in a merged Nigerian bank. The organizational culture comprises mission traits, consistency, involvement, and adaptability. The performance variables include employee commitment, job satisfaction, and employee retention (Denison & Neale, 1998; Yilmaz & Ergun, 2008).

A quantitative methodology was most appropriate because the study analyzed the relationship between the independent variables of organizational culture and the dependent variables of organizational performance. Quantitative research helps measure an objective reality and code subject responses manipulated into statistical analysis (Cooper & Schindler, 2008, p. 164). A qualitative methodology was not suitable because a qualitative study explores knowledge about events by collecting data about participants' lived experiences (Cooper & Schindler, 2008, p. 162).

Qualitative data are subjective and vulnerable to bias and misinterpretation from open-ended questions. Statistical data from the quantitative study helped measure the significant relationship between organizational culture and performance variables. The study surveyed a sample of employees of a merged Nigerian bank in Abuja. The location for the study was a merged bank in Abuja, the FCT of Nigeria. The population for the study included all bank employees in the Nigerian bank.

1.11 SIGNIFICANCE OF THE MERGER STUDY

The current study is unique because the research was concentrated on the relationship between organizational culture and performance in a merged

Nigerian bank. Prior studies focused on merged companies within the United States in different organizational settings (Johnson, 2007; Peete, 2007). Organizations need to align cultural traits to performance expectations to achieve employee commitment and higher performance (Badrtalei & Bates, 2007; Coffey, 2005; Harford, 2005). The research findings can be applied to any organization that intends to undergo a merger or maybe already in the merger and acquisition process. The study may help policymakers formulate merger policies and procedures to maintain organizational stability and economic growth. The data from the study may assist in theoretical discussions relating to merger theories of different organizations. Information from the research may be used to integrate human resource values into organizational values. Organizational leaders may use the results from the study to refine their leadership strategy toward diversified business processes, joint ventures, and partnership projects.

1.12 SIGNIFICANCE OF THE MERGER STUDY TO LEADERSHIP

The study provides information to help leaders reduce failure strategies in merged organizations. Organizations intending to merge sometimes make assumptions about potential benefits such as business diversification, maintaining a competitive advantage, and increasing their customer base (Brahy, 2006; Lang, 2008). Meeting merger objectives requires leadership practices and organizational structures that support strong culture. Transformational leadership practices support a strong culture that influences merger success (Xenikou & Simosi, 2006). After a merger, the study provided essential leadership strategies and cultural traits for realizing desirable performance outcomes. The research findings provided effective merger strategies for organizational leaders to manage culture integration and maintain a high level of organizational performance. The study findings may help beginners, and experienced leaders enhance their managing strategies for past and future merger processes. By analyzing the study's conclusions, leaders in various organizations can exercise knowledge sharing, shared understanding, and commitment to achieving professional and personal goals within a merger environment. Shared knowledge and commitment might enhance business development, talented employee retention, and organizational sustainability through an increase in performance rate. The information from the study may help theorists link executive leadership and the societal transformation process during a merger and acquisition to maintain high performance and business profitability.

1.13 NATURE OF STUDY

The study used quantitative correlational and regression research to examine the relationship between organizational culture and performance in a merged bank in Abuja, the FCT of Nigeria. The benefits of using correlational and regression analyses include correlation helps to identify the strength of relationships, and the regression helps identify the dependence between the study variables. Hence, the quantitative correlational and regression method was appropriate because the study identified the significant relationships and dependencies between organizational culture and performance variables in a merged Nigerian bank. The banking industry was selected for the study due to the increase in merger waves since the 2000s in the global banking sectors (Aburime & Uche, 2008; Agboola, & Salawu, 2008; Koetter, 2008; Rodriguez, 2008). Several merger failures have been reported in the telecommunication and banking industry (Kanter, Raffaelli, & Raymond, 2004; Rodriguez, 2008). The study may help organizational leaders to manage culture integration during pre-merger and post-merger to avoid merger challenges such as culture clashes. The data collected from the study may serve as a baseline for future organizational mergers incorporating culture in the merger process. The Denison Organizational Culture and Performance (DOCP) survey instrument was used to collect data on the independent culture variables that comprise the cultural traits of (a) mission, (b) consistency, (c) involvement, and (d) adaptability (Denison & Neale, 1998; Yilmaz & Ergun, 2008). The dependent performance variables include the following: (a) employee commitment, (b) job satisfaction, and (c) employee retention. The survey method was used to access the merged banking company's directors, managers, and employees. A total of 220 participants were used, comprising ten directors, ten managers, and 200 employees. Voluntary participants signed and submitted consent forms before responding to the survey questions.

Unlike a qualitative study, quantitative research is standardized. A qualitative method was not helpful in the study because the research purpose analyzed the relationship between organizational culture and performance, a process that involves independent and dependent variables. Qualitative research focuses on exploring themes, experiences, and attitudes that emerge during the research process. Using a qualitative method was not suitable for the research objective that focuses on relationships among culture and performance variables. Using the DOCP survey instrument helped identify the study's cultural traits and measure the corresponding performance variables. The study identified and analyzed the data gathered from the participants who responded to the invitation to survey. The DOCP survey instrument has a strong foundation with proven effectiveness in several local and global organizations (Denison, Janovics, Young, & Cho, 2006; Nazir & Lone, 2008). The Denison Organizational Culture Model and the survey instrument are based on Denison and Neale's 20 years of research practice (1998). The model identified the four cultural traits as (a) mission, (b) consistency, (c) involvement, and (d) adaptability. Organizations need to manage these cultural traits (Denison, 2006; Yilmaz & Ergun, 2008).

In the study of 170 firms in Russia, the Denison model reflected a significant correlation between the four cultural traits and organizational effectiveness (Fey & Denison, 2003). A study of 150 executives from six private organizations in India found that organizations with strong cultures increase sales, reserves, and profit compared to weak cultures (Fey & Denison, 2003). The study of 764 organizations by Denison and Mishra (1995) provided evidence of a significant relationship between cultural traits and organizational performance of return on assets and sales growth.

The quantitative correlational and regression study findings are transferable to other settings and populations. The results from the survey might assist organizational leaders with different strategies to manage cultural traits in a merged environment to enhance performance. The stratified random sampling method enabled generalizations from the sample to other populations. Generalizing the research findings might help local and global organizational leaders decide on future mergers and existing mergers towards performance enhancement. Each cultural trait was represented with three indexes for 12 indexes in the model. The components of the mission traits include strategic direction, intent, goals, and objectives. The consistency traits are core values, agreement, coordination, and integration. Involvement traits comprise empowerment, team orientation, and capability development. Adaptability traits include creating change, customer focus, and organizational learning (Andreadis, 2009; Denison, Janovics, et al., 2006). A total of 12 indexes were covered on the 60-item DOCP survey instrument, where five survey items represent each index.

The cause of most merger failures relates to organizational leaders not integrating cultures to suit the new organization (Effects of Organizational Culture, 2002). The emergence of a new organization from the merger process creates three possible cultural attributes: perceived objective, dominant culture, and unique cultures (Schein, 1999). The above three attributes are like the cultural traits identified by Denison, Janovics, et al. (2006). First, the perceived objective relates to the mission that the organizational leaders use to expand the customer base and diversify products and services. Second, the dominant culture relates to the adaptability of the new environment to accept change. Third, the unique culture refers to consistency and involvement in team orientation to maintain core values. A quantitative analysis helped identify if the cultural traits meet the theoretical objectives of the organizational leaders. The research questions set forth below helped to direct the research study.

1.14 RESEARCH QUESTIONS AND HYPOTHESES

Research questions help provide an inquiry with a research purpose and guide for conducting the study, ensuring the investigation of the correct variables (Creswell, 2005). The purpose of the research study was to examine the relationship between organizational culture and performance in a merged bank in Abuja, the FCT of Nigeria. Organizational culture traits functioned as the independent variables: mission, consistency, involvement, and adaptability. Employee commitment, job satisfaction, and employee retention were performance-dependent variables.

Lack of employee commitment decreased job satisfaction, and high employee turnover has been significant problems in most merged organizations, such as the banking and telecommunication industries (Appelbaum, Gandell, Yortis, Proper, & Jobin, 2000; Badrtalei & Bates, 2007). Lack of employee commitment results in significant loss of revenue and merger failure (Badrtalei & Bates, 2007; Coffey & Tombari, 2005; Harford, 2005). Bank employees often search for new opportunities rather than alternative means to enhance job performance (Valant, 2008).

The research questions and hypotheses focused on the relationship of the four cultural traits to three performance variables. The hypotheses were presented in the form of a H_o null component and H_a alternative hypotheses. The null component indicated no existence of a statistically significant relationship, and the alternative component revealed a statistically significant relationship (Vogt, 2007). The research questions and hypotheses for the study included the following:

Research Questions and Hypothesis:

Research Question 1: What is the relationship between organizational culture traits of mission, comprising consistency, involvement, and adaptability, and employee commitment performance in a merged Nigerian bank?

H_o1: There is no significant relationship between organizational cultural traits of mission, consistency, involvement, and adaptability, and employee commitment performance in a merged Nigerian bank.

H_a1: There is a significant relationship between organizational culture traits of mission, consistency, involvement, and adaptability, and employee commitment performance in a merged Nigerian bank.

Research Question 2: What is the relationship between organizational culture traits of mission, comprising consistency, involvement, and adaptability, and job satisfaction performance in a merged Nigerian bank?

H_o2: There is no significant relationship between organizational culture traits of mission, consistency, involvement, adaptability, and job satisfaction performance in a merged Nigerian bank.

H_a2: There is a significant relationship between organizational culture traits of mission, consistency, involvement, and adaptability and the job satisfaction performance in a merged Nigerian bank.

Research Question 3: What is the relationship between organizational culture traits of mission, comprising consistency, involvement, and adaptability, and employee retention performance in a merged Nigerian bank?

H_o3: There is no significant relationship between organizational culture traits of mission, consistency, involvement, and adaptability and employee retention performance in a merged Nigerian bank.

H_a3: There is a significant relationship between organizational culture traits of mission, consistency, involvement, and adaptability and employee retention performance in a merged Nigerian bank.

1.15 THEORETICAL FRAMEWORK

The advancement in cultural knowledge and the corresponding relationship to the organizational performance provided the theoretical framework for the study. Transformational leadership theory, equity theory, motivation theories, and Denison's corporate culture model explained the importance of culture and performance within merged organizations.

Transformational Leadership Theory

Transformational leadership is a theory of leadership where leaders work with their employees, teams, and followers beyond their immediate self-interests to recognize the need for a new vision and change. Transformation leadership theory helps to guide the change by inspiring, influencing, and executing the difference in a cycle with committed teams. This change in self-interest elevates the team's levels of maturity and ideals, especially in a merger and acquisition environment. This transformational leadership theory shows the importance of organizational culture during organizational change (Emery & Barker, 2007).

Effective Transformational Leadership

Effective transformational leadership inspires people to attain remarkable results. It provides workers the autonomy over jobs and decision makings. Some of the fundamental qualities of transformational leadership are inspirational, where the leader inspires workers to find improved ways of accomplishing a goal. Transformational leaders mobilize people into groups to improve morale and get work done.

Equity Theory

Equity theory is one social psychological theory that focuses on establishing a fair distribution of resources to both relational partners, such as in a merger and acquisition process. Some social psychological theories are equity, emotion, justice, and exchange theories. Equity theory (Adams, 1965), justice theory (Parris, Hegtvedt, Watson, & Johnson, 2014), and exchange theory (Lawler, 2001) detail the constitutive relationship between emotion and social structure. The study explores the equity theory related to mergers and acquisitions. Hence, equity is determined by comparing the ratio of costs and benefits for each person or partner. Like the justice theories, equity theory was first developed in the 1960s. Equity theory shows that perceptions of fairness are an essential factor that helps manage and treat employees equitably (Anderson & Patterson, 2008).

Similarly, equity theory relates to the perceptions of fairness in job and employees' motivation that might affect participants' behavior and job performance (Adams, 1965; Mowday, 1991). Equity theory helps to predict that individuals are likely to experience negative emotions when they perceive inequity in their relations with others. Initially, the equity theory predicted that individuals would experience un-generalized distress, whether they were under-benefited or over-benefited. Still, later scholars stated that anger was more likely in the former, whereas shame was more likely to be experienced in the latter.

Equity theory recommends that individuals estimate the ratio of their input and outcomes for the parties involved (Adams, 1965). Inputs are the employee's contributions, such as education, skills, performance, and work experience. At the same time, outcomes relate to what the employees receive in exchange for their contributions, such as wages, promotions, and career development opportunities. When there is an imbalance between inputs and outcomes, employees might reduce the discrepancy by adjusting their approaches, contributions, and outcomes to restore the balance between the two ratios. Hence, the social-psychological perspectives reveal that emotions are shaped by existing social and structural arrangements. They also demonstrate emotions' ability to contribute to and disrupt different conditions. Therefore, equity theory assumes that the perception of equity, fairness or net gains over the interaction affects emotions that the individuals are embedded in, such as during the pre-merger and post-merger processes.

Denison Organizational Culture Model

Denison's organizational culture model used the four cultural traits to analyze cultural relationships on organizational outcomes, emphasizing sales increase, assets, and quality of products and services (Denison & Neale, 1998). The four cultural traits are composed of four features: mission, consistency, involvement, and adaptability. Because the Denison Organizational Culture Model focused on financial performance, the study may link the model with identifying cultural relationships on employee commitment, job satisfaction, and employee retention performance.

Organizations that inherit environments where employees perceive unfairness and inequality experience employee lack of commitment, intent to leave, and low performance (Anderson & Patterson, 2008). Transformational leadership and equity theories were the theoretical schools and foundations to support the study. Leaders might integrate organizational culture by aligning the new vision and shared assumptions such as values and norms (Bass & Avolio, 1994). Transformational leadership theory enables leaders to accept culture integration after an organizational merger to help promote employee commitment and job satisfaction. The theories helped analyze corporate culture and performance within a banking company that has experienced a merger and acquisition. The study connected critical management areas such as culture, performance, transformational leadership, and equity theory.

The concept of organizational culture started over 130 years ago with anthropologists and sociologists. Taylor, 1871 defined culture in his book *Primitive Culture* as morals, laws, customs, behaviors, and knowledge (Schein, 1992). The current literature in the era of innovative technology and business globalization relates to the integration and sharing of Edward's cultural components that make up the culture concept. The concept of culture differs among scholars. Anthropologist Williams 1958 explained cultures with symbols (Higgins, 2001). Williams believed that every culture has a different shared scope that requires explanation. Williams's meaning of society's culture was not evident from Taylor's categorical culture perspective. According to Hall (1959), the concept of culture relates to language and communication. The three forms of communication-related to culture are formal, informal, and technical. Hall stated that cultural conflict results from an inability to integrate culture between two organizations due to the non-integration of the three types of communication.

The constant failures of organizational mergers, business globalization, and technological advancement have caused the culture to become an important factor necessary for measuring an organization's performance. Many researchers are finding ways to enable leaders and managers to integrate organizational cultures to achieve organizational goals. The various perceptions of Taylor in 1871, Williams in 1958, and Hall in 1959 described the different angles of culture research. Many researchers have performed empirical studies to determine effective corporate cultures. Other researchers have used questionnaires to survey organizational members to determine the cultural influence on organizational performance (Denison, 2006; Gillespie, Denison, Haaland, Smerek, & Neale, 2008; Weber & Camerer, 2003).

The results from prior studies support the idea that corporate cultures differ between organizations. Weber and Camerer (2003) developed a theoretical model of corporate cultures using the concept of shared knowledge within an organization. They examined how corporate cultures are mingled among employees, managers, and top leaders. Weber and Camerer (2003) concluded their research that good communication and knowledge sharing led to increased productivity. Lack of communication and understanding reduces productivity in organizations, leading to lower performance levels (Chew & Sharma, 2005). Similarly, Denison (2006) developed an organizational culture model that portrayed culture as a critical factor that affects organizations' effectiveness. The model comprises four cultural traits with 12 indexes that help measure culture and performance factors in organizations.

As organizations move into ever more diverse and sophisticated innovations in high technology, leaders and employees will likely face issues with high-volume projects and meeting target deadlines (Bayer & Gann, 2006). Executives also must be concerned with producing quality products, gaining customer satisfaction (Dutta & Dutta, 2009), employee retention (Pickett, 2005), and high organizational performance (Gillespie et al., 2008; Kirkbride, 2006; Liu & Chen, 2008). Each of these challenges relates to personal and organizational performance factors. The Denison organizational cultural model is comprehensive enough to respond to these factors. The growth and sustainability of most organizations depend on employees' commitment and effective leadership practices. Effective culture management during a merger process might increase performance levels to achieve organizational sustainability (Nadolska, & Barkema, 2007; Sull, 2007). The present study used empirical data from the survey instrument to analyze organizational culture traits of mission, adaptability, consistency, and involvement with employee commitment, job satisfaction, and employee retention performance.

1.16 MOTIVATIONAL THEORIES

Motivation Theories

Motivation is a state of mind with energy and enthusiasm which drives an employee to work in a certain way to attain set goals. Motivation is the energy that causes people to work with a higher commitment. Motivation decodes into a human's behavior as a driving force behind human actions during pre-merger and post-merger processes. Various forces guide people's motivations. It is essential to confirm that every organizational team member is motivated and meets project expectations. Numerous psychologists have studied human behavior and explained different motivational theories. These motivational theories drive how people behave and what motivates them. Thus, motivation theory is a way of looking at a person's motivation and how this influences their behavior. Motivation is vital in society but very relevant to business and management. Motivation is the primary factor in committing employees to attain more productivity. The six theories of motivation are:

- Abraham Maslow's Theory of Hierarchical Needs
- Hertzberg's two-factor Theory
- McClelland's Theory of Needs
- Vroom's Theory of Expectancy
- McGregor's Theory X and Theory Y
- Alderfer's ERG Theory

The study explores two theories of motivation: Abraham Maslow's Theory of Hierarchical Needs and McGregor's Theory X and Theory Y, as it applies to merger and acquisition.

McGregor's Theory X and Theory Y

Theory X and Theory Y relate to human work motivation and management theories. Douglas McGregor formed them while working at the MIT Sloan School of Management in the 1950s and developed further in the 1960s. McGregor's work. This theory is rooted in motivation theory and Abraham Maslow's works, which created the hierarchy of needs. The hierarchy of needs theory clarifies humans' five essential requirements. This hierarchy of conditions could be applied in the business context during pre-merger and post-merger.

In terms of theories X and Y, the Hawthorne plant in the 1920s conducted the Hawthorne experiment. The experiment applied the use of reasoning and its procedures to understand human behavior. The experiments underscored

Rosenthal's and Rasnow's reflection, which states that the application of scientific investigations of human behavior shows how human behavior complexity. In the workplace experience, the Hawthorne effect is essential in constructing scientific knowledge (Gillespie, 2008). There are different implications of this experiment in the workplace. First, the investigation has greatly disagreed in meaning and its application. This scenario has attracted serious scrutiny in its history. The Hawthorne experiment has enhanced the performance of specific individuals who cannot correctly intervene in situations through ill-defined variables, such as during the merger and acquisition process.

Theory X Managers

The manager believes that most of his employees are self-centered and self-conscious. They are only motivated by physiological and safety requirements and are openly indifferent or uncaring when it comes to the organization's needs that they are employed (Hardy, 2010). The team lacks good ambition and has little workplace creativity and problem-solving abilities. As a result, they dislike their job and will try all means to avoid it. The team avoids taking responsibility. These managers, therefore, tend to be authoritarian.

Theory Y Managers

In contrast to Theory X managers, Theory Y managers trust employees. They believe that most individuals are better performers in a favorable work environment. This is because most of the employees' creativity and commitment help meet the requirements of the organization they work for (Gabriel, 2009). Theory Y managers believe that most individuals take responsibility and accountability and are self-disciplined. Finally, according to Maslow's hierarchy of needs, they think that most people are motivated by different conditions.

Human Relations Movement

The Human Relations Movement grew from the Hawthorne Studies. A group of Harvard researchers, headed by Elton Mayo, conducted a series of experiments on worker productivity in 1924 at the Hawthorne plant of Western Electric Company in Illinois. These experiments have come to be known as the Hawthorne studies. The Hawthorn Experiment was based on interviews conducted several decades around the Hawthorn studies. This was a reanalysis of the original research in 1935. The study proved that employees need supportive supervision and group dynamics to allow positive job performance.

People think that average employees want to be directed by management, while Theory Y believes that the key to committing employees is to satisfy them in their jobs. Theory X thinks people don't like responsibility, while Theory Y people seek and accept responsibility under the right circumstances.

McGregor's Theory X and Theory Y Assumptions

Based on McGregor's Theory X, most people dislike work, have to be punished before working, and prefer to be directed. I find this statement to be false. The motivator in our society is money and power. This pushes employees to work harder and gain independence from their managers. Theory Y states that work is a natural activity, people are capable of self-direction, and the typical employee can seek responsibility. I believe this to be true. I have worked with several managers that have allowed me to work independently and seek additional responsibility within my tasks. I prefer a manager that applies the Theory Y approach. It enables me to feel comfortable with the possibility of growth within an organization without being micro-managed or reprimanded if I complete a project incorrectly.

Maslow's Theory of Hierarchical Needs

Abraham Maslow's hierarchy of needs is among the best-known theories of motivation. Maslow's theory states that people's actions are motivated by particular physiological needs. Abraham Maslow assumed that a person is motivated when all the person's needs are fulfilled. People often work to contribute and use their skills more often than money and security. Below is the Maslow's Theory hierarchy of needs:

Physiological needs: relates to the basic requirements for existence such as food, water, sleep, air, clothing, sex, and shelter.

Safety needs relate to safety, such as protection from threats and dangers from job loss or property loss.

Social needs: relates to the need for affiliation, association, and relationship.

Self-esteem needs: relates to the need for respect and recognition.

Self-actualization needs: relates to the opportunity for self-actualization, personal development, professional development, learning, and creative work.

Motivation and Job Performance

Motivation is the desire to perform a task or service to accomplish a goal. It's the essential element in setting and attaining business objectives and attaining organizational performance. Motivation is one of the driving forces behind human behavior. A person's accomplishment consists of three principal fundamentals: motivation, skill, and tools. Individuals' reason depends on their desires and how their work surroundings please them. Proficiency is a function of a person's ability and the Job training the person is given. Qualifications, in turn, depend on psychological and physical ability, knowledge, and education. The tools used for a specific job allow individuals to increase their ability to improve Job Performance. The tools depend on the job, but computer systems are often used for knowledge workers. Maslow's and McClelland's Need Theories: state that the job performance model of motivation is a tool used to explain how motivation influences job behaviors and performance broadly. The employees at the workplace are likely to develop implicit expectations of behavioral reciprocity from leaders and coworkers because reciprocity is the dominant value of social exchange in collective cultures. This belief enhances the individual's perception of a warm climate in the workplace (Ali, Tang, Rolf, & Mir, 2019).

Organizational Culture Relationship to Motivation

Organizational culture plays a vital role in maintaining the motivation level among employees in organizations. An employee exhibits more commitment and efficiency at work when there is a match between the individual's motivation and the organizational culture. Thus, organizational culture is crucial in determining the success of the organization. It is the ecosystem in the workplace through the interaction of employees at work. Organizational culture could be learned in the social environment, and it encourages innovative behavior among members of the organization. It serves as a mixture of knowledge, belief, art, morals, and habits of people. It helps an organization create a culture among the employees and provide a framework for motivational factors. Hence, organizational culture helps enhance the employee's level of motivation in the organization.

As organizational culture integrates the members of a group, employees can participate and involve in the organizational activities and decisions. This helps create positive motivation within the organization, and the management believes that their employees are capable of decision-making. According to Contiu, Gabor, and Oltean (2012), employees become inefficient and costly to the organization without motivation.

Employers need to invest in providing more benefits to aid the process of employee motivation, promotion, transfer, job growth, job enrichment, and training (internal and external sources). In this perspective, the organization must be more responsive to the needs of the employees, thus increasing their level of motivation. Organizational culture is a part of what integrates company teams; therefore, employees need the chance to participate in the organization to improve positive motivation. The management must believe that their employees can make decisions and control the situation. Therefore, employees need to understand an organizational culture to contribute to the organization's success.

Motivation Influencers

The two motivational influences are Individual inputs and Job context.

Individuals Input bring individual inputs to the table themselves, such as their work ethic, personal reward system, goals, job knowledge, etc.

Job Context is what the job itself offers to the individual about motivations. These inputs are organizational culture, reward systems, supervisory support, physical environment, etc. Both sets of inputs allow individual skills to be utilized within the job context's limitations to be fulfilled in an employee's motivated behaviors and, ultimately, job performance.

Top Management Improving Performance through Motivation

The employer or top management could offer motivations and job contextual inputs to enhance the performance model. This could improve an individual's motivation and overall organizational performance. Two theories of motivation are Maslow's need hierarchy and McClelland's need theory.

Maslow's notion of a proponent or stair-step hierarchy of five levels of needs has not stood up well under research.

McClelland believes that motivation and performance vary according to the strength of an individual's need for achievement. High achievers prefer moderate risks and situations where they can control their destiny. Top managers should have an increased demand for power coupled with a low need for affiliation with the work and family conflict values model.

Two Approaches Management could use to Enhance Motivation

Mechanistic approach is used to identify the most efficient way to perform a job. Employees are trained and rewarded to achieve their positions accordingly.

Motivational Approaches are techniques such as (job enlargement, job rotation, job enrichment, and job characteristics model) to improve employees' affective and attitudinal reactions and behavioral outcomes.

Intrinsic motivation is driven by the opportunity rewards of a sense of meaningfulness and a sense of choice. The accomplishment rewards a sense of competence and a sense of progress. The purpose of task completion is driven by meaningfulness and progress, whereas feelings of choice and competence revolve around the tasks one performs at work. Managers specifically lead for meaningfulness, choice, competence, and progress by inspiring and modeling, empowering, delegating, supporting, coaching, and rewarding.

Motivation Implications for Management

The perception of fair organizational processes leads to increased affective commitment in employees (Jehanzeb & Mohanty, 2020). Similarly, Morales-Sánchez and Pasamar, 2020, stated that the two types of motivation, extrinsic and intrinsic motivation, contribute to employee commitment. Motivation is triggered by outside factors when an action is taken for the external benefits it can have, such as economic rewards, and generally brings short-term gains (Guillén et al., 2015). Therefore, extrinsic motivation refers to a benefit, utility, or external advantage suitable for practical purposes such as subsistence and physiological needs, security, power, etc. On the other hand, intrinsic motivation refers to commitments acquired because they are inherently agreeable or exciting; that is, they trigger an internal reward. This reward depends on the values and interests of each person; in other words, intrinsic motivations refer to something received internally that causes pleasure or satisfaction. These motivations unfold when agents learn, improve their abilities, and thus acquire competence and satisfaction (Guillén et al., 2015; Morrison & Szumilo, 2019).

1.17 ASSUMPTIONS

The quantitative correlational and regression study used a culture and performance survey to gather data. Participants shared their beliefs and assumptions regarding employee commitment, job satisfaction, and employee retention performance in a merged banking company in the survey. Three assumptions underlying the research study were acknowledged. First, the participants' experience in the study represented the merger experience between two cultures. Unless the participants have had merger experience, the responses to the survey questions may have lacked meaningful substance. Second, the participants were assumed to respond to the survey questions honestly and truthfully. While such honesty cannot be guaranteed, because of the purpose of the study, the participants may have wanted to facilitate the merger process for other companies.

Third, the validity of the survey instrument was suitable to cover facets of organizational cultural traits and organizational performance variables. The assumptions helped accomplish the research objectives by gathering relevant cultural traits and performance information. The need for relevant merger information might have enhanced the leaders' decisions during the pre-merger and post-merger processes. Collecting data from participants who experienced the merger in a Nigerian bank helped to provide accurate information relating to cultural traits and performance variables. The ability of the participants to provide honest responses helped collect unbiased data for statistical analysis.

1.8 SCOPE OF STUDY

The scope of the quantitative correlational and regression study was limited to a merged bank in Abuja, the FCT of Nigeria. The sample was 220 employees drawn from different sample segments within the ten branches and head office of the merged bank in Abuja. The various components of the model were the directors, managers, and employees. The sample employees included both men and women currently working in the merged Nigerian bank in Abuja. The sample was randomized for selection into the three segments. The selection process guarded the design against potential bias from the volunteer participants. Although the research participants consisted of volunteers from the total population and may not represent a true cross-section of the total population, statistical inferences to establish relationships among the volunteer participants were judged unlikely to threaten the results.

1.19 LIMITATIONS

Identifying research limitations helps specify potential weaknesses of a study (Vogt, 2007). Past studies showed that culture is a complex concept to analyze and measure (Schein, 1992). The complexity and nature of culture comprised one of the study's limitations. The quantitative correlational and regression method provided data that helped analyze the relationship between culture and organizational performance. Neither correlation nor regression analyses can be interpreted as establishing cause-and-effect relationships. Correlation indicates the strength of relationships, and regression reveals dependence between variables. Determining the variables' support and the power of the correlation between culture and performance helped to predict and indicate the relationship of the variables for the study.

A limitation also consisted of the attitudes of the participants toward taking surveys. The merged Nigerian bank's directors, managers, and employees represented the research subjects. Because the study was limited to participants who agreed to respond to the survey voluntarily, the survey responses depended on the subjects' willingness to participate. The study's limitations included the economic and political conditions of the country of Nigeria. Disruptions in the economic and political situations of the country or the merged bank itself could affect the results of the study.

1.20 DELIMITATIONS

The presence of delimitations narrows the scope of the research study (Creswell, 2005). The study involved employees of the merged bank in Abuja, the FCT of Nigeria. The merged bank has numerous locations across the country of Nigeria. Due to time constraints, the population for the study was narrowed to all bank employees in one merged bank in Nigeria. The sample was composed of 10 directors, ten managers, and 200 employees. A clear description of the Abuja bank may allow for greater generalization. If the research population was extended to other developing and developed countries in Africa, Europe, and the United States, the research findings could have broader generalizability. Another delimitation to the study was using four independent variables for organizational culture and three dependent variables for organizational performance. The selected independent variables included mission, consistency, involvement, and adaptability, while the dependent variables included employee commitment, job satisfaction, and employee retention. The study did not investigate other aspects of organizational culture and organizational performance, such as human resource culture, recruitment, career management, shareholders return, customers' satisfaction, and quality of products and services that impact organizational performance outcomes.

1.21 SUMMARY

Organizational mergers are increasing due to technology advancement and dynamic environments in most organizations (Sung & Gort, 2006). Organizational culture might relate to the success or failure of merged companies. Mergers that ignore corporate cultures might result in low productivity and high employee turnover (Gordon, 2008). With so many organizations undergoing mergers and a lack of cultural integration, most mergers still fail (Atkinson, 2005). Several studies have explained that unsuccessful integration of organizational cultures in merged organizations contributes to low performance (Terranova, 2007), and bankruptcy (Coy, Thornton, Arndt, Grow, & Park, 2005; Kanter et al., 2004), and high employee turnover (Gordon, 2008). The study focused on analyzing the relationship between organizational culture and performance in a merged bank in Abuja, the FCT of Nigeria. The cultural traits for the survey include mission, consistency, involvement, and adaptability as the independent variables, while employee commitment, job satisfaction, and employee retention represent the performance-dependent variables. The theoretical framework that underscored the present study was founded on transformational leadership theory, equity theory, and Denison's organizational culture model. Chapter 1 explains the reasons why companies enter mergers and acquisitions. Whatever reason a company ascertains to fit its goals is a valid option, but it is best only to choose one strategic rationale for each acquisition. If a company selects multiple rationales simultaneously, the company could risk losing focus. Concentrating on one reason for a merger would keep the company on track to achieve the target goals. Chapter 2 provides a detailed review of the organizational culture, merger, and performance literature. The relationship of a merger on organizations, leadership, and productivity is discussed.

1.22 CHAPTER 1 STUDY QUIZ QUESTIONS

Question 1. Which of the following best defines the meaning of a merger?

A. The complete combination or absorption of one company by another, where the acquiring company stops, and the acquired firm continues to exist as a separate entity.
B. The complete combination or absorption of one company by another, where the acquiring the company maintains its identity and the acquired firm stops existing as a separate entity.
C. The incomplete combination or absorption of one company by another, where the acquiring company maintains its identity and the acquired firm stops existing as a separate entity.
D. None of the above

Question 2. Which of the following is the correct meaning of culture?

A. The patterns and without a characteristic of human behavior.
B. The patterns and characteristics of human performance.
C. The patterns and characteristics of human behavior.
D. The designs and skills of human performance.

Question 3. Culture is one collective term of religion, beliefs, social norms, arts, customs, and _________ that people possess.

A. Habits
B. Problems
C. Issues
D. Challenges

Question 4. ___________is one of the most important concepts within sociology because sociologists recognize that it plays a crucial role in our social lives

A. Performance
B. Social
C. Culture
D. Management

Question 5. Culture is an umbrella term that involves the ______________, community, and norms found in human societies, as well as the knowledge, beliefs, and habits of the people in groups.

A. Social behavior
B. Culture skills
C. Social skills
D. Social activity

Question 6. Humans acquire culture through the learning processes and socialization that come from diverse cultures across societies.

A. True
B. False

Question 7. Which of the following is the correct definition of acquisition?

A. When one company purchases fewer assets of another company's shares without control of that company.
B. When a company does not purchase assets but only the liability of another company.
C. When one company purchases most or calls another company's shares to gain control of that company.
D. None of the above

Question 8. Purchasing more than 50% of a target firm's stock and other assets allows the acquirer to make ____________ about the newly acquired assets without the approval of the company's other shareholders.

A. Promotions
B. Learning
C. Decisions
D. Culture

1.23 CHAPTER 1 STUDY QUIZ SOLUTIONS

1. B
2. C
3. A
4. C
5. A
6. A
7. C
8. C

1.24 CHAPTER 1 EXERCISES

1. Define a merger and acquisition (M&A)?
2. What are the different types of mergers?
3. What are the advantages and disadvantages of mergers?
4. Describe the purpose of a merger and acquisition.
5. How is a merger different from an acquisition?
6. What is the pre-merger and post-merger process?
7. What is a McGregor's Theory X and Theory Y?
8. What is Maslow's Theory of Hierarchical Needs?
9. What is an Equity Theory?
10. What is a Transformational leadership theory?

NOTES

1. Rodriguez, A. (2008). Mergers and acquisitions in the banking industry: The human factor. *Organization Development Journal*, 26(2), 63–73. Retrieved from Business Source Complete database.

2. Becher, D. A., & Campbell, T. L. (2005). Interstate banking deregulation and the changing nature of bank mergers. *Journal of Financial Research*, 28(1), 1–20.

3. Aburime, U., & Uche, C. (2008). Impact of share capitalization on bank profitability in Nigeria. *European Journal of Scientific Research*, 19(3), 438–452. Retrieved from Academic Search Complete database.

4. Ezeoha, A. E. (2005). Increasing incidence of poverty in Nigeria: An impact assessment of the government's economic reform programme. *Journal of Social Development in Africa* (Zimbabwe), 22(2), 112–131.

5. Ezeoha, A. (2007). Structural effects of banking industry consolidation in Nigeria: A review. *Journal of Banking Regulation*, 8(2), 159. Retrieved from ABI/INFORM Global database.

Chapter 2

Review of the Literature

2.2 DOCUMENTATION

The literature search began with a historical review of organizational culture and performance. A search for peer-reviewed sources from ProQuest and EBSCOhost databases was conducted. A context search was limited to mergers and acquisitions, banking, telecommunication, and global mergers. The literature review included 243 (Okoro, 2010).

Table 2.1 shows the 243 sources reviewed and is categorized by topics used to build the research study. Of the 243 total sources used in the report, a total of 207 or 85% were published from 2005 to 2009, while 36 or 15% reflected germinal research (Okoro, 2010). The total individual searches from 2005 to 2009 on various topics yielded the following: organizational culture (56), organizational performance (40), mergers (70), and leadership (41). Germinal searches before 2005 on various topics yielded the following: organizational culture (10), organizational performance (6), mergers (13), and

Table 2.1. Summary of Literature Review by Search Topic

Theoretical concepts and Search topics	*Journals, peer-reviewed articles, and periodicals*	*Books, Internet dissertations, and reports*	*Total*	*Resources before 2005*	*Resources 2005 to 2009*	*Total*
Organizational Culture	57	9	66	10	56	66
Organizational Performance	43	3	46	6	40	46
Mergers	76	7	83	13	70	83
Leadership	44	4	48	7	41	48
Total Literature Reviewed	220	23	243	36	207	243

leadership (7). Figure 2.1 represents the graphical literature map for the study. A literature map helps to display the research literature by topic and enables readers to understand the focus and importance of the study (Creswell, 2005).[1] The nature of the study requires a detailed literature review to reveal any knowledge gap in the research purpose. Chapter 2 was developed around the germinal theories, recent studies, and the purpose statement of the study (Okoro, 2010).

2.3 HISTORICAL PERSPECTIVE OF ORGANIZATIONAL CULTURE

Despite extensive research on organizational culture, researchers have different views on culture definition (Behery & Paton, 2008; Coffey & Tombari, 2005).[2] Several researchers described organizational culture as work values, ideologies, philosophies, and beliefs of formal and informal processes that integrate organizational workers into a coherent whole (Cooke & Rousseau, 1988; Schein, 1992).[3] Organizational culture can be described as shared meaning, way of life, beliefs, symbols, rituals, and myths among people (Balthazard, Cooke, & Potter, 2006; Coffey & Tombari, 2005).[4]

Culture can be seen to focus on the values, assumptions, and beliefs of individuals in groups (Schein, 1992). The shared leadership styles, processes, procedures, customs, and rituals among members in groups make up the organizational culture (Coffey & Tombari, 2005; Schein, 1992). A shared organizational culture influences firms' ability to adapt to change (Xenikou & Simosi, 2006).[5] Organizational culture relates to the ways companies manage their employees while considering why individuals act in a certain way in the work environment (Rosenberg, 2005; Zhang & Tansuhaj, 2007). Similarly, organizational culture can be seen as the structure of organizations that originates from members' assumptions, beliefs, and values (Cooper, Densten, Gray, & Sarros, 2005). Culture can reflect employees' shared beliefs and expectations of how duties can be performed (Cartwright & Cooper, 1993). Schein (1992) stated that organizational culture includes objective and subjective aspects. The objective aspect involves company location, artifacts, and environmental setting. The subjective aspect involves beliefs and shared values within the organization (Schein, 1992).

In the organizational setting, culture can be defined as members' beliefs and expectations (Schein, 1992). Balthazard, Cooke, and Potter (2006) stated that cultural norms influence organizational members' performance. Organizational culture was categorized into three aspects: culture direction, culture intensity, and culture integration (Cooke & Rousseau, 1988). Culture direction indicates the specific styles of thinking, behaving, and feeling adopted by an organization to succeed and realize set goals. Culture intensity suggests how organizational members commit to one particular system over others (Alavi, Kayworth, & Leidner, 2006; Cuong & Swierczek, 2008). Culture integration portrays how organizational divisions share a common culture (Alaranta & Henningsson, 2008; Freeland, 2005; Lai & Lee, 2007). Similarly, Yilmaz and Ergun (2008) recognized four cultural traits: involvement, adaptability, consistency, and mission. Yilmaz and Ergun's study concluded that the four traits of culture exert a positive influence on a firm's performance. Integrating the four culture traits may help organizations attain superior firm performance over an imbalanced combination of the factors (Denison, Haaland, & Goelzer, 2004; Effects of Organizational Culture, 2002; Mitleton-Kelly, 2006; Yilmaz & Ergun, 2008). Most researchers have argued over some organizational cultural elements of definition and measurement (Behery & Paton, 2008). Prior studies agreed that culture contributes to how employees adapt and fit into the organizational structure (Alston & Tippett, 2009).

Organizational culture and organizational performance relationships have attracted several researchers since the early 1980s (Chew & Sharma, 2005; Cooke & Rousseau, 1988; DeHilal, Wetzel, & Ferreira, 2009; Dounis, 2008). The outcome from prior researchers has suggested that organizational culture contributes to the factors that determine organizational performance (Chew & Sharma, 2005; Pike, 2006; Schein, 1992). Similarly, Schein (1992) argued that culture is among the factors that influence work performance in organizations. Jing and Graham's (2008) empirical results reflected that cultural values significantly influence economic development. In a recent study of personnel management and the effects of culture on organizations, Chew and Sharma (2005) concluded that strategic personnel management has a positive relationship with financial performance. The positive relationship between human resource management and performance relates to culture integration and employee commitment to organizational activities (Tyler, Stanley, & Brady, 2006). Chew and Sharman's results reflect that adequate integration of an organization's leadership value profile with strategic human resource management might enhance a high level of financial performance. Sharman's argument was supported by Luna-Arocas and Camps (2008), who explained that human resource culture in organizations positively relates to performance.

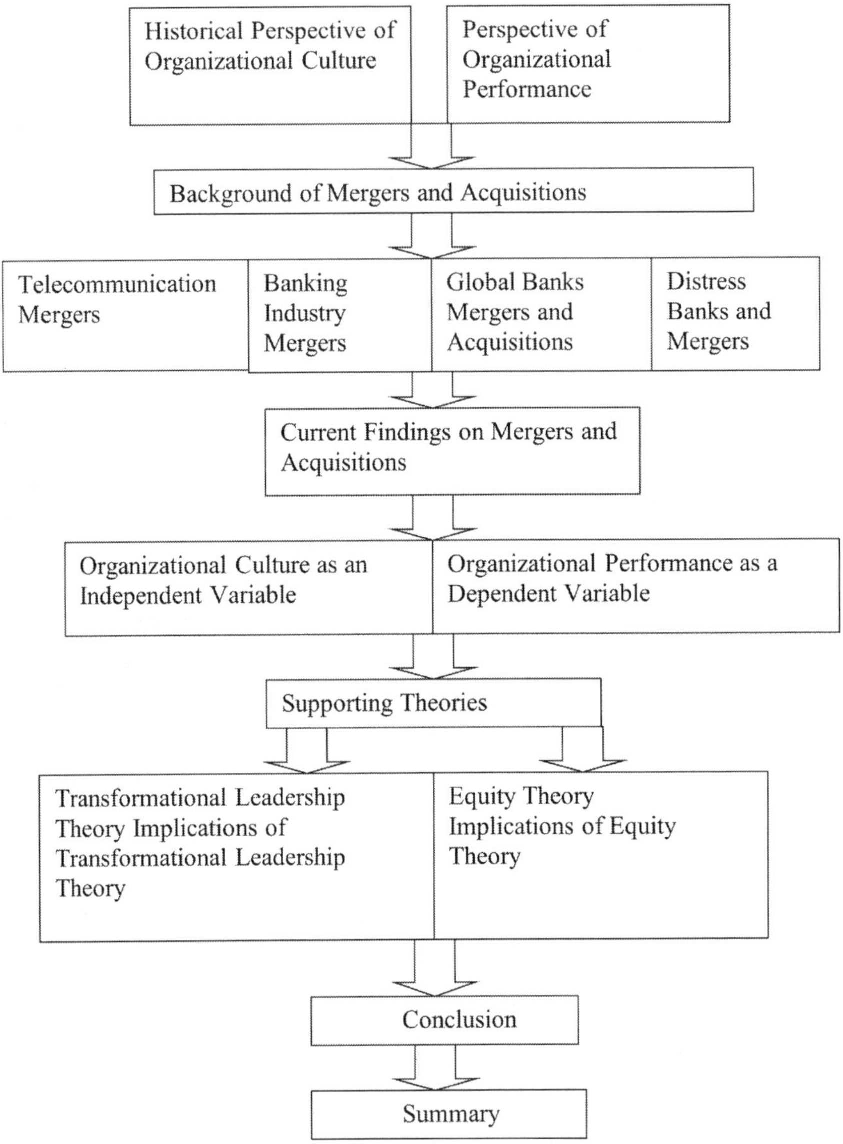

Figure 2.1. Literature Review Map

Figure 2.1 demonstrates the variables of the literature review map while highlighting the historical perspective of organizational culture, organizational performance, and the background of mergers and acquisitions for various industries (Okoro, 2010). The competing values framework (CVF) provides a practical way for managers to understand, measure, and change the organizational culture (Kinicki & Kreitner, 2009). The CVF indicates that organizations vary along two fundamental dimensions or axes: The first dimension is how an organization focuses its attention and efforts on internal dynamics and employees or outward toward its external environment and its customers and shareholders. The second dimension is the organization's preference for flexibility and discretion or control and stability. Integrating these two axes creates four types of organizational cultures, including different core values and criteria for assessing organizational effectiveness: Clan, Adhocracy, Hierarchy, and Market.

2.4 CATEGORIES FOR ASSESSING ORGANIZATIONAL EFFECTIVENESS

The four categories for assessing organizational effectiveness are clan culture, Adhocracy Culture, Market Culture, and Hierarchy Culture.

Clan Culture

The Clan culture has an internal focus and values flexibility rather than stability and control. Clan cultures resemble family-type organizations in which effectiveness is achieved by encouraging collaboration between employees. In addition, clan cultures are very "employee-focused" and strive to instill cohesion through consensus and job satisfaction, and commitment through employee involvement. Clan organizations devote considerable resources to hiring and developing their employees, and they view customers as partners. An example of a strong clan culture organization is Badger Mining Corporation

Adhocracy Culture

Adhocracy culture: a culture that has an external focus and values flexibility. Adhocracy cultures foster the creation of innovative products and services by being adaptable, creative, and fast to respond to changes in the marketplace. Adhocracy cultures do not rely on centralized power and authority relationships. They encourage employees to take risks, think outside the box, and experiment with new ways of getting things done. This culture is well suited for start-up companies, those in industries undergoing constant change, and those in mature industries that need innovation to enhance growth. An example of a strong adhocracy culture organization is Apple, W. L. Gore & Associates, Inc., and Intel.

Market Culture

Market culture has a strong external focus and values stability and control. Market cultures relate to competition and a strong desire to deliver results and accomplish goals. Customers and profits took precedence over employee development and satisfaction and rewarded people who had results. An example of a market culture organization is the Mayo Clinic

Hierarchy Culture

Hierarchy culture has an internal focus and values stability and control over flexibility. Hierarchy cultures have an inner compass, which produces a more formalized and structured work environment and values stability and control over flexibility. Hierarchy cultures are characterized by reliable internal processes, extensive measurement, and the implementation of various control mechanisms, and they are likely to use total quality management (TQM) programs. Effectiveness is likely to be assessed by efficiency, timeliness, and reliability of producing and delivering products and services. An example of a hierarchical culture organization is Exelon and Dell.

2.5 THE AGE OF HUMAN AND SOCIAL CAPITAL

Human capital and social capital have a relationship because human capital represents the workers employed by a company. In contrast, the colonial capital involves the education and training of the workers to increase the social capital in the area. Thus, human capital is the productive potential of knowledge and actions. Positive and negative interactions between business, society, and individuals are vital to good decision-making involving human and social capital. However, social and human capitals are more subjective than other capitals, such as financial, natural, manufactured, and intellectual (Kinicki & Kreitner, 2009). This can make the prioritization, quantification, and potential monetization of social and human capital open to challenges from various stakeholders.

Human Capital—is the knowledge, skills, and attributes of the workforce and others across the value chain that contribute to a successful organization.

Social Capital—is the value added by the organization's products, services, and activities to wider communities. The relationships of individuals and groups of people internally and externally, and between the organization, its value chain, and the diverse communities and locations where it operates. Hence, organizations can integrate human and social capital impacts and dependencies. For example, an organization uses training and skills to conduct its recruitments. Therefore, social capital is the productive potential of strong, trusting, and cooperative relationships.

The Five Human Capital Outcomes

1. Leadership/managerial practices: delivering performance feedback and instilling confidence.
2. Workforce optimization: guiding and sustaining the use of people's talents on the job.
3. Learning capacity: the organization's overall ability to learn and improve.
4. Knowledge accessibility: the ease of sharing ideas and knowledge.
5. Talent engagement: the ability to retain and engage the best talent.

How to Build Human and Social Capital

Social entrepreneurship calls for organizations to achieve two bottom lines; one measures financial performance, and the other is the company's success in meeting social goals. Organizations could find innovative ways to solve society's problems that are not being addressed by the market or the public sector.

2.6 THE ETHNOCENTRIC IN ETHNIC GROUPS

Ethnocentric is overlooking the potential of different ethnic groups as inferior to others. This approach was developed during the two World Wars. The system has not been shed off for decades, even in the aftermath of civil rights movements around the globe. For decades, the Western world has been thought to be superior to other nations. This approach or perception has stalled several development issues in developing countries. Organizations founded in the west tend to employ top managers from their home countries because of the superiority complex. Thanks to globalization, there is a need for cheap labor in Europe, and it is the opposite in Asian and African countries. Cheap delivery is available. The challenge is whether to move the job to the peoplc or people for the job (Leach, 2006). This scenario has led multinational companies to replicate their cultures in the local community worldwide. Toyota Company started as a Japan-based automobile company. Today is the world-leading automobile company with its famous production system that relies on Japanese culture.

Toyota automobile company believes in its Japanese approach to manufacturing. In 1953, the company introduced its methods and traditions in America when General Motors went down. Toyota failed to integrate

Japanese practices and culture into the American workforce. The company had to change its strategy and train employees within their respective countries to achieve profitability and product acceptance into the market. Toyota case study has initiated the establishment of training facilities and exchange programs by all the multinational companies around the globe (Diller, 2010). This attempts to transmit a business culture and perception to all the company branches in different countries.

Ethnocentric can also be expressed in terms of religion. Islam phobia has been on the rise since the invasion of America into Iraq. This has led to mixed reactions within the religious groups in America. In the Muslim world, the opposite is witnessed. This trend led to the 9/11 attack on the American twin towers. Organizations and companies can overcome this practice through cultural integration and adaptability to the workplace's different mindsets. Social cultures are perceptions and beliefs that a specific community believes in. The practice has social merits and demerits. What is right and wrong within society? When rolling business in a new location, organizations need to bear these facts. It is, therefore, of importance to foster cultural beliefs between the company and the local community (Tierney, 2007). A new manager should be conversant with the local language and challenges for the business's success. The language barrier is a significant challenge for several employees in the Diaspora.

Perceptions and Morals

Culture is a trend followed by the community and social organizations. Perceptions and morals impact a community by culture forging an effective practice within the organization. Companies worldwide have set visions and goals in line with the company's cultural practices. An excellent example is that the Coca-Cola bottling company has a well-laid down business structure replicated worldwide. The company operates within a set tradition. Professionals refer to it as organizational culture. The approach has merits and demerits quickly spotted within the corporate management structure. Employees' educational level determines organizational structure. The unavailability of a skilled workforce in a particular region will define organizational culture. The company may opt to ship in employees from different countries with the much-needed skills and culture. Multinational companies are applying this trend in their expansion strategy. In Europe, Toyota, Peugeot, and BMW automobiles have merged to produce cars cheaply and efficiently. The merged companies offer their expertise in the different departments. This helps integrate skills and culture from the other companies and continents.

Politics Influence Culture

Politics influences culture in several ways. The business culture will depend on a country's political undertone. If a country is experiencing a stable political situation, this gives room for developing and nurturing organizational cultural beliefs. If only political stability could be attained worldwide (Gay, 2003). Then all businesses worldwide would have to adopt a single strategy that will later form what is called business culture.

Economic challenges have become more frequent around the world. Organizations have closed doors and restructured their plans to remain aloof during these hard financial times. Cultures formed by the different organizations have been interrupted by this trend to adopt new cultures. New challenges call for new approaches to win the game, which has brought a global financial situation (Siapera, 2010).

Companies around the world need new markets for their products. The result can be achieved through globalization. Companies should open doors in different countries with unique cultures. This will foster cultural exchange and integrate new ideas into the business. In the development of a business cultural idea and perception, all the different cultures and beliefs surrounding the company should be in cooperated to achieve an acceptable culture across all nations of the globe.

2.7 ROGERS LAW OF DIFFUSION OF INNOVATIONS THEORY

Diffusion of Innovations Theory

Communications professor Everett Rogers first explained the Law of Diffusions of Innovation in his 1962 book Diffusions of Innovations. Diffusion is how the innovation of a new product is communicated amongst the participants in a social system or market.

An organization could choose to adopt the laggard category to gain acceptance of a new information system. In this category, the organization has employees' peers demonstrate how the change has helped them and bring pressure to bear from other adopters. The innovatory type might hinder the rollout of a new information system. A successful enterprise IT system needs the top-down imposition of policies, procedures and standards that provides how transactions could be done with the supporting information identified, stored, and shared. As a result, senior management supports the adoption of enterprise IT by threatening penalties for nonconformance.

Rogers Law of Diffusion of Innovation Model

Roger's theory indicated that a company could split the people in any market into five groups based on their mindset. Diffusion of innovations is a theory that explains what rate new ideas and technology spread. Diffusion is a macro process involved in spreading a new product from its source to the users. Adoption is a micro process that focuses on the phases through which users decide when to accept or reject a new product (Idea to Value, 2021).

1. *Innovators*: People who are open to risks and the first to try new ideas. An example is buying a new Apple Watch as a forward thinker. People at this stage make up about 2.5% of the total market.
2. *Early Adopters*: People interested in trying new technologies and establishing their utility in society. An example is opinion leaders in a market, who could influence others. People at this stage make up about 13.5% of the total market.
3. *Early Majority*: People who strive to use innovation within their environment. They wait to see Early Adopters' actions before they are confident enough to try an innovation. People at this stage make up about 34% of the market.
4. *Late Majority*: People who wait until the innovation has been developed before entering the new products in the market. They are more risk-averse than the Early Adopters and Early Majority as they remain for the invention to be proven quality. People in this stage make up about 34% of the market and are more resistant to trying innovations.
5. *The Laggards*: People who act last in the market innovation often refuse to try new technology. They want to remain in their comfort zone and retain what they already have. They are doubtful to adopt an innovation unless they are obliged to. People in this stage make up about 16% of the market. For example, those who still use legacy IT systems based on Windows XP or earlier Windows versions, despite those systems being unsupported.

Consequently, Innovators and Early Adopters make up about 16% of the total market, and together with the Early Majority, makeup about 50% of the market, more open to innovations. The latter Late Majority and Laggards, about 50%, are more resistant. Assessing these stages, the Diffusion of Innovation Model helps pre-merger and post-merger companies to access their people's culture and habits. The wealth of a company does not determine what category they fit into. Some big companies are unwilling to invest in new technologies, and some small startups are laggards in specific processes (Idea to Value, 2021).

2.7 Diversity Climate

Diversity climate refers to organizational members' attitudes and perceptions toward people from cultural groups other than their own. Diversity climate relates to corporate members' attitudes and perceptions toward people from cultural groups other than their own. These attitudes and perceptions are manifested in the practices and behaviors of individuals in the organization. Design a model with methods and procedures for analyzing diversity and implementing a cultural diversity training program. The variety of any organization can affect the way people operate in any business. The company can be affected by its employee's ethnicity, gender, age, and socioeconomics.

Ten Barriers to Successfully Implementing Diversity Initiatives

According to (Kinicki & Kreitner 2009), obstacles and challenges in managing diversity. The text list Ten barriers to successfully implementing diversity initiatives:

1. *Inaccurate stereotypes and prejudice*, Communication between employees from different cultures may encounter unforeseen difficulties and possible communication disturbances due to cultural factors such as problems in Communication due to the denial of cultural differences, cultural patterns of thinking, and ethnocentric arrogance.
2. *Ethnocentrism* is the difference in management styles of employees from different countries. Some people prefer democratic and participative management styles (North America, Northern Europe), and people from eastern and developing countries are more used to the authoritarian, paternalistic methods.
3. *Poor career planning*, Differences in the formulation of problems and making decisions. The current procedures adopted in the company must reflect the values, attitudes, and behaviors that are inherent to employees participating in the process of solving problems. The multi-cultural team can work effectively only with mutual understanding between its members, the essence of collective interaction.
4. *In an unsupportive and hostile working environment* for diverse employees, Potential conflicts can arise due to differences in motivation. The motives of employees are determined mainly by their social situation and marital status. For example, people from developing countries value material needs and the need for security (this relates to the general standard of living and welfare). In contrast, people from many western industrialized countries mainly desire self-development and achieving ambitious goals in life.

5. *Lack of political savvy* on the part of diverse employees
6. *Difficulty in balancing career* and family issues
7. Fears of reverse discrimination
8. *Diversity* is not seen as an organizational priority
9. *The need to revamp the organization's performance* appraisal and reward system
10. *Resistance to change.* Communication between employees from different cultures may encounter unforeseen difficulties and possible communication disturbances due to cultural factors: Differences in socio-cultural competence and personnel development. Socio-cultural managerial competence requires certain flexibility, which is expressed as follows: Acceptance of other cultures, understanding of their cultural interdependence, Openness, and tolerance in the process of cultural Communication, and Ability to change approaches of personnel management due to cultural diversity.

Influencing Ethical Behavior

An organization can influence ethical behavior in employees in several ways. The organization can influence ethical behavior by offering rewards to employees to promote ethical behavior. An organization can also provide its employees with ethical standards to solidify the relations between employees and management. A combination of ethical training programs and self-discipline is also crucial as it gives a basis for making complex decisions in an honest relationship. An organization can also influence ethical behavior by emphasizing the expected behavior.

This will be achieved by closing any gap between actual actions and everyday actions. If employees know the right thing to do, they will strive to do it right. New employees should be taught the present virtuous values in an organization. Managers are required to explain the importance of an organization during the orientation of new employees. This is a powerful way of influencing and promoting ethical behavior because new employees can observe the actions of current employees in an organization.

Essentially, ethics programs are meant to affect how people think about and address ethical issues that arise on the job and Sets of formal and informal standards of conduct that people use to guide their behavior at work. The standards are based on the core values such as honesty, respect, and trust, but they also can be learned directly from the actions of others. For example, what people see their organizational leaders, managers, and coworkers do on the job can influence their views of acceptable or unacceptable behavior.

2.6 Perspective of Organizational Performance

Organizational performance relates to the outcome of culture integration involving effective sets of values, beliefs, and behaviors (Rose, Kumar, Abdullah, & Ling, 2008). Many researchers have argued that culture integration impacts organizational performance (Chow & Liu, 2007; Collins & Smith, 2006; Terranova, 2007; Xenikou & Simosi, 2006). Organizations that effectively manage change and culture integration positively affect organizational performance. The mergers and acquisitions process exposes the new organization to multiple cultural challenges.

Some authors have argued that culture positively links to performance (Cambra-Fierro, Polo-Redondo, & Wilson, 2008; Chen, 2008; Weinzimmer, Franczak, & Michel, 2008). Recent studies noted the importance of culture and performance, whereby culture serves as a variable for research purposes (Chen, 2008; Rose et al., 2008; Weinzimmer et al., 2008; Zhu & Huang, 2007). The research conducted by Rose et al. (2008) discovered that culture positively affects productivity advancement, employees' commitment, and performance. Similarly, Weinzimmer et al. (2008) portrayed that fully integrated organizational culture predicts performance at different levels in their review.

Other factors that affect performance include high operating costs (Paliwal, 2007), the change process (Pollitt, 2007; Risher, 2007), and task implementation (Sull, 2007; Ungan, 2007; Zollo & Meier, 2008). Developing organizational culture enhances the performance outcomes of total quality management (Joiner, 2007). Weinzimmer et al. (2008) recommended future research on integrating organizational behavior and strategy perspectives on culture related to performance. Weinzimmer et al. (2008) suggested that consistent research results on the culture-performance link may help leaders and managers to integrate cultural attributes that influence organizational performance.

Having mentioned the influence of culture on performance, Smith (2008) noted that organizations are successful when they successfully integrate culture into the work environment. Organizations that incorporate culture might enable high financial returns, satisfied employees, and increased organizational performance (Cervantes, 2008; LaHuis & Avis, 2007; Pickett, 2005). Many organizations have linked culture and performance to enhance performance effects (Hennart & Zeng, 2005; Weinzimmer et al., 2008; Yilmaz & Ergun, 2008). Since organizational culture may improve organizational performance, culture might be ineffective in some other aspects of organizational settings (Rose et al., 2008; Schraeder & Simpson, 2006). Researchers undergo organizational culture research assuming that organizational cultures might help improve organizational performance (Peloza & Papania, 2008;

Weinzimmer et al., 2008). Xenikou and Simosi (2006) explained three types of cultural orientations that predict organizational performance effectiveness: humanistic orientation, achievement orientation, and adaptive orientation.

Humanistic Orientation

Humanistic orientation shows the "human relations movement" in the workplace, such as teamwork, self-actualization, empowerment, creative thinking, joint decision making, and social support (Xenikou & Simosi, 2006). Chew and Sharma (2005) explained that strategic human relations management impacts organizations towards employees' commitment and organizational performance. In support of Chew and Sharma (2005), Xenikou and Simosi (2006) stated that organizations that encourage culture integration strive to improve teamwork, coordination, and efficient use of resources to realize high-level organizational performance.

Achievement Orientation

The achievement orientation refers to the assumptions, values, processes, goal setting, and organizational objectives for achieving a high level of performance (Dewhurst, 2009; Xenikou & Simosi, 2006). Organizations that integrate a cultural norm may help achieve efficiency, motivate employees, and provide feedback on employees' performance (Xenikou & Simosi, 2006). The use of input and motivational tools helps to promote individual and group feelings within the work environment.

Adaptive Orientation

Adaptive orientation refers to the relationship that organizations employ during internal and external environmental challenges. Organizations under mergers face a culture-performance link related to contingency factors in a competitive environment (Kotter & Heskett, 1992). Kotter and Heskett suggested that cultural integration might help organizations adapt to external challenges and enhance long-term performance.

Kotter and Heskett (1992) concluded that lower performance in organizations could be attributed to the inability to maintain culture integration within the business environment. Organizational leaders might help to improve organizational performance through cultural adaptation and integration (Shimoni, 2008). The use of capability and incentive systems helps predict knowledge-related performance (Chow & Liu, 2007). Linking the literature review of culture and performance to organizational mergers, the following section focuses on the background of mergers and acquisitions.

2.7 Background of Mergers and Acquisitions

The mergers and acquisitions process enables control and ownership changes within organizational resources (Chen, 2008; Kiymaz & Baker, 2008; Leland, 2007; Luo, 2005; Romeo & Dick, 2005). Organizations expand their product, services, and growth by merging (Sung & Gort, 2006; Vandergriff, 2007). Prior studies showed that about 56% of mergers in the United States fall below expectations (Atkinson, 2005; Dyer et al., 2004; Pultz, 2005).

Analyzing how merger failure impacts organizations' performance contributes to the effect of culture integration during merger transformation (Ness, 2005; Valant, 2008). Mergers and acquisitions increased by 50% from 2004 to $1.2 trillion (Shay, 2006). Shay noted that the increase showed the highest trend since 2000. Global mergers and acquisitions increased to $1.3 trillion in 2006, showing a 40% increase from 2005 (Shay, 2006). In support of Shay, Berman (2006) stated that U.S. merger activity reported $475 billion in May 2006, showing the highest trend since 2001.

Researchers in the 2000s have investigated recent mergers and observed that mergers and acquisitions (M&A) contribute to growth in the global economy (Badrtalei & Bates, 2007; Brahy, 2006; De Mattos, Salciuviene, & Lewis, 2007; Iyer & Miller, 2008; Vaughn, 2008; Vermeulen, 2005). In the study of culture compatibility in banking mergers, De Mattos et al. (2007) reflected those cultural differences contributed to the underperformance of several mergers. De Mattos et al. study indicated a significant lack of research on the implications of cross-cultural compatibility on banks' integration during cross-border M&A.

Contrary to mergers contributing to growth, Ranft and Marsh (2008) suggested that alliances outperform mergers by helping organizations share knowledge and enhance performance. An empirical study conducted by Ranft and Marsh (2008) found that alliances outperform acquisitions in new market transformation because alliances share governance and knowledge without transferring ownership and control. Alliances avoid the substantial implementation costs incurred by ownership transfer involved in the merger process.

To improve merger performance, De Mattos, Salciuviene, and Lewis (2007) suggested two important merger implications during the M&A process. First, organizations should assess intending merger companies' culture before implementing the merger process. The second is that banks should use social controls to manage the integration process to eliminate the cultural impacts between the merger companies. De Mattos et al. (2007) specified that cultural assessment includes the fit between the merging companies, while the social controls include the strategy to coordinate the transition teams of participants from both merging companies during the merger implementation. Similarly, Iyer and Miller (2008) noted that merger strategies need to include factors that motivate participants to implement significant changes in the organizational activities.

The 1960s–'70s mergers were primarily of the conglomerate or vertical type that involved a merger of companies in an unrelated field of products and services (Badrtalei & Bates, 2007; Cartwright & Cooper, 1993). In contrast, during the 1980s the '90s, the wave of mergers was a horizontal type that involved mergers of companies in related fields of product or services (Badrtalei & Bates, 2007; Cartwright & Cooper, 1993; Shahrur, 2005). With the increase in vertical and horizontal mergers, about 55 to 75% of mergers fall below expectations (Kanter et al., 2004).

Some of the failed mergers include Daimler–Benz and Chrysler in 1998 (Vlasic & Stertz, 2000), WorldCom and MCI in 1998 (Fealy & Kompare, 2003; Kanter et al., 2004), and Compaq–DEC and Quaker Oats–Snapple (Fealy & Kompare, 2003). The main reason for the failures of these mergers can be linked to the differences in organizational cultures (Fealy & Kompare, 2003). Brahy (2006) stated that organizations need cultural integration to allow mergers to succeed.

Badrtalei and Bates (2007) explained the effects of culture in the mergers in the auto industry because of their study. The auto industry has a long history of horizontal mergers. Some of the successful mergers in the auto industry are Chrysler–Jeep in 1987, Renault–Nissan in 1999, and Ford–Volvo in 1999 (Badrtalei & Bates, 2007; Feast, 2003). In contrast, the unsuccessful mergers that failed to meet merger expectations in terms of recovering total investment in the auto industry included Ford Motor and Jaguar in 1993, General Motors and Saab in 1992 (Feast, 1998), Volkswagon, Lamborghini, Bentley, and Bugati (Feast, 2003), and Daimler–Chrysler in 1998.

The leading cause of most merger failures has been the tendency of organizations to concentrate only on the "hard" data of financial and economic information while neglecting the integration of organizational cultures, often called "soft" issues (Badrtalei & Bates, 2007; Cartwright & Cooper, 1993). "Soft" issues represent the people in the organization, and "hard" data represent the financial and strategic fit of the merger. The distinction between "hard" data and "soft" issues creates a complex problem in a merged environment. As a result, cultural integration has been separated from strategic fit to identify performance in organizations (Cartwright & Cooper, 1993).

The rapid increase in organizational mergers and resultant failures relate to leaders lacking the strategies to make the merger process succeed. Cultural clash in most merger environments contributes to leaders' challenges (Rosenberg, 2005). Cultural conflict involves the employees' low level of commitment and cooperation (Pooley, 2005), higher turnover rate (Gordon, 2008), reduction in performance (Lytle & Timmerman, 2006), and a drop in shareholder worth (Rosen, 2006).

Several studies argued that culture clash contributed to the failure of many mergers, acquisitions, and joint ventures (Baughn & Finzel, 2009; Elashmawi, 1998; Gebler, 2009). The merger of two companies involves bringing together two different cultures that might create threats to merger implementations. The Booz Allen Hamilton survey (Larsson & Lubatkin, 2001) concluded that cultural integration contributed to the merger success of most organizations, even more than strategic and financial factors.

Researchers continued to argue that post-merger integration affects the success or failure of organizational mergers (Dyer et al., 2004; Epstein, 2004; Hopkins, 2008; Hubert & Van, 2006; Quinlan, 2008). Epstein suggested five factors that might contribute to merger success to provide solutions for merger success. Those five factors include the following: (a) neutral integration strategy, (b) strong culture integration, (c) communication between senior management, employees, and customers, (d) implementation, alignment, and risk management, and (e) employee retention and customer satisfaction. Epstein emphasized that the merger between J. P. Morgan and Chase Manhattan Bank in 2000 was successful due to awareness and implementation of Epstein's five critical factors for post-merger integration. Epstein concluded that lack of cultural integration contributes to the constant failure of most organizational mergers. The following section focuses on reviewing mergers in telecommunication and banking industries as a concentration of the study.

2.8 PRE-MERGER AND ACQUISITION

The pre-merger and acquisition phase, also called the (Pre-M&A) is a process when the integration transaction is conceived and negotiated by the top-level executives of an organization. The shareholders and regulators shall legally approve the merger transaction during this phase. Thus, mergers and acquisitions bring two or more companies together to maximize synergies to ensure that the arrangement works as expected in terms of value, culture, and mission accomplishment. The process of pre-merger involves five categories:

1. Vision integration
2. Strategy integration
3. Planning integration
4. Pre-merger integration
5. Pre-merger deliverables

Vision Integration

The vision integration is integrating the two companies in an agreed time frame to enable the acquirer company to realize targeted revenue and cost synergies quickly.

Integration Strategy

The integration strategy is the process that allows the formation of the merger board and steering committee to manage and implement multiple concurrent integration work such as the following:

- Achieving interaction targets through exemplary implementation and fitted financial control
- Effective and consistent communication
- Issue escalation and resolution
- Continuing business operations without disruption
- Progress reporting to all stakeholders
- Integration Planning

Planning Integration

The planning integration is the process of drafting activities between the signing and closing of the merger. The draft is usually aimed at planning the first 100 days of the post-close for each workstream. The plan identifies post-signing work that can start early at pre-close.

Pre-Merger Integration

The pre-merger integration is the process of identifying the comprehensive list of projects within each work activity. The process helps assess internal and external staffing requirements, establish a calendar by functional area, specify the tasks that will be done pre-close, and kick off each activity or task.

Pre-Merger Deliverables

The pre-merger deliverables involve the daily transition updates and issue escalation process. The process helps to identify sub-projects within each task, identify issues and risks, approach and engage the appropriate resources

2.9 POST-MERGER INTEGRATION

The four types of post-merger integration are absorption merger, symbiosis merger, preservation merger, and holding. Each type of post-merger needs requires an adequate process to attain the set goals. Post-merger is unifying two companies, their assets, people, tasks, and resources to develop more valuable towards realizing efficiencies and synergies, DealRoom (n.d). Figure 2.2 portrays the need for firms to adopt the six steps to post-merger integration which include organizational processes, purchasing, production, marketing, supply chain management, and HR culture. According to a McKinsey study, mergers, and acquisitions challenges cause deals to fail and result in the inability to extract true value from deals (Doherty, Engert, and West, 2016).

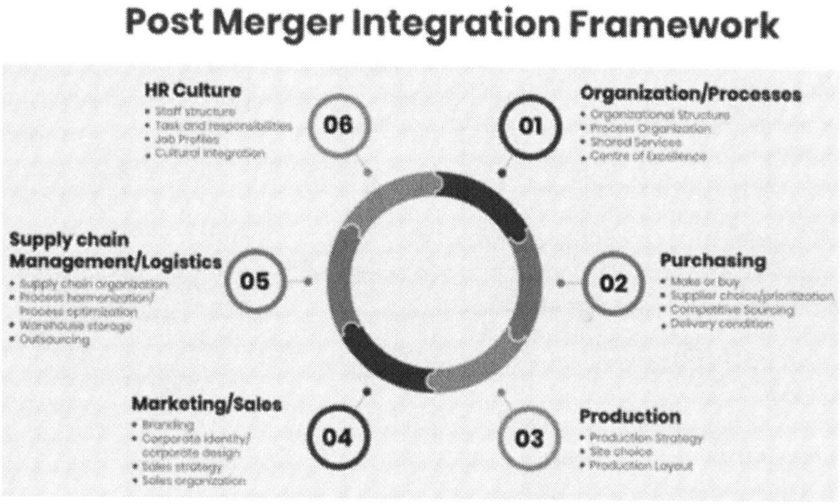

Figure 2.2. Post-Merger Integration Framework

Types of Post-Merger and Acquisition Integration

There are four types of post-merger and acquisition integration.

Absorption Merger—is when the acquiring company completely absorbs the target company, including all processes, organizations, and procedures.

Symbiosis Merger—occurs in some regions of the merger process to help meet the goals of the merger or acquisition.

Preservation Merger—is when the target company is mainly kept at self-governing of the merger company, and some integration may occur with financial information.

Holding—is when the acquiring company holds ownership of the target company, but they do not integrate.

Post-Merger Checklist

The post-merger checklist includes the task of helping stabilize the merger process. The process consists of hiring processes for short- and long-term needs, redundancies, turnover, employee retention, information technology integration, systems merging, migrations, tracking employee performance, and other tasks.

Post-Merger Questionnaire

The post-merger questionnaire helps identify the needy areas and the merger performance status. The post-merger integration questionnaire allows companies to understand and align goals. The post-merger integration plan includes the followings:

Hiring Process

The hiring process could be for short-term needs or long-term needs. The hiring also includes reviewing the benefits and compensation of all employees in the merged organization.

Overlap and Redundancies

The overlap and redundancies are cleaned up to reduce waste and be more efficient in daily activities. The process involves securing top employees, layoffs, and severance forms.

Technology Integration

Technology integration helps to reorganize the business processes. This includes new organizational charts, customer relations management CRM, enterprise tools, and merging the entire systems.

Employee Performance

The post-merger integration process includes the training plans, employee review documents, and human resources management systems.

The Importance of Post-Merger Integration for Businesses

The complexity of post-merger centers on the various integration of each element from merging companies which contribute to the success of M&A. The reasons why post-merger is a critical factor to merger success include the following:

Relationship Between Business and Technology

Digital assets are the pillar for developing, maintaining, and monetizing customer relationships. It provides the opportunity to automate operations and processes, save costs and reduce overhead expenses.

Post-Merger Allows Employees to Succeed in Their Roles

While developing value for the organization. The digital age contributes to the driving forces behind growth activity in several businesses. In the past, companies entered mergers to realize economies of scale, increase customer base, and negotiate power. These days, companies enter mergers to expand the relationship between business and technology. According to Bain & Company's Corporate M&A Report 2020, companies are shifting toward scope deals. The goal of a scope deal is to extend business capabilities and modernize operating models to achieve new revenue streams through innovation. Approximately 60% of all 2019 mergers and acquisitions were classified as scope deals instead of just 41% in 2015. Among technology companies, that number increased to 82%. With enterprises shifting operations to bloom in a digital world, their integrations and technology assets are vital components during the merger. Without the proper stakeholders in place and the correct tools to support their efforts, complementing the information technology atmospheres of separate entities is bound to fail.

2.10 TELECOMMUNICATION INDUSTRY MERGERS

Telecommunication mergers have increased with the expectation of diversifying products and services and maintaining competitive advantage (Kanter et al., 2004). Janjua, Noor, and Khan (2008) and Kanter et al. (2004) emphasized that the Telecommunication Act of 1996 enabled long-distance telecommunications providers such as Label Distribution Protocol (LDPs) to compete in the service market with the local exchange carriers (LECs). The LDPs automatically generates and exchanges labels between routers. Each router locally generates labels for its prefixes and will then advertise the label values to its neighbors. LDPs include AT&T, WorldCom, and Sprint and the LECs include Qwest Communications, SBC Communications, and General Telephone Electric (GTE). The increase in telecommunications market competition gave rise to advancements in technology through digital technologies, new fiber optics, and 3G protocols (McNurlin & Sprague, 2006). While the competition rate increased, companies were undergoing M&A to sustain the market challenges. Some of the market challenges include increased customer base, product diversification, and quality services in the local and global market (Anderson & Billou, 2007; Coy, Thornton, Arndt, Grow, & Park, 2005; Kanter et al., 2004). In 1996, telecommunication mergers totaled $77 billion in value (Kanter et al., 2004). Some telecommunication mergers failed to meet target expectations, such as maintaining a competitive advantage (Kanter et al., 2004). The WorldCom and MCI merger in 1998 failed due to the loss of key executives and unsuccessful culture integration (Kanter et al., 2004). The merger failure pushed WorldCom–MCI to declare bankruptcy in 2002 (Coy et al., 2005; Kanter et al., 2004).

Despite the WorldCom–MCI merger failure, the rate of telecommunications mergers in the 2000s increased. In 2004, Cingular Wireless acquired AT&T Wireless Communications (Coy et al., 2005), Sprint acquired Nextel in 2005, SBC Communications and AT&T merged in 2005, and Verizon and MCI merged in 2005 as well (Pultz, 2005). With the wave in telecommunications mergers, Pultz (2005) stated that 2005 represented a pivotal year of M&A activity in the telephone industry in the United States. In 2007, AT&T Wireless and Cingular entered another merger with the main focus of acquiring more subscribers than other competitors (Duffy, 2007). Pultz (2005) noted that the most crucial mergers and acquisitions events in the 2000s might profoundly affect the entire market structure by 2010. Table 2.2 shows the most prominent mergers in the telecommunication industry in the United States for the past ten years, as listed by Duffy.

Table 2.2. The 10 Largest U.S. Telecom Carrier Mergers and Acquisitions

No.	*Telecommunication Carrier*	*Value*	*Year*
1	AT&T/BellSouth	$86 billion	2007
2	SBC/Ameritech	$56 billion	1999
3	Bell Atlantic/GTE	$53 billion	2000
4	AT&T Wireless/Cingular	$41 billion	2004
5	Sprint/Nextel	$35 billion	2005
6	Qwest/US West	$35 billion	2000
7	WorldCom/MCI	$30 billion	1998
8	Alltel/private equity	$27.5 billion	2007
9	SBC/Pacific Telesis	$16.5 billion	1997
10	SBC/AT&T	SBC/AT&T	2005

2.11 Banking Industry Mergers

The Riegle--Neal Act of 1994 contributed to the dynamic change in the banking industry due to the removal of barriers to interstate banking (Becher & Campbell, 2005; Rodriguez, 2008). The Riegle--Neal Act of 1994 is an American banking law that initiated a significant transformation in the U.S. banking system. The Act gave the banks the flexibility to operate interstate branches compared to a prior operation that was limited and resulted in smaller banks across the nation (Rodriguez, 2008). With the Act of 1994, the small banks of the American banking system transformed into larger banks through mergers and acquisitions. The enactment of the Riegle–Neal Act created the expansion of the American banking system into bigger banks that can operate interstate and globally.

In the 1990s, the merger waves in the banking industry condensed the number of U.S. bank-holding companies (Rodriguez, 2008). The removal of restrictions on interstate banking enabled many banks to merge with other banks within the United States (Becher & Campbell, 2005). The merger process helped reduce inter-state banking operating costs while increasing diverse workforce challenges. Rodriguez (2008) examined the mergers and acquisitions in the banking industry with a focus on the human factors before the merger was completed. Mergers in banks cause employees to display behaviors, hopes, beliefs, and expectations from the merger transition.

The constant wave of mergers between banks creates new opportunities for future profits and market growth (Azofra, Olalla, & Olmo, 2008; Hagendorff, Collins, & Keasey, 2007). The possibilities for new growth involve national banks merging and acquiring smaller banks to maintain a competitive advantage and gain market share. With the rate of merger transactions increasing, less attention is paid to the employees of the target bank to be acquired (Rodriguez, 2008). The non-inclusion of human factors during the merger contributes to most merger failures (Antila & Kakkonen, 2008; Rodriguez, 2008). Most of the unsuccessful mergers resulted in an initial plan lacking strategies to communicate the change objectives to the target company's employees. The most successful mergers incorporated human factors into the system and addressed problems as they arose (Antila & Kakkonen, 2008). An analysis of merger failure demonstrated that employees' key issues, such as benefits, salaries, and pensions, were not addressed (p. 207).

Appelbaum, Gandell, Yortis, Proper, and Jobin (2000) stated that good communication contributes to merger success in their study of mergers and acquisitions. Sharing information and communicating with employees significantly influences the merger process. The influences involve the integration of new culture, change approach, and expectations of the employees (Appelbaum, Gandell, et al., 2000, p. 649). The lack of communication and employee-employee relationship encourage rumors within the organization, thus affecting the credibility of top management (p. 650). Effective communication from the top management is a vital factor in keeping employees informed of the merger process.

Appelbaum, Gandell, et al. (2000) stated five common reactions employees display during pre-merger and post-merger. These shared reactions included (a) loss of identity, (b) lack of information and anxiety, (c) obsession with survival, (d) lost talent, and (e) family repercussions (p. 675). The employees might perceive layoffs as a byproduct of the merger process. Leaders need to consider employees' situation because unsecured employees might not cope with the changes, thus impacting the merger process and organizational performance.

Allred, Boal, and Holstein (2005) stated that most merged organizations face challenges and link their failure to economic issues. The cause of most merger failures relates to lack of fit (Allred et al., 2005). The lack of fit requires that organizations evaluate their cultural fit before merging with another firm. Cartwright and Cooper (1993) concluded that the success or failure of any merger relates to the ways organizational cultures are integrated. Many cultural differences tend to create more merger problems, while fewer cultural differences help mergers succeed (Cartwright & Cooper, 1993).

Cultural differences arise when employers and employees have different perspectives on the organization's merger intent. Cartwright and Cooper recommended that merged organizations identify business philosophies and leadership styles to fit the merged company cultures (p. 76). Most organizational mergers create different synergies that require different strategies to achieve success (p. 79). The review of the banking industry mergers shows that apart from economic issues, organizations should integrate human factors into merger strategies.

2.12 GLOBAL BANK MERGERS AND ACQUISITIONS TRENDS

The trend in global bank mergers and acquisitions has been on the increase. Among the countries that experienced a high wave of bank mergers include U.S. banks (Rodriguez, 2008), German banks (Koetter, 2008), Taiwan (Lin, 2005), Austrian banks (Herbst, 2008), Malaysian banks (Radam, Baharom, Dayang-Affizzah, & Ismail, 2009), Nigerian banks (Aburime & Uche, 2008), and Indian banks (Jayadev & Sensarma, 2007). German bank mergers and acquisitions have increased since the early 1990s (Koetter, 2008). Germany's number of banking institutions has declined by 35% since 1997 (CEPR, 2005). The decline in the number of banks relates to the consolidation and

M&A among banks rather than to bank failures (Porath, 2006). The success of the merged German banks remains a matter of debate among the financial institutions. Koetter (2008) identified two criteria that might help achieve merger success. The requirements included, first, that the merged banks should display efficiency levels above the non-merged banks and, second, that the merged banks should show efficiency changes between merged banks and non-merged banks.

Lin (2005) studied the effect of bank mergers on efficiency in Taiwan. The study used data from 46 commercial banks in Taiwan from 1997 to 1999. Lin concluded that integrating different cultures during a merger might help to reduce the bank's efficiency cost. Bank mergers that incorporate different cultures might help to improve innovations from legacy practices. A merger between homogeneous banks might revert to old cultures, delaying improvement (Lin, 2005). Lin stated that small banks in Taiwan would benefit from the merger process and thus improve in performance from mixing with experienced banks. In 2007, Austria experienced higher merger waves than in the last 20 years (Herbst, 2008). Foreign financial investors penetrated the Austrian market and increased the merger opportunities. Among the closed merger, deals in the US private Cerberus Capital of Austria's fourth-largest bank BAWAG/PSK for €3.2 billion in 2007, Rasperia/STRABAG for €1.3 billion, BayernLB/Hypo Alpe Adria Group for €1.6 billion, and France Telecom/Mideuropa for €1.4 billion (Herbst, 2008). As most merger processes relate to combining two or more companies to strengthen market positions to boost productivity and market share, Malaysian banks' mergers differed (Radam et al., 2009).

The bank mergers in Malaysia were necessitated by a mandatory instruction from the central bank, known as Bank Negara Malaysia (BNM). The process of business globalization contributes to the banking industries facing a dynamic and competitive operating environment. Malaysia's banking institutions were encouraged to merge to enhance operational efficiency and innovation in the financial sector (Radam et al., 2009). The Malaysia consolidation program in 2000 involved the merger of 58 banks into ten anchor banking groups, comprising commercial, financial, and merchant bank groups (Radam et al., 2009). Similarly, the Nigerian banks were mandated by the Central Bank of Nigeria (CBN) to perform bank consolidation and mergers to meet the minimum required share capital (Aburime & Uche, 2008). The Governor of CBN, Professor Charles Soludo, announced in 2004 that the banking sector needed reform to meet the increased minimum share capital of N25 billion which is approximately US$195 million. The mandatory requirement was established to eliminate the distress in the existing Nigerian banks.

Aburime and Uche (2008) examined the impact of share capitalization on bank profitability in Nigeria. Data analysis for the study used 98 banks from 1989 to 2004. The result of the study found a significant effect of share capitalization on Nigerian banks' profitability from 1989 to 1991. From 1997 to 2004, there was no significant effect on share capitalization on bank profitability. The no significant impact indicates that the new minimum share capital of N25 billion was inappropriate in improving bank productivity and eliminating distressed banks in Nigeria (Aburime & Uche, 2008). Despite the monetary authorities' efforts to regulate the banking industry through mandatory consolidation and mergers, most Nigerian banks are still in distress (Ezeoha, 2005, 2007; Toby, 2006). The distressed position in which the banks find themselves relates to the following challenges: increased regulatory constraints, slow economic growth, and excessive government intervention. Toby (2006) stated other distressed banks' problems include default loans, poor management, maturity mismatches, fraud and conflict of interest, insider abuses, political instability, and corruption. Ezeoha (2007) concluded that Nigeria's bank consolidation and mergers lacked empirical backing. Ezeoha (2007) accepted some positive effects of bank consolidation but argued that such benefits might not apply to third-world countries like Nigeria. Ezeoha (2007) further stated that Nigeria needed to address other background economic problems to help meet consolidation problems. These background problems relate to corporate cultures, information technology in the merged banks, employee commitment, deplorable infrastructure, and rebuilding public trust in the country (Ogba, 2008).

The mandatory consolidation and mergers in Malaysian and Nigerian banks relate to forced mergers rather than market-driven mergers. Mann and Kohli (2008, 2009) analyzed the synergistic gains from forced bank mergers and market-driven mergers. Mann and Kohli (2008) stated that market reaction to forced mergers is adverse, while it remains favorable for market-driven mergers. Like market reaction, forced mergers have less value to organizational profitability in merged banks (Mann & Kohil, 2008, 2009). The market drives mergers' help to provide a competitive advantage with long-term profitability in merged banks. Jayadev and Sensarma (2007) studied the banking industry in India about transformation and consolidation since the adoption of liberalization, privatization, and globalization in 1991. With the dynamic technological changes and low performance of the Indian banks, Narsimaham Committee-II recommended mergers and acquisitions to strengthen the banks (Jayadev & Sensarma, 2007). The main objective of bank mergers in India relates to economies of scale, diversification, and global penetration.

Jayadev and Sensarma (2007) concluded that forced mergers do not add value to the merged banks concerning shareholders' wealth and financial performance as expected by the market. The consolidation in the Indian banks occurred through forced mergers that focused on global competition and economies of scale and scope. Jayadev and Sensarma (2007) suggested that the government encourage banks to initiate mergers by themselves instead of forcing mergers on banks. The ability of banks to create mergers may enable expected synergies to allow merging organizations to derive expected benefits (Jayadev & Sensarma, 2007).

2.13 *MERGER AND ACQUISITION DEALS WORLDWIDE (2015–2021)*

The number of mergers and acquisitions has been consistent with about 50,000 global mergers per year between 2015 and 2019, but COVID-19 contributed to the significant downturn in 2020 (see Figure 2.3). According to a report by Accenture on the pandemic's impact on the M&A market, the count of mergers decreased by 12% and 3%, respectively, and merger values have reduced by 47%. The scale of the COVID-19 crisis is unmatched, triggering global responses from organizations and governments towards quick resets of the equity markets.

The drop in 2021 is consistent with another economic downtown, where the decline in merger value of about 50%. Liquidity is stood at a premium, valuations fluctuate, and credit tightens. However, the decrease is mostly in more extensive mergers, whereas smaller mergers continue as businesses drop assets and distressed businesses seek M&A as answers to their challenges.

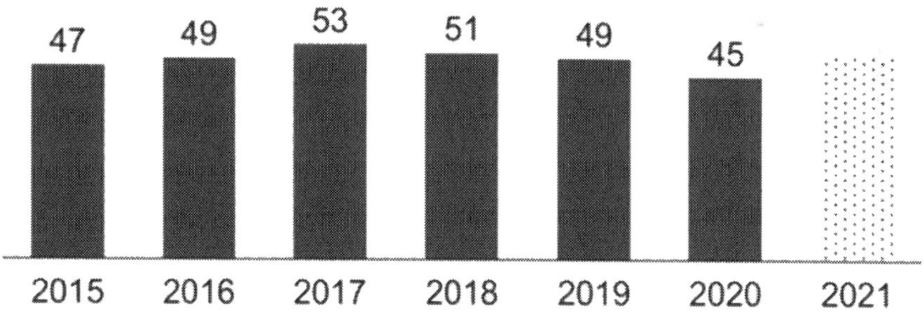

Figure 2.3. Number of M&A Deals Worldwide (2015–2021)
Source: Institute of Mergers, Acquisitions, and Alliances (IMAA)

2.14 DISTRESSED BANKS AND MERGERS

Koetter (2008) explained that a distressed bank should not be the acquirer in the merger process but rather should be the merger target because bank mergers with distressed banks as the acquirers have less chance of success

(Koetter, 2008). When the distressed bank is the acquirer, the merger might face more challenges to achieving merger success (Koetter, 2008). The German savings and cooperative bank merger assessment revealed that geographical location and distressed banks' involvement might predict the merger's success or failure. In contrast, mergers with distressed banks as the targets might benefit in the short run. Mergers may not disrupt a country's financial system while trying to eliminate the availability of distressed banks. Carbonara and Caiazza (2008) studied cross-border mergers and acquisitions between Italian and East European banks. The study evaluated the factors that can contribute to cross-border merger operations' success. Most cross-border mergers often fail due to heterogeneous environments with different legal and cultural-related issues (Carbonara & Caiazza, 2008).

The cultural issues can be addressed by integrating the organizational structure, values, leadership styles, and information flow into the merger strategies. Carbonara and Caiazza (2008) suggested three stages to address the cultural issues: the first is to identify the gaps in the perception of organizational vision, values, structure, management practices, and behaviors. The second is to bridge the holes in the cultural process. The third is to incorporate the findings into a plan, communicate, and implement involving employees in shared values, expectations, and performance.

2.15 GAPS IN LITERATURE

A review of the literature from 1959 to 2009 did not reveal any gap in the literature on the relationship between organizational culture and performance in merged organizations. A review of the germinal literature suggested that possible cultural differences arise when employers and employees have different perspectives on the intent of the organization's merger. From the germinal studies, the belief emerged that potential relationships exist between employee retention status and perceived job satisfaction. Germinal literature portrayed that top-level management pays less attention to the issue of culture during the merger and acquisition process. Germinal research supports those possible relationships in organizational cultural traits of mission, consistency, involvement, and adaptability and organizational financial performance such as sales increase, assets, and quality of products and services. The objective of the current research study was to determine the level of the relationship between the organizational cultural traits (mission, consistency, involvement, and adaptability) and performance (employee commitment, job satisfaction, and employee retention). The present study, which occurred in a merged Nigerian bank within a developing country, was unique because of the focus on cultural traits' relationship to organizational performance rather than financial performance.

2.16 CURRENT LITERATURE ON MERGERS AND ACQUISITIONS

Mergers and acquisitions are ongoing processes in most organizations. Researchers have conducted studies on mergers in several industries such as the auto industry (Badrtalei & Bates, 2007) and the truck industry (Reiskin, 2006). Studies have also been conducted on mergers in the high tech industry (Network World, 2008), accounting firms (Valant, 2008), and the telecommunication industry (Sidener & Kinsman, 2008). Other studies have focused on the banking industry (De Mattos, Salciuviene, & Lewis, 2007), laboratory firms (Weber & Camerer, 2003), private sectors (Field & Peck, 2003), and professional industries (Dunham & Davis, 2008). Finally, studies have focused on operating companies (Sung & Gort, 2006) and global mergers (Elashmawi, 1998; Shay, 2006). The increase in the merger process has generated several challenges to making mergers a success and meeting target expectations. For instance, the auto industry has experienced mergers that meet expectations and mergers that failed (Badrtalei & Bates, 2007). The same merger implication applies to other sectors trying to exceed expectations in merger performance.

Despite the failure rate in prior mergers, leaders in the auto industry still lack the strategy to sustain new and current mergers (Badrtalei & Bates, 2007; Rhodes-Kropf, Robinson, & Viswanathan, 2005). The most cited factors contributing to merger failures relate to organizational culture, nationality, personalities, and technological systems (Feast, 2003). Having mentioned several factors that contribute to a merger failure, the study focused on the relationship between organizational culture and performance in a merged Nigerian bank. While the rate of M&A keeps growing, several researchers identified the two types of mergers as vertical and horizontal (Badrtalei & Bates, 2007; Brouwer, 2008; Sung & Gort, 2006; Vlasic & Stertz, 2000). One of the specific examples of a horizontal merger in the auto industry that failed was the $36 billion mergers of Daimler–Chrysler in 1998 (Mateja, 2001). The Daimler and Chrysler companies had high-performance rates in terms of shareholder value before entering a merger. Before the merger, Chrysler's stock was at $84 dollars per share. After the merger, the stock value experienced a continuous drop in price to $37.75 in 2000.

The decrease in the financial performance of the Daimler–Chrysler company initiated the shutdown of six auto plants and employee lay-offs in the United States (Mateja, 2001). Vlasic and Stertz (2000) described the merger of Daimler–Chrysler as the horizontal "merger of equals" with higher expectations for growth in the auto industry. The result of the merger was the opposite of the expectations, thus leading to the retiring of top American executives, a lay-off of employees, and voluntary resignations (Vlasic & Stertz, 2000). The decrease in Daimler–Chrysler profitability and drop in stock price was caused by three factors (Feast, 2003). The first factors were the external factors relating to the competitive supply of new models by other auto manufacturers. The second factors were the internal factors relating to leaders' decisions governing the new organization. The third factor was the cultural barrier as the biggest uncertainty that caused the merger company operations to be inefficient (Feast, 2003).

Sung and Gort (2006) studied the effects of the horizontal merger on performance in the operating companies and concluded that such mergers failed to meet expectations. The study compared a merged company's performance with that of non-merged companies as the control group. Sung and Gort (2006) concluded that merged operating companies outperformed non-merged companies only in the short run. The short-run benefits decreased as the post-merger time interval lengthened. Comparing total factor productivity between merged and non-merged companies showed no significant increase. The merged operating companies increased total cost, reduced economies of scale, decreased productivity, and reduced shareholder worth in the long run.

Like Feast's (2003) culture barrier on merger performance, Brahy (2006) noted that most merger failures could be attributed to the problem of cultural integration. The increase in market globalization enables growth in international alliances that face cultural conflicts (Allert & Innes-Brown, 2005; Brahy, 2006; Brock, 2005). Brahy concluded that culture integration directly relates to international mergers' business performance. Rodriguez (2005) noted that organizations should include cultural integration into process compatibility during the merger to encourage success. Compatible process and culture integration play significant roles in organizational success and employees' commitment (Garver, 2006). Weber and Camerer (2003) researched merger failure in two laboratory firms due to conflicting organizational cultures. Weber and Camerer (2003) concluded that the performance of two merging firms decreases due to conflicting cultures. The inability of merging firms to integrate organizational cultures increases the possibility of merger failure. Weber and Camerer (2003) further maintained that firms still enter mergers because the potential of cultural conflicts and merger failures are underestimated. Weber and Camerer's (2003) experiments supported the hypothesis that cultural differences in organizations lead to a constant reduction in performance. Cultural differences and high turnover rates after mergers contribute to increased cultural conflicts and employees' discontent (Weber & Camerer, 2003). In an attempt to enhance merger performance,

Badrtalei and Bates (2007) suggested eight factors that might help achieve merger success in organizations.

The eight factors, according to Badrtalei and Bates (2007), that might help mergers to succeed include (a) no partnership of equals, (b) avoiding arrogance, (c) inevitable change, (d) culture, (e) communications, and (f) viewing employees as assets of organizations, (g) employees' involvement, and (h) timing. Ficery, Herd, and Pursche's (2007) study identified six most common mistakes that might cause mergers to fail. Among the six factors are the following: (a) broad or narrow synergies, (b) wrong opportunity timing, (c) insufficient incentives, (d) lack of talented employees, (e) culture mismatch, and (f) wrong process. Dunham and Davis (2008) researched the significant trends in professional mergers and acquisitions literature published from 1996 through 2003. The merger rate in the banking and telecommunication industries has increased since the 1990s (Baranes & Flochel, 2008; Kanter et al., 2004; Michalakelis, Dede, Varoutas, & Sphicopoulos, 2008; Valant, 2008).

Researchers noted that technology is one of the factors affecting merger policies and procedures. Since cultural conflict affects merger firms, other factors contributing to merger performance include advancements in technology. Advances in technology enable merger participants to conduct business via automated systems, networking, and the Internet. Technological advancements allow organizations to streamline their values and processes during M&As (Dunham & Davis, 2008). As the merger rate of organizations continues to rise, the changes in technology to improve the current work process becomes more complex. The advancements in technology create new responsibilities, values, and techniques that challenge merger performances (Dunham & Davis, 2008). These values relate to organizational culture, which was the study's primary purpose: to identify the relationship between organizational culture and performance. Researchers have continuously argued that organizational culture within the banking and telecommunication industries has focused mainly on product diversification, growth, and market competition (Baranes & Flochel, 2008; Michalakelis et al., 2008; Sung & Gort, 2006; Valant, 2008). Even though 56% of mergers in the United States are falling below expectations, merger rates are still increasing (Atkinson, 2005; Dyer et al., 2004; Pultz, 2005). Table 2.3 displays the technology industry's most significant mergers and acquisitions in 2008 as listed by Network World (2008). The continuous increase in the number of mergers in the technical sectors supports the need to identify ways to meet expectations and achieve merger success. The most significant number of M&As in 2008 amounted to $65 billion. These mergers involved information technology service companies specializing in networking, hardware, wireless technology, and security services (Network World, 2008).

Some of the technology industry mergers listed in Table 2.3 include the Verizon Wireless–Alltel merger in 2008. This merger increased the number of subscribers to 80 million to overtake AT&T with a current subscriber count of 71 million (Network World, 2008). The Oracle–BEA merger in 2008 focused on being the strategic software vendor of choice and leader in the competitive middleware market, as noted by Oracle CEO Larry Ellison during a conference call with investors (Smith, 2008). BEA Systems, Inc. was a company that specialized in enterprise infrastructure software products which was wholly acquired by Oracle Corporation on April 29, 2008. BEA began as a software company, founded in 1995 and headquartered in San Jose, California. It grew to have 78 offices worldwide at the time of its acquisition by Oracle. The Hewlett-Packard (HPQ) and Electronic Data Systems (EDS) merger called HP–EDS in 2008 was to help HP triple the size of its services and gain a better competitive advantage over IBM (Network World, 2008). HP, the world's largest technology company, provides printing and personal computing products and IT services, software and solutions that simplify the technology experience for consumers and businesses. HP completed its acquisition of EDS on Aug. 26, 2008.

CenturyTel, an Internet Service provider and a local exchange carrier, merged with Embarq, resulting in increasing the number of their access lines to 8 million broadband subscribers from 2 million, increasing the number of video subscribers to 400 thousand, and expanding coverage from 25 to 33 states (Network World, 2008). Brocade Communications Systems (BRCD), a network equipment maker, and Foundry Networks (FDRY), an Ethernet technology company, merged in 2008 to form Brocade–Foundry. The merger

Table 2.3. The 15 Tech Industry's Largest Mergers and Acquisitions in 2008

Tech Industry	***Value***	***Year***
Verizon Wireless–Alltel	$28.1 billion	2008
HP–EDS	$13.9 billion	2008
Oracle–BEA	$8.5 billion	2008
CenturyTel–Embarq	$5.8 billion	2008
Brocade–Foundry	$2.6 billion	2008
Microsoft–Fast Search and Transfer	$1.2 billion	2008
Sun–MySQL	$1 billion	2008
AT&T–Centennial Communications	$944 million	2008
BMC Software–BladeLogic	$800 million	2008
Symantec–MessageLabs	$695 million	2008
Gores/Siemens–Enterasys	$550 million	2008
McAfee–Secure Computing	$465 million	2008
HP–LeftHand Networks	$360 million	2008
Sophos–Utimaco	$314 million	2008
Ciena–WorldWide Packets	$290 million	2008

increased revenue growth and offered a lower price point to customers (Network World, 2008). In addition to investigating the high rate of increase in high tech industries mergers, in a dissertation, Johnson (2007) investigated the effects of culture on performance in merged Air Force Duty and National Guard personnel. The study concluded that cultural commonality influences organizational performance. Johnson's findings supported Denison, Haaland, and Goelzer (2004) and Weber and Camerer (2003) that organizational performance correlates with the overall culture. Johnson's study was limited to military sectors and may not generalize to other industries. Prior studies have overlooked the construct of organizational culture as one of the reasons for merger failures (Johnson, 2007).

2.17 *CURRENT TRENDS ON MERGERS AND ACQUISITIONS (2020–2022)*

The volume of mergers and acquisitions has mostly remained consistent with about 50,000 global deals yearly between 2015 and 2019, but recently in the COVID-19 era, it showed a significant decline in 2020 (see Figure 5). According to a report by Accenture on the pandemic's impact on the M&A market, the number of merger deals decreased by 12% and 3%, respectively. Nevertheless, M&A deals increased in 2021. According to Deloitte's M&A Trends Survey, about 61% of dealmakers adopted M&A activities to return to pre-COVID-19 levels after 12 months. Thus, the 2022 M&A trends are increasing to help companies pivot to mergers and acquisitions faster. The M & M&A market is strong, with current M&A trends indicating an upcoming run. Exploring insights from corporate and private equity firm dealmakers could help companies anticipate obstacles, adapt to evolving regulations, and innovate their M&A strategy.

Several variables relative to organizational culture enable employees to fit into the organization and be productive (Behery & Paton, 2008). Leaders and managers have the responsibility to maintain and enhance organizational performance. To maintain a high level of organizational performance, cultural integration is increasing, especially in the merger companies with multiple cultures in the same environment (Behery & Paton, 2008; Terranova, 2007). Prior studies showed that organizational culture has several independent variables (Behery & Paton, 2008; Denison & Neale, 1998; Yilmaz & Ergun, 2008). The four cultural traits identified by Denison and Neale include mission, consistency, involvement, and adaptability, which were used for the study. Other cultural variables include the four dimensions of culture integration identified by Behery and Paton (2008), including system fairness, system satisfaction, system importance, and system feedback.

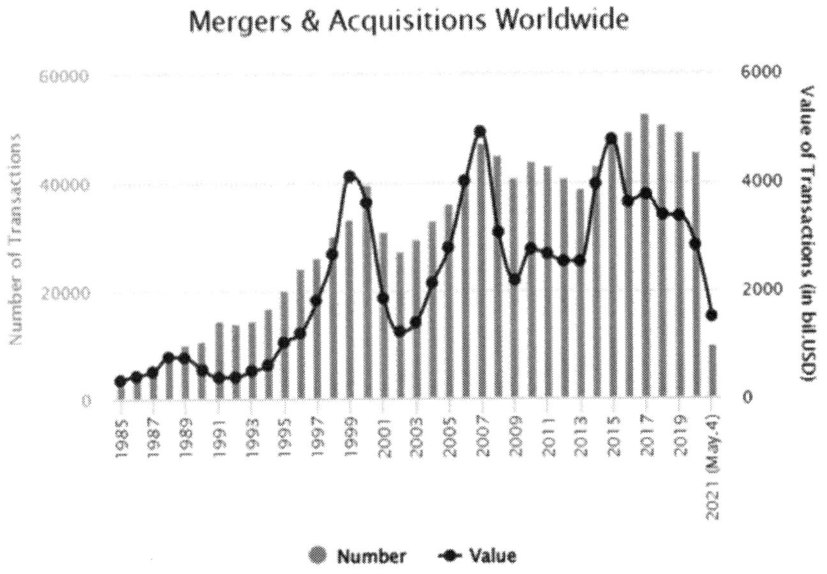

Figure 2.4. Mergers and Acquisition Deals Worldwide
Source: Institute of Mergers, Acquisitions, and Alliances (IMAA).

System Fairness

For organizational employees to be effective and productive, the organization needs to adopt culture integration that allows accuracy and fairness (Alston & Tippett, 2009; Caligiuri & Day, 2000). Otherwise, employees might exhibit less effort devoted to duties. Lack of system fairness contributes to non-commitment to new processes, lack of interest, and less effort to enhance performance or resolve issues (Caligiuri & Day, 2000).

System Satisfaction

Information and knowledge sharing allow employees to understand the new system and process within organizations (Behery & Paton, 2008). Employees tend to feel committed and engaged when they shape the organizational future (Behery & Paton, 2008). The extent to which employees perceive a good fit within the organization influences employee commitment, job satisfaction, culture integration, and job performance (Behery & Paton, 2008). Perceived system satisfaction with cultural integration may be linked to the frequency of performance reviews, reality alignment, addressing personal needs, and resolving work-related inequalities (Caligiuri & Day, 2000).

System Importance

Organizations need links between formal and informal control mechanisms to match organizational outcomes and culture (Behery & Paton, 2008). System importance needs to enable culture and performance fit to allow people to agree on a shared priority towards fulfilling an expectation (Behery & Paton, 2008; Terranova, 2007). Organizations integrating cultural values to identify system importance might enhance both project and merger success (Terranova, 2006).

For example, merging two firms with anticipation of market diversification might be good system importance. Other factors might contribute to the system acceptance for the merger to succeed, such as shared cultural values. Identifying the significant and desirable shared values contributes to organizational culture variables (Behery & Paton, 2008).

System Feedback

Timely and valued feedback helps an organization to build strong culture integration. Performance feedback positively impacts motivation, commitment, productivity, and job satisfaction (Behery & Paton, 2008). Many employees might want to know how they perform through performance recognition and rewards systems. Feedback should be appropriate and specific to enable managers and employees to understand the job process clearly (Behery & Paton, 2008). Having emphasized different culture variables, the study used organizational culture as an independent variable to focus on the four dimensions of culture integration relating to mission, consistency, involvement, and adaptability.

2.17 ORGANIZATIONAL PERFORMANCE AS A DEPENDENT VARIABLE

The literature found several organizational performance variables that enable an organization to measure productivity in terms of employees' commitment, job satisfaction, turnover rate, shareholder returns, and organizational growth (Behery & Paton, 2008; Rothman, 2008; Weinzimmer, Franczak, & Michel, 2008). Several researchers have observed that leaders and managers are responsible for maintaining organizational performance (Behery & Paton, 2008; Peloza & Papania, 2008; Rose et al., 2008). Behery and Paton's study showed that organizational performance is linked to employee commitment, job satisfaction, and staff turnover. Farrell, Oczkowski, and Kharabsheh (2008) used the market and learning orientation concepts to examine the five factors of business performance. The business performance variables are related to product quality, increase in sales, return on investment, customer retention, and overall performance. Farrell et al. (2008) concluded that international joint venture organizations with market orientation have a more positive relationship with organizational performance. The global joint venture with a learning orientation has a more positive relationship with return on investment (Farrell et al., 2008).

The study used the three variables of organizational performance: employee commitment, job satisfaction, and employee retention (Behery & Paton, 2008; Denison & Neale, 1998; Yilmaz & Ergun, 2008). Employee commitment refers to how employees are dependable (Tay, 2009). Job satisfaction relates to the positive job-related emotions experienced by employees within the company. Employee retention involves the tendency of employees to leave the company.

Employee Commitment

The feeling of responsibility of employees within the organizational goals and values relates to their commitment (Bambacas & Patrickson, 2008; Tay, 2005). Previous studies suggested that organizational commitment links to organizational culture (Chang & Huang, 2005; Cooper-Hakim & Viswesvaran, 2005; Tay, 2009). Cultural integration might help to enhance organizational commitment to align employee commitment with organizational goals (Beard, 2007; Yao & Wang, 2008). The study used employee commitment as an organizational performance-dependent variable to determine the relationship on culture in a merged banking company.

Job Satisfaction

Job satisfaction refers to employees' positive emotional state regarding experiences and perceptions (Anderson & Patterson, 2008; Greenberg & Baron, 2008; Warr, 2007). Organizational culture has a positive relationship with job satisfaction (Ghazzawi, 2008). Luna-Arocas and Camps (2008) confirmed that job satisfaction might be enhanced when employees are equitably rewarded. The study used job satisfaction as an organizational performance-dependent variable to determine cultural relationships in the merged banking industry.

Employee Retention

Several studies reflected that organizational commitment and job satisfaction positively impact employee turnover (Benson, 2006; Caligiuri & Day, 2000; Freund, 2005; Indridason & Wang, 2008). Inadequate cultural integration and inappropriate employee fit in organizations might increase the rate of turnover among employees. The research study focused on employee retention as an organizational performance-dependent variable on culture integration in a merged banking company

2.19 SUPPORTING THEORIES

Leadership is culturally dependent and varies within organizational cultural forces (Alas, Tafel, & Tuulik, 2007). Early leadership theories were created from behavioral and situational traits to form a change-oriented approach (McLaurin, Bushanain, & Amri, 2008). The leadership process thus involves ways to influence followers (Erkutlu, 2008; Laohavichien, Fredendall, & Cantrell, 2009). For the past 50 years, considerable research has been conducted on leaders' abilities to influence their followers successfully. Early leadership research concentrated on identifying successful leaders' personal characteristics, such as those that create so-called born leaders and traits of influential leaders. As most organizations cannot predict success from individual characteristics, leadership researchers tend to identify behaviors that can improve followers' performance (Howell, Neufeld, & Avolio, 2005; Luthans & Youssef, 2007).

Early leadership behavior researchers described leadership behaviors in terms of roles and styles of leaders (Kahn, 1964). Some of the behavioral leadership models are contingency and path-goal leadership. The contingency model supports the assertion that the leadership style depends on the situation. The path-goal leadership model integrates situational and expectancy variables theory to describe employees' motivation.

Prior studies have criticized that incorporating behavioral leadership models in organizational change has not been successful (Bass & Avolio, 1994; Laohavichien, Fredendall, & Cantrell, 2009). Due to the criticisms, Bass created transformational and transactional leadership from existing behavioral leadership. Transformational leadership was designed to help radical organizational change, and transactional leadership to help improve incremental change (Bass & Avolio 1994). Transformational leadership theory was used for the study to identify the management of culture within a merged environment.

Transformational Leadership Theory

The transformational leadership model helps to promote collective decision making, employee empowerment, and higher performance (Atkins & Turner, 2006; Avey, Hughes, Norman, & Luthans, 2008; Kest, 2006; Konorti, 2008;

Trim & Lee, 2008). Transformational leadership enables leaders to provide intellectual stimulation and empowerment that enable followers to perform tasks effectively (Bass & Avolio, 1994; Kirkbride, 2006; Walumbwa, Lawler, Avolio, Wang, & Shi, 2005). Theories of transformational leadership relate to values, emotions, and leadership that encourage creativity in employees (Garcia-Morales, Matias-Reche, & Hurtado-Torres, 2008).

Recent studies showed that transformational leaders perform better than transactional leaders in managing different groups and cultures (Emery & Barker, 2007; Kest, 2006; Xenikou & Simosi, 2006). Transformational leadership theory continues to be a vital topic for researchers (Kest, 2006; Vallejo, 2008; Xenikou & Simosi, 2006). The study by James Burns popularized transformational leadership theory (Kest, 2006). Transformational leadership supports the idea that leaders should share knowledge and conveys organizational vision to their followers (Kest, 2006).

The vision of merged organizations might require a change in the organization. The demand in today's global and market competition requires organizations to use transformational leadership styles to motivate followers. Transformational leaders encourage followers to improve productivity, team values, and growth by responding to job challenges (Burns, 1978; Kest, 2006). Leaders acting as advisors in a merged group may allow the opportunity to build trust and show sensitivity to different cultural perceptions within the group. Improving knowledge sharing within the merged firms may enhance productivity (Olson, Parayitam, & Twigg, 2006; Zou & Ghauri, 2008). Transformational leadership theory supports the need for organizational leaders to integrate culture into a business environment (Xenikou & Simosi, 2006). Culture contributes to the business success or failure, depending on the leadership styles and practices (Valant, 2008; Xenikou & Simosi, 2006). The M&A of organizations requires that two merging companies integrate two cultures to form one acceptable culture.

In studying transformational leadership and cultural effects on performance, Xenikou and Simosi (2006) investigated the interrelation between transformational leadership, culture, and outcomes. The results from their research reflected that adaptive culture orientations directly impact performance. The same study portrayed that transformational leadership indirectly relates to performance. Most organizational effectiveness is linked to transformational leadership and culture (Xenikou & Simosi, 2006).

Several studies reflect that cultural orientation links to organizational performance (Denison & Mishra, 1995; Rose et al., 2008; Weinzimmer, Franczak, & Michel, 2008). Bass and Avolio (1994) portrayed that transformational leadership qualities help organizations reach performance expectations. Leadership roles affect the change process in organizations (Dulewicz & Higgs, 2005; Green, 2007). Some management ideas fail due to neglected organizational culture (Smith, 2008). The values and beliefs of leaders affect decision-making and problem resolutions (Shivers-Blackwell, 2006).

Leadership styles and actions play a major role in the merger implementation process within organizations. Several authors have posited that organizational leadership is vital to integrating organizational culture to fit merger firms (Green, 2007; Tucker, Turner, Barling, Reid, & Elving, 2006; Xenikou & Simosi, 2006). Leaders are change agents for organizations and should develop good relationships with employees to enhance employee commitment to the merger implementation process.

Chew and Sharman (2005) explained the elite value profile as an organization's power centered at the apex to relate culture and performance to leadership. The leadership profile shares the same shape as the profile, emphasizing force authority (Chew & Sharman, 2005). Chew and Sharma's study recommended that organizations going into M&A need to adopt the leadership value profile. The profile includes strategic human resource management effectiveness to enable a high level of financial results. The integration of organizational culture depends on leaders such as chief executive officers (Lainema & Lainema, 2007). The results of a study conducted by Sheraton and Sterns Corporate Management (SSCM) (2002) supported the belief that 80% of top-level management pay less attention to the issue of culture during the M&A process (Hon, 2002). Leaders who ignore the impact of culture changes in organizations face a potentially chaotic situation (Green, 2007). Leaders of organizations need to identify strategies to combine organizational cultures to enhance successful mergers. Leadership involves directing, motivating, and aligning people toward an organizational goal (Xenikou & Simosi, 2006).

Organizational leaders help to manage change in organizations. The merger process is one of the processes of change in organizations. Some steps to change the process include recognizing the need for change, assessing the organization's goals, and institutionalizing the change (Trim & Lee, 2008). Assessing the organizational plan requires benchmarking with other organizations' performance and environmental factors (Brown, Jones, & Leigh, 2005). Institutionalizing changes involves motivating employees to create innovative ideas for job commitment and change implementation. Transformational leadership has moved from an internal leadership style to a broader focus to accommodate external factors (Dulewicz & Higgs, 2005; Walumbwa, Avolio, & Zhu, 2008). The transformational leadership style focuses on maintaining operational efficacy in different environments. Organizations under mergers or restructuring need the transformational leadership style to assess and renew organizational vision (Singh, 2008). The transformational leadership style might help transform organizations and followers both during and after the merger process (Limsila & Ogunlana, 2008).

The Implication of Transformational Leadership Theory

The study's transformational leadership theory implications relate to how leaders implement change in a merged organization. Application of the theory involves creating opportunities for change, assessing organizational goals, and institutionalizing changes through employee motivation. The impact of transformational theory on the proposed research study included the following: (a) a leadership focus on a broader view to accommodate different cultures of merged organizations, and (b) a rapid increase in organizational mergers and frequent merger failures might need a transformational change with a different leadership approach. The third impact was (c) the banking industry in Nigeria might need a transformational leadership style to redirect policies, integrate cultures, and motivate employees for successful merger implementation.

Equity Theory

Equity theory relates to treating employees within a fair and equitable structure to receive similar roles and responsibilities (Adams, 1963, 1965). People working in organizations perceive levels of inputs and outcomes to compare with other employees. For example, input relates to the time, resources, knowledge, and effort to complete the job, while outcome relates to the compensation, recognition, and rewards for the job completed. Studies on fairness perceptions in predicting organizational performance concluded that perceived negativity and interaction might determine employee reactions (Horvath & Andrews, 2007; Mowday, 1991; Parish, Cadwallader, & Busch, 2008). Organizational fairness in decisions, compensation, and promotion are components of equity theory perception. Perceptions of fairness help build relationships among managers and employees to enhance job satisfaction, commitment, and performance (Anderson & Patterson, 2008; Carr, 2007). As research on equity and justice perceptions continue, researchers have argued that employees' reactions are influenced by perceptions of ways to achieve outcomes (Allen, Takeda, & White, 2005; Anderson & Patterson, 2008; Fadil, Williams, Limpaphayom, & Smart, 2005; Mowday, 1991). The employees' perceptions of fairness relate to organizational outcomes and commitment (Anderson & Patterson, 2008). The appropriate strategies to achieve employee job satisfaction, commitment, and retention during the organizational merger process link equity theory to the study. Hence, the perception of fairness is an important factor in the management and motivation of employees (Okoro, 2010).

During a merger process, organizations require participants' commitment to meet target expectations such as quality service and increase in production.

One part of merger strategies might reduce the workforce while asking the remaining employees to maintain a higher workload. Employees retained after the merger might perceive merger actions as inequitable due to more responsibilities with non-matching compensation.

According to Leavy (2005), employees who perceive inequitable balance might take action to eliminate the situation. For instance, employees can reduce working hours, refuse to share knowledge with new employees from the merger process, and expend less effort on job responsibilities. Employees who perceive inequitable balance might leave the organization, resulting in the loss of talented employees (Leavy, 2005). The loss of talented employees might impact merger organizations during the crucial merger integration, preventing essential knowledge sharing to employees during the merger process.

Implications of Equity Theory

The study's equity theory implications relate to how leaders in merged organizations might measure employee perception of inputs and outcomes. Different employees might have different values and expectations from their job. Job security and satisfaction might be a threat for employees who survived the merger in a merged environment. Determining ways and processes to retain employees within a fair and equitable structure becomes a challenge for leaders because employees might be required to perform multi-tasking jobs in a merged environment. Employees with different experiences and qualifications doing the same position might have different perceptions of outcomes on various jobs achieved. Employees' perceptions of work done and corresponding outcomes might be incorrect, and a fairness process is required in a merged organization to correct such perceptions. Establishing a fairness process might include recognizing employees' contributions and offering rewards and promotions to adhere to equitable balance. Such recognition might boost employees' morale regarding change commitment, job satisfaction, and employee retention while meeting the merged organization's expectations.

2.20 SUMMARY

The literature review provided the information necessary for integrating organizational cultures in merged companies to improve performance. Many researchers have argued that cultural integration affects organizational performance (Chow & Liu, 2007; Terranova, 2007; Xenikou & Simosi, 2006). Findings showed a rapid increase in organizational mergers despite the merger failures, especially in the banking and telecommunication industries

(Aburime & Uche, 2008; Coy et al., 2005; Kanter et al., 2004; Rodriguez, 2008; Valant, 2008). A successful merger can be improved when leaders and managers involved in the merger process integrate organizational cultures successfully (Weber & Camerer, 2003; Lai & Lee, 2007; Wriston, 2007). Banking and telecommunication industries mergers have reflected some issues, as researchers have continuously argued that organizational culture in the environment focuses mainly on product diversification, growth, and market competition (Baranes & Flochel, 2008; Michalakelis et al., 2008; Sung & Gort, 2006; Valant, 2008). Most mergers in the banking and telecommunication industries might meet target expectations and improve performance when organizational culture integration is included in the merger process.

A literature review resulted in findings that demonstrated that most organizational mergers fail due to inadequate cultural integration among the merging companies (Atkinson, 2005; Dyer et al., 2004; Ness, 2005; Pultz, 2005). From the findings in the review, the research study examined the relationship between organizational culture and performance in a merged bank in Abuja, the FCT of Nigeria. The literature review provided the historical and theoretical perspective on organizational culture, performance, and merger activities to create a framework for the research methodology. Chapter 3 describes the research methodology for the study to cover data collection, research design, and data analysis for reliability and validity. The research methodology will enable readers to understand the research questions and hypotheses and how the study may determine if a relationship exists between the organizational culture and organizational performance in a merged Nigerian bank.

2.21 CHAPTER 2: STUDY QUIZ QUESTIONS

Questions 1. Which of the following best describes an organizational culture?

A. It is a system of individual plans and actions that helps individuals understand which behaviors are and are not appropriate within an organization.
B. It is a system of shared assumptions, values, and beliefs that helps individuals understand which behaviors are and are not appropriate within an organization.
C. It is a system of shared individual plans and beliefs that helps the company understand which behaviors are not appropriate for their employees.
D. All of the above

Questions 2. Cultures can be a source of competitive advantage for organizations.

A. True
B. False

Questions 3. Which of the following makes an effective organizational culture?

A. Outcome Orientation
B. People Orientation
C. Team Orientation
D. All of the above

Questions 4. A company possess _______________if the workplace culture relates to the culture in a family.

A. adhocracy culture
B. clan culture
C. market culture
D. hierarchy culture

Questions 5. A company possess ____________________ if the company emphasizes creativity and innovation.

A. adhocracy culture
B. clan culture
C. market culture
D. hierarchy culture

Questions 6. A company possess ____________________ if the company emphasizes creativity and innovation.

A. adhocracy culture
B. clan culture
C. market culture
D. hierarchy culture

Questions 7. A company possess ____________________ if the company emphasizes values and accomplishes tasks quickly and efficiently.

A. adhocracy culture
B. clan culture
C. market culture
D. hierarchy culture

Questions 8. A company possesses ________________ if the company emphasizes predominantly focuses on creating a fixed organizational structure through the implementation of specific processes and introduction of multiple levels of power and responsibility.

A. adhocracy culture
B. clan culture
C. market culture
D. hierarchy culture

2.22 CHAPTER 2: STUDY QUIZ SOLUTIONS

1. B
2. A
3. D
4. B
5. A
6. A
7. C
8. D

2.23 CHAPTER 2 EXERCISES

1. What is a research literature review?
2. What is organizational culture?
3. What is organizational performance?
4. What is an employee commitment?
5. What is job satisfaction?
6. What is the pre-merger and post-merger process?
7. What are the categories for assessing organizational effectiveness?
8. What is a post-merger integration?
9. Which strategy do leaders need to achieve a merger success?
10. What is a diverse climate?

ENDNOTES

1. Creswell, J. W. (2005). *Educational research: Planning, conducting, and evaluating quantitative and qualitative research* (2nd ed.). Columbus, OH: Merrill Prentice Hall.

2. Behery, M. H., & Paton, R. A. (2008). Performance appraisal: culture fit and organizational outcomes within the U.A.E. *Journal of American Academy of Business, Cambridge*, 13(1), 166–176. Retrieved from ABI/INFORM Global database.

3.Schein, E. H. (1992). *Organizational culture and leadership* (2nd ed.). San Francisco: Jossey-Bass.

4. Coffey, C., & Tombari, N. (2005). The bottom-line for work and life leadership: Linking diversity and organizational culture. *Ivey Business Journal Online*, 1–7. Retrieved from ProQuest database.

5. Xenikou, A., & Simosi, M. (2006). Organizational culture and transformational leadership as predictors of business unit performance. *Journal of Managerial Psychology*, 21(6), 566–579. Retrieved from ABI/INFORM Global database.

Chapter 3

Methodology

3.1 METHODOLOGY

The purpose of the study was to analyze the relationship between organizational culture and performance in a merged bank in Abuja, the FCT of Nigeria. The continuous increase in merger failures and the resultant high employee turnover and non-commitment in the banking industry provided the opportunity to conduct the research study. The study examined the relationship between organizational cultural traits composed of mission, consistency, involvement, and adaptability as independent variables concerning performance as the dependent variable. The performance variables for the study included employee commitment, job satisfaction, and employee retention. Chapter 3 discusses research design, its appropriateness, population sample, and data collection and analysis. The characteristics and size of the sample are identified, along with a discussion of the instrumentation, confidentiality, and data collection process for the present study.

3.2 RESEARCH METHOD AND DESIGN APPROPRIATENESS

The rationale for selecting the quantitative correlational and regression design method is that a correlation helps measure the strength of the relationship between two or more variables. A regression helps to reveal the dependence between the variables. The research aimed to determine the relationship between organizational culture and performance in a merged Nigerian bank. Using a quantitative correlational and regression design helped accomplish the study goal by examining the covariation and degree of association of the four cultural traits and the three performance variables.

Using the correlational design helped explain the relationships between cultural traits and associated performance variables. The use of regression analyses helped examine the combined association of multiple independent variables of mission, consistency, involvement, and adaptability on each performance-dependent variable of employee commitment, job satisfaction, and employee retention. The appropriateness of using both the correlational and regression design relates to analyzing relationships among the study criterion and predictor variables.

A correlational design helps predict variables and analyze the relationship among the variables (Creswell, 2005).[1] Using a correlational design enabled statistical correlation tests to explain and measure the degree of association between two or more variables. Correlations can be either positive or negative. Positive correlations signify that the increase in one variable links to the rise in another variable, while a decrease in one variable links to the reduction of another variable. Negative correlations signify that the increase in one variable does not link to the reduction of another variable.

The regression analyses enabled inferential statistics to describe the variables' relationship insignificance, validity, and certainty. The correlational and regression analyses helped associational statistics to establish the significant relationships between the study's cultural traits (mission, consistency, involvement, and adaptability) and organizational performance (employee commitment, job satisfaction, and employee retention). Neither correlation nor regression analyses can be interpreted as establishing cause-and-effect relationships. Correlation indicates the strength of relationships, and regression reveals dependence between variables. It helps to compare the selected correlational and regression design to other available research designs such as experimental, survey, ethnographic, and exploratory/explanatory mixed-method methods.

Experimental designs focus on using interventions to influence an outcome for one group and another (Creswell, 2005). An exploratory research design was not appropriate for the study because the research did not compare different groups relative to an outcome. The study did not involve any intervention to manipulate the participants in the study.

Survey design focuses on studying trends for a population. The survey research design might be cross-sectional or longitudinal (Creswell, 2005, p. 397). A cross-sectional survey design was appropriate because the design focused on collecting data about current attitudes, opinions, or beliefs relating to cultural traits and organizational performance. In contrast, a longitudinal survey design enables the study of individuals over a period (Creswell, 2005). The current research did not study individuals over a specific period.

Ethnographic research design helps study a group of individuals in a unique environment to provide an account of events (Creswell, 2005). The ethnographic method was not appropriate for the study because it did not involve observing participants in their environment. Survey questions were distributed to participants to gather data that helped to analyze the relationship between cultural traits and performance variables in the studied bank.

Exploratory and explanatory mixed-method design requires gathering qualitative and quantitative data to explore a phenomenon and test relationships found in qualitative data (Creswell, 2005). The study used quantitative correlational and regression design to measure the strength of the relationship and predict dependence between the study variables. Even though the mixed methods design was not used, the correlational and regression design examined the significant relationship between organizational culture traits and organizational performance.

3.3 TWO TYPES OF RESEARCH QUESTIONS

There are two types of research questions in analyzing problems: exploratory and explanatory.

1. explanatory research explains why certain events work in a particular way
2. exploratory analysis explores a problem that is not clearly defined.

Explanatory Vs. Exploratory Research Questions

Explanatory research—helps a researcher to understand and explain the topic generally. Researchers use explanatory research when they want to explain why a particular phenomenon happens. Explanatory research attempts to explain why certain phenomena work in a certain way. Explanatory research identifies research studies that answer the "why question" and link different ideas to understand the nature of cause-and-effect relationships. Hence, explanatory research analyzes problems and explains the patterns of relationships between variables.

An example is when a researcher wants to carry out an explanatory study of why people have an addiction to smartphones. In that case, the study will explain the reasons behind peoples' addiction and the factors that contribute to the addiction. Some examples of explanatory research are:

- In-depth interviews
- Literature research
- Case studies
- Focus group research

Exploratory research—explores, investigates, and analyzes the general phenomenon or a problem that is not clearly defined. While exploring the research problem, it does not propose final or conclusive solutions to existing problems. Instead, the researcher starts with general concepts to get ideas about approaching the research subjects, what methods to use, and what type of data to collect. Researchers usually perform exploratory research to test the feasibility of conducting an extensive study on a particular topic. Hence, exploratory analysis helps to conduct research for problems at a preliminary stage where the researcher could change direction according to new insights from the study.

There are different types of exploratory research methods.

- Primary research methods involve surveys, polls, interviews, focus groups, and observations.
- Secondary research methods involve literature research, online research, and case study research.

The exploratory research studies do not have a proper structure, but it uses several steps to identify the problem, create the hypothesis, and conduct further research.

Quantitative Research Questions

Quantitative research questions are objective questions that provide detailed knowledge about a research topic. The data collected are numerical that can be analyzed statistically. Quantitative research questions imply that researchers want to gather information about variables that quantify or measured. Quantitative research questions help identify trends and patterns to make logical sense of the research topic. The data collected could be generalized to the entire population and help make data-driven decisions.

Types of Quantitative Questions

There are three types of Quantitative Research Questions

1. Descriptive Research Questions
2. Comparative Research Questions
3. Relationship-based Research Questions

Descriptive Research Question

Descriptive research questions help gather a customer's view or attitude about variables to measure. Descriptive research questions focus primarily on one group and one variable.

Hence, descriptive research questions are inquiries that researchers use to collect quantifiable data about the characteristics of research subjects. These questions seek responses that reveal existing patterns like the research subjects.

Comparative Research Question

Comparative research questions help analyze the difference between two or more groups based on one or more dependable variables. The number of variables depends on the need of the research. The comparative research question asks the respondents, "what is the difference in" a dependent variable between two or more groups.

Relationship-based Research Questions

Relationship-based research questions are quantitative research questions when a researcher identifies trends, causal relationships, or associations between two or more variables. IT relates to an experimental research design. Relationship-based research questions help examine the cause and effect between two variables where a variable could be responsible for the impact on the other variable. Relationship-based research questions do not need to distinguish between causal relationships, trends, or associations. An example is "What is the relationship" between independent and dependent variables between two or more groups.

3.4 RESEARCH QUESTIONS AND HYPOTHESES

Research questions imply a relationship to be checked (Creswell, 2005). The research questions focused on the relationship between organizational culture and performance in a merged bank in Abuja, the FCT of Nigeria. Organizational culture traits comprise mission, consistency, involvement, and adaptability, functioning as independent variables. In contrast, employee commitment, job satisfaction, and employee retention were performance-dependent variables.

The research questions and hypotheses focused on the relationship between the four cultural traits and performance related to employee commitment, job satisfaction, and employee retention. The hypotheses were presented in the form of a Ho null component and Ha alternative hypotheses. The null component indicates no existence of a statistically significant relationship, and the alternative component indicates an existence of a statistically significant relationship. The research questions and hypotheses for the study included the following:

Research Question 1: What is the relationship between organizational culture traits of mission, comprising consistency, involvement, and adaptability, and employee commitment performance in a merged Nigerian bank?

Ho1: There is no significant relationship between organizational culture traits of mission, consistency, involvement, and adaptability, and employee commitment performance in a merged Nigerian bank.

Ha1: There is a significant relationship between organizational culture traits of mission, consistency, involvement, and adaptability, and employee commitment performance in a merged Nigerian bank.

Research Question 2: What is the relationship between organizational culture traits of mission, comprising consistency, involvement, and adaptability, and job satisfaction performance in a merged Nigerian bank?

Ho2: There is no significant relationship between organizational culture traits of mission, consistency, involvement, adaptability, and job satisfaction performance in a merged Nigerian bank.

Ha2: There is a significant relationship between organizational culture traits of mission, consistency, involvement, and adaptability and the job satisfaction performance in a merged Nigerian bank.

Research Question 3: What is the relationship between organizational culture traits of mission, comprising consistency, involvement, and adaptability, and employee retention performance in a merged Nigerian bank?

Ho3: There is no significant relationship between organizational culture traits of mission, consistency, involvement, and adaptability and employee retention performance in a merged Nigerian bank.

Ha3: There is a significant relationship between organizational culture traits of mission, consistency, involvement, and adaptability and employee retention performance in a merged Nigerian bank.

3.5 POPULATIONS AND SAMPLING FRAME

A population comprises people with similar characteristics that distinguish them from other groups (Creswell, 2005). The population for the study included all bank employees in the sample Nigerian bank. The sample for the analysis comprised the 220 employees from each segment of the sample. The different segments of the sample included the directors, managers, and employees. The sample employees were both men and women currently working in the merged Nigerian bank in Abuja. The current employees were used as the research population because they participated in the merger and thus experienced the merger's impact on their daily activities. A sampling frame was required because the total population would be too large for the research study. A sample frame helps generalize population characteristics, participants' availability, and desired rigor (Cooper & Schindler, 2008[2]; Creswell, 2005).

The sample of 220 employees was drawn from the merged bank's population, which includes ten branches, regional offices, and head office, due to the time constraints for the study. Each branch has one manager, about 100 employees, and 14 directors. The sample was composed of 10 directors, ten managers, and 200 employees. The merged bank in Abuja was selected because of the geographical spread and extensive branch network after consolidation and merger with other banks in 2004. The sample chosen merged bank emerged from the consolidation of nine other banks. A representative sample of the 220 employees was determined to be 50% of the directors, 100% of the managers, and 20% of the employees of the merged bank in Abuja. The approach was consistent with the concept of Cooper and Schindler (2008), who suggested that when the sample size approaches 120, the sample standard deviation becomes an excellent statistical estimate. The representative sample of the different segments was determined to be significant based on the ability to generalize back to the population.

A stratified random selection was used to draw the sample of 220 employees from an alphabetized list of employees from a merged bank in Abuja, the FCT of Nigeria. Using stratified sampling ensured representation of the critical subgroups of the population. The sample was randomized for selection into the three segments. The selection process guarded the design against potential bias from the volunteer participants. Although the research participants consisted of volunteers from the total population and may not represent a true cross-section of the total population, statistical inferences to establish relationships among the volunteer participants were judged unlikely to threaten the results. Banking employees were chosen because the employees, managers, and directors participated in the merger process and have knowledge of the organizational structure, culture, and daily operations. Selecting the sample of 220 employees reduced the impact of the activities on the company under study. The characteristic of the sample included men and women over 18 years of age and currently employed in the merged Nigerian bank.

3.6 GEOGRAPHIC LOCATION

The total population for the study included all the bank employees in the merged bank selected for the study with a sample of 220 employees. The purpose of the study was to examine the relationship between organizational culture and performance in the merged Nigerian bank. A merged Nigerian bank was chosen because most Nigerian banks are in distress, despite the mandatory consolidation and merger process in 2006. The mandatory consolidation and merger emerged to meet the CBN minimum share capital of N25 billion, which is approximately US$195 million. The increase in the merger waves since the 2000s in the global banking sectors necessitated a study in the banking industry (Aburime & Uche, 2008; Koetter, 2008; Rodriguez, 2008)[3]. Because Nigeria is a developing country, the data collected from the study may help address the merger challenges while reducing the distressed bank situations in the country. Abuja is the federal capital territory and is in the northern region. The selection of a merged bank in Abuja provided an excellent representation since most banks have most of their branches and head offices in Abuja.

3.6 INFORMED CONSENT AND CONFIDENTIALITY

An informed consent form was designed for the study to be signed by voluntary participants. The consent form provided participants the background information on the research and the purpose, procedure, risks, and benefits of participating. The participants were advised that participation was voluntary and that they could withdraw at any time if they chose not to participate in the study without any penalty or loss of benefits. The consent forms were distributed via electronic email and a hand delivery system to the participants. The electronic email and hand-delivered consent forms were read, signed, and returned to a collection box by voluntary participants. A copy of the survey instrument was distributed only to the participants that signed and returned the consent forms. The consent form required voluntary participants to be 18 years or over to be eligible to participate.

The study ensured confidentiality to all participants by assigning a code number to each consent form and survey instrument, thereby providing complete anonymity. A letter requesting access to the premises was sent to the bank's managing director in Abuja, the FCT of Nigeria. A signed permission letter from the merged bank in Abuja indicated permission to use the bank premises as a research location. The survey instrument did not ask for information to identify a participant, such as names, phone numbers, and personal identification numbers. All signed consent forms and survey questions completed by voluntary participants are in possession of the researcher and will not be shared with any other individual. The electronic transcriptions of the survey were secured in an external storage device and fingerprint Jet Flash drive to maintain confidentiality and access through a password protection system. To ensure confidentiality, the manually completed surveys were archived in a safe box and are scheduled to be destroyed three years after completion of the study.

3.7 DATA COLLECTION AND INSTRUMENTATION

Data collection is collecting and measuring data on variables of interest in an established logical manner that enables a researcher to answer stated research questions, test hypotheses, and evaluate outcomes. Data is one of the most valuable resources in every business. The more information one gathers about customers, vendors, and stakeholders helps to understand their interests and needs. This understanding helps organizations meet and exceed customer expectations and attain goals. Hence, setting and achieving goals include more significant focus, excellent direction, increased productivity, enhanced performance, and higher motivation levels. Therefore, setting goals in pre-merger and post-merger sets the pace for specific and measurable mindsets, habits, and confidence to drive daily actions.

Primary Data Collection

Primary data relates to the data one collects rather than the data previously gathered and recorded by another party. Primary data is information obtained directly by the researcher from a source and serves as the first party to use the set of data collected. Hence, first-party data is the information collected directly from the audience, online data, and customer relationship management system through surveys and other sources. First-party data is different from second-party and third-party data. Thus, second-party data is the first-party data of another company. A researcher could purchase second-party data directly from the organization that collected it or other sources.

Quantitative vs. Qualitative Data

The primary data can be divided into two categories: quantitative and qualitative.

Quantitative data—relates numerically, such as numbers, quantities, and values. It is very objective and reliable. Quantitative data describes things in concrete and easily measurable. When researchers analyze quantitative data, they may uncover insights that could help understand the audience—for example, the number of customers who bought a particular product.

Qualitative data—is descriptive rather than numeric and less easily measurable than quantitative data. Qualitative data contain descriptive views, phrases, and opinions. An example is an online review of a customer for a product. Qualitative data helps explains the "why" behind the quantitative information data reveals.

DOCP survey instrument

The DOCP survey instrument was used to collect data for the study. A consent form requesting survey participation was distributed to a sampling of employees via electronic email and a hand delivery system. A list of the merged bank employees was collected from the bank management to allow random distribution based on employees' last names. The participants were required to sign the form to indicate voluntary participation in the survey. Administering the survey involved random allocation to the participants involved in the merger to complete a 15- to 20-minute survey. Other alternatives to helping with a survey included post office mailing and online survey administration. The study used electronic email and a hand delivery system to enable easy survey distribution and data collection. Electronic email and a hand delivery system enabled immediate receipt and eliminated the need for mailing to avoid delay and loss of packages in transit. The hand delivery system enabled the participants to complete the survey and return it immediately to allow a high response rate.

A simple data-coding procedure was used to transfer the raw data to the Microsoft Excel spreadsheet program and SPSS software for data analysis. For example, the gender used the value of "1" for males and "2" for females under demographics. For the culture and performance survey questions, the Likert-type closed-ended value ranging from 1 (strongly disagree) to 5 (strongly agree) and 1 (negligible) to 7 (extremely high) was used, respectively. Using the closed-ended type of survey enabled responses to be limited to the study's research problem (Cooper & Schindler, 2008). The culture and performance survey questions were appropriate for the correlational design selected. The data collected from the survey helped to explain and measure the degree of association between the four cultural traits and performance variables. Statistically analyzing the data collected helped answer the research problem of identifying the relationship between organizational culture and performance in a merged Nigerian bank. Finally, the data collected were secured and achieved in an external hard drive and fingerprint

Jet Flash drive to maintain confidentiality and access through a password protection system.

The instrument for the study was Denison Organizational Culture and performance (DOCP) survey instrument. The DOCP survey instrument was appropriate for the proposed research because the components of the survey used the cultural traits and performance questions related to the research problem. The DOCP survey was developed after over 20 years of research on culture and performance linked to the Denison Organizational Culture Model (Denison, Haaland, et al., 2004). An examination of the existing DOCP survey instrument by Denison, Haaland, et al. revealed that the instrument has a strong research foundation with proven reliability and validity. The components of the instrument include a model with four critical traits of organizational culture (Kotter & Heskett, 1992).[4]

These four traits include mission, consistency, involvement, and adaptability. The formation of the Denison Organizational Culture model used three indexes to measure each of the four traits totaling 12 indexes in the instrument (Denison & Neale, 1998). Figure 3.1 shows a graphical illustration of the 12 indexes that link the model to the survey instrument. To explain the components of the four culture traits, the mission trait includes the indexes of (a) strategic direction and intent, (b) goals and objectives, and (c) vision. The consistency trait consists of the indexes of (a) core values, (b) agreement, and (c) coordination and integration. The involvement trait includes the indexes of (a) empowerment, (b) team orientation, and (c) capability development. The adaptability trait consists of the indexes of (a) creating change, (b) customer focus, and (c) organizational learning (Denison & Neale, 1998).[5]

The survey shows 69 questions composed of 60 questions on organizational culture, three questions on organizational performance, and six demographic questions. The cultural traits aspect used the Likert-type scale ranging from 1 (strongly disagree) to 5 (strongly agree). The performance aspect used the Likert-type scale ranging from 1 (negligible) to 7 (extremely high). Demographic questions were used to classify the participants for the study. Prior researchers have used the Denison Organizational Culture model to validate their research. For example, in a dissertation by Johnson (2007), the Denison Organizational Culture Model was used to identify the effects of culture on performance in merged Air Force Active Duty and National Guard Personnel. Johnson's study supported Denison's Organizational Culture Model in stating that the more two cultures differ in the organization, the more the organizational performance diminishes (Denison, Janovics, et al., 2006).

3.8 VALIDITY AND RELIABILITY

Correlational research needs measurement instruments that will provide high validity and reliability. Identifying substantial correlations between two or more variables is possible only if the study can measure the variables with a reasonable degree of validity and reliability (Leedy & Ormrod, 2005, p. 194). Quantitative studies might achieve reality if the measurement tools are accurate and can measure the study intent (Reynolds, Livingston, & Wilson, 2006). The survey instrument needs to be valid and reliable to enable the study to provide an accurate assessment of research participants Creswell, 2005).

The reliability of a survey instrument refers to the accuracy of the measurement. A reliable survey question provides similar results when repeated to similar samples or populations (Vogt, 2007). The DOCP survey instrument was administered to a sample of 35,474 participants from 160 different firms to maintain the stability and reliability of the survey questions (Denison, Haaland, et al., 2004; Denison, Janovics, et al., 2006). DOCP survey instrument has been tested for reliability to show consistency over organizational culture and performance over repeated use.

The validity of a survey instrument refers to the extent to which the measure correlates with the underlying study. The validity of a research instrument relates to the scope to which the instrument measures the research variables (Leedy & Ormrod, 2005). The validity of an instrument means the measure for the questions being investigated and the appropriateness of the design to reach accurate conclusions (Vogt, 2007). The validity of a survey instrument relates to internal and external factors.

Internal validity

Internal validity relates to the link between independent and dependent variables (Creswell, 2005). DOCP survey instrument has been tested using Cronbach's alpha and factor analysis to predict the validity measures and acceptable levels of consistency in various research scales (Denison, 2005; Denison, Haaland, et al., 2004). Factor analysis is a correlational technique that analyzes beyond the Cronbach's alpha measurement (Vogt, 2007). The validation of the instrument was based on a varied sample of 35,474 participants from 160 different firms (Denison, Haaland, et al., 2004; Denison, Janovics, et al., 2006). The four independent variables were clustered into three sub-categories to get 12 indexes. Each of the 12 indexes had five survey questions to ensure that related items were together. The test established the validity of the 60 survey questions and 12 five-item indexes as measures of the four fundamental cultural traits to predict organizational effectiveness.

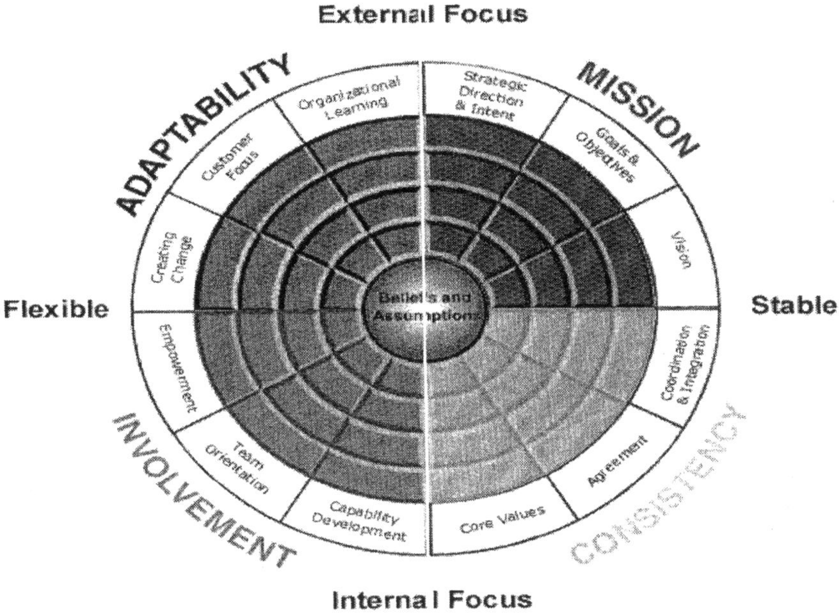

Figure 3.1. Denison organization culture model

Source: From "Denison Organizational Culture Model Survey," by D. R. Denison and W. S. Neale, 1998, Ann Arbor, MI: Aviat. Copyright 1998 by Denison Consulting. Reprinted with permission.

The validity study used three phases representing (a) factor analysis model, (b) homogeneity data, and (c) correlation between the cultural model and organizational performance. The result from the three phases showed the following results.

Phase one calculated the coefficient alphas for each of the 12 indexes used in the survey instrument. The alphas showed an acceptable level of internal consistency ranging from 0.70 to 0.85 for each of the 12 indexes and 0.87 to 0.92 for the inner characters of the four traits (Denison, Janovics, et al., 2006). The alpha consistency ranges met the scientific standard for acceptable reliability and showed a relationship among the cultural elements in the survey instrument (Denison, Janovics, et al., 2006).

Phase two reflected sufficient homogeneity within the survey at an acceptable level of 0.77 to 0.89 (Denison, Janovics, et al., 2006). They selected homogeneous samples to allow researchers to control factors that might influence relationships between research variables (Creswell, 2005). The test confirmed participants' ratings of cultural traits as measured by the items in the survey to allow organizational level aggregation. Phase three results reflected that culture and performance are strongly connected with an average correlation of 0.58. The analysis ascertained the criterion relationship of the cultural traits in predicting organizational effectiveness.

Other studies reported a Cronbach alpha of 0.91 with subscales ranging from 0.80 to 0.88 (Mezzich, Ruiperez, Yoon, Liu, & Zapata-vega, 2009) and a Cronbach's alpha of 0.82 with subscales ranging from 0.71 to 0.93 (Yang & Cipolla, 2007). All were above 0.70, the minimum threshold for the internal consistency reliability in social science research (Vogt, 2007). The study aimed for a total Cronbach's alpha of about 0.80 while acknowledging lower levels of Cronbach's alpha of 0.70 (Vogt, 2007). To enhance the validity and reliability of the proposed study, the SPSS package was used to calculate the figures for Cronbach's alphas on the traits of organizational culture and performance variables applied to the survey instrument. The results from the analyses validated that the DOCP survey questions measured the four cultural characteristics of the research study. Removing the 12 indexes significantly affected the organizational culture model. Organizations that score high on one of these traits would likely score high on the others (Denison, Janovics, et al., 2006). The four cultural traits were sufficiently autonomous to be classified as independent variables. The measures of organizational effectiveness in the validation test supported that organizational culture is closely related to organizational performance.

External validity

External validity relates to the generalization of a research study to other related settings and populations (Creswell, 2005). For the study to be beneficial to local and global organizations entering mergers and acquisitions towards achieving organizational performance, the study would need to show a high level of external validity (Lissitz & Samuelsen, 2007). External validity is the degree of practical use versus the appropriateness of the study. For example, the data collected by prior users of the survey instrument covered 35,474 participants from 160 organizations (Denison, Janovics, et al., 2006). The study showed significant correlations between organizations, thereby raising the confidence level of the external reliability of the study (Denison, Janovics, et al., 2006).

3.9 DATA ANALYSIS

The SPSS statistical package was used to conduct the data analysis for the study. The statistical analysis addressed the research questions and tested the hypotheses to establish a relationship between organizational culture traits and organizational performance in a merged Nigerian bank. The plan followed a three-step statistical process: (a) descriptive, (b) associational, and (c) inferential. Descriptive statistics were used to describe and summarize data. Associational statistics were used to determine how variables are associated. The inferential statistics helped conclude the populations using the samples drawn for the study. Correlational and regression analyses do not allow the interpretation of cause-and-effect relationships.

Descriptive Statistics

The use of descriptive statistics involves the measure of central tendency and frequency such as mean, mode, median, range, variance, and standard deviation (Vogt, 2007). Using descriptive statistics helped summarize the data collected on the cultural traits and the output variables. Vogt (2007) stated that descriptive statistics help to summarize extensive data with one number. Using descriptive statistics helped explain the relationship's characteristics with table and graphical approaches.

Associational Statistics

The correlation coefficient and multiple regression analysis referred to the associational statistics and helped establish the significant relationships among the cultural traits (mission, consistency, involvement, and adaptability) and organizational performance (employee commitment, job satisfaction, and employee retention). A correlation coefficient is a measure of association between variables that ranges between -1.00 and +1.00 (Vogt, 2007). Positive correlation between the responses ranges between 0 and +1; no correlation means zero, while -1 indicates negative correlation. The two-tailed analysis of the Pearson correlation r values was used to determine the study's cultural traits and performance relationship.

Inferential Statistics

The multiple regressions analysis was used as the inferential statistics to determine the significant predictors among the independent variables when applied to the prediction dependent variables of organizational performance at the $p < .05$ significance level. The multiple regressions were appropriate for the study because each dependent (output) variable was explained using a combination of independent (predictor) variables. Unlike simple linear regression, multiple regressions extend to two or more independent variables (Weiers, 2005). Using ANOVA with three or more independent variables might be complex (Vogt, 2007). The use of multiple regression made the analysis of 10 to 15 independent variables easier (Vogt, 2007).

3.10 SUMMARY

Between the traits of organizational culture and organizational performance participants in a merged bank in Abuja, the FCT of Nigeria, there were three research questions with three hypotheses, which focused on relationships between organizational culture traits and performance in a merged bank in Abuja. The instrument for the proposed study was Denison Organizational Culture and Performance (DOCP) survey. Formation of the Denison Organizational Culture Model uses three indexes to measure each of the four cultural traits, totaling 12 indexes in the instrument. DOCP survey instrument used a 5-point Likert-type scale, which Cooper and Schindler (2008) posited as being more practical in scientific analysis and most frequently used. A sample size of 220 was used for the study with a mixture of 200 employees, ten managers, and ten directors. The approach was consistent with the concept of Cooper and Schindler (2008), who suggested that when the sample size approaches 120, the sample standard deviation becomes an excellent statistical estimate. The SPSS statistical package was used to test the null hypotheses and compute the statistical analysis for the study. The study followed a three-step process to analyze the data collected using descriptive statistics, correlation analysis, and multiple regression analysis. Chapter 3 explained the data collection method, informed consent, and confidentiality procedures for the study. Chapter 4 includes an analysis of data collected and results from the survey.

3.11 CHAPTER 3 STUDY QUIZ QUESTIONS

Question 1. Which of the following best describes a methodology?

A. The study of research methods or contextual framework choices that researchers use to conduct a study that comprises the abstract analysis.
B. The study of research methods or contextual framework choices that researchers use to conduct a study comprises the theoretical analysis of the body of methods and principles associated with a branch of knowledge.
C. The academic study methods that researchers use to conduct a study
D. None of the above

Question 2. A ________________ is a complete set of people with a specialized set of characteristics

A. Sample
B. Population
C. Method
D. Methodology

Question 3. A _____________ is a subset of the population.

A. Sample
B. Population
C. Method
D. Methodology

Question 4. _________________ is the process where a researcher obtains and maintains, the permission of a person or authorized representative to participate in a research study.

A. Informed consent
B. Informed skills
C. Skills consent
D. Practical consent

Question 5. The process where a health care provider trains a patient about the risks, benefits, and alternatives of a given procedure or intervention relates to one of the followings?

A. Informed practice
B. Informed consent
C. Skills consent
D. Practical consent

Question 6. _______________ in research is not discussing information provided by an individual with others and presenting findings so individuals cannot be identified.

A. Management
B. Knowledge
C. Confidentiality
D. Motivation

Question 7. The __________ of a research study relates to how well the results among the study participants represent true findings among similar individuals outside the study.

A. validity
B. result
C. analysis
D. data

Question 8. ___________________ is a process of identifying, examining, cleansing, transforming, and modelling data with the aim of discovering useful information.

A. Validity
B. Methodology
C. Data storage
D. Data analysis

3.12 CHAPTER 3 STUDY QUIZ SOLUTIONS

1. B
2. B
3. A
4. A
5. B
6. C
7. A
8. D

3.13 CHAPTER 3 EXERCISES

1. What is a research methodology?
2. What is a qualitative and quantitative study?
3. What is a research question?
4. What is a research hypothesis?
5. What are a population and a sample?
6. Define informed consent?
7. What is confidentiality in a research study?
8. What is data collection?
9. What is data analysis?
10. What is research validity and reliability?

NOTES

1. Creswell, J. W. (2005). *Educational research: Planning, conducting, and evaluating quantitative and qualitative research* (2nd ed.). Columbus, OH: Merrill Prentice Hall.

2. Cooper, D. R., & Schindler, P. S. (2008). *Business research methods* (10th ed.). Boston: Irwin.

3. Rodriguez, A. (2008). Mergers and acquisitions in the banking industry: The human factor. *Organization Development Journal*, 26(2), 63–73. Retrieved from Business Source Complete database.

4. Kotter, J., & Heskett, J. (1992). *Corporate culture and performance*. New York: Free Press.

5. Denison, D. R., & Neale, W. S. (1998). *Denison organizational cultural model survey*. Ann Arbor, MI: Aviat.

Chapter 4

Results

4.1 CORRELATION AND REGRESSION ANALYSIS

Correlation and Regression

Correlation and Regression are the two standard techniques for investigating the relationship between two quantitative variables. Correlation and Regression are the two-analysis based on multivariate distribution. A multivariate distribution is explained as a distribution of multiple variables.

Correlation Analysis

Correlation is the analysis to know the association or the absence of the relationship between two variables "x" and "y." Spearman's correlation coefficient rho and Pearson's product-moment correlation coefficient are the two most popular correlation coefficients. Hence, correlation is a statistical measure that establishes two quantities' co-relationship or association. Correlation is mainly used to represent the linear relationship between two variables. Correlation can be positive or negative. This means that when two variables move in a unilateral direction, that shows an increase in one variable and a corresponding increase in another variable and vice versa. The increase in a variable is deemed to be positively correlated. In comparison, if the two variables move in different directions, an increase in one variable will decrease another variable and vice versa. Then, the decrease in variable shows a negative correlation.

Regression Analysis

Regression is the analysis using an independent variable numerically related to the dependent variable. Regression analysis predicts the value of the dependent variable based on the known value of the independent variable if the average statistical relationship between two or more variables. Regression analysis is a reliable method of identifying which variables impact a topic of interest. The regression process helps determine which factors matter most, which elements could be ignored, and how the factors influence each other.

Two critical variables in the regression analysis are as follows:

The Dependent Variable—Dependent variable is the main factor in a regression analysis study that the researcher needs to understand and predict.

Independent Variables—Independent variables are the factors in a regression analysis study where the research hypothesizes an impact on the dependent variable.

Hypothesis Test of Correlation

The hypothesis test of a correlation coefficient is used to test whether there is a linear relationship between the variables in the population. The null hypothesis means that the population correlation coefficient equals 0.

The Meaning of Research Results

The research results section represents the core findings of a study obtained from the methods applied to collect and analyze data. The result presents these findings in a logical sequence without interpretation bias. The result sets the stage for adequate interpretation and evaluation in the discussion. The primary purpose of the Results section is to break down the data into sentences that show its significance to the research questions.

The Results section appears third in the section sequence in most scientific papers. It follows the presentation of the Methods and Materials and is presented before the Discussion section, although the Results and Discussion are presented together. This section answers the fundamental question, "What did you find in your research?"

Contents of the Research Results

The Results section includes the findings of the study. The findings include:

- Data presented in text, tables, charts, graphs, and other figures
- A contextual analysis of the data explaining its meaning

- Data that relates to the central research questions
- Secondary findings such as subgroup analyses, outcomes, etc.
- The most relevant results to the research question are stated in the beginning

Ways to Organize Results

Results are logically presented in the Result section. The logical and precise method of organizing research results is to provide them with the research questions. Each research question presents the type of data that addresses that research question.

Why does an Organization use Regression Analysis?

- Regression analysis helps to use a statistical method that can be leveraged across an organization to establish the degree to which independent variables influence dependent variables.
- Regression analysis helps to analyze research results to yield valuable, actionable, and business insights from research analysis.

4.2 RESEARCH RESULTS

The quantitative correlational and regression study aimed to examine the relationship between organizational culture and performance in a merged Nigerian bank. The investigation involved identifying if a significant relationship between organizational culture and performance existed in the studied merged bank. To enable the analysis, the study tested the traits of organizational culture on performance in 220 employees of a merged bank in Abuja. The objective of the entire research study focused on three research questions and three alternate hypotheses with corresponding null hypotheses. The research questions helped guide the study by examining if a relationship exists between organizational culture and organizational performance. The quantitative correlational and regression research sought to answer the following three research questions and test the corresponding alternative and null hypothesis:

Research Question 1: What is the relationship between organizational culture traits of mission, comprising consistency, involvement, and adaptability, and employee commitment performance in a merged Nigerian bank?

H_o1: There is no significant relationship between organizational culture traits of mission, consistency, involvement, and adaptability, and employee commitment performance in a merged Nigerian bank.

H_a1: There is a significant relationship between organizational culture traits of mission, consistency, involvement, and adaptability, and employee commitment performance in a merged Nigerian bank.

Research Question 2: What is the relationship between organizational culture traits of mission, comprising consistency, involvement, and adaptability, and job satisfaction performance in a merged Nigerian bank?

H_o2: There is no significant relationship between organizational culture traits of mission, consistency, involvement, adaptability, and job satisfaction performance in a merged Nigerian bank.

H_a2: There is a significant relationship between organizational culture traits of mission, consistency, involvement, and adaptability and the job satisfaction performance in a merged Nigerian bank.

Research Question 3: What is the relationship between organizational culture traits of mission, comprising consistency, involvement, and adaptability, and employee retention performance in a merged Nigerian bank?

Ho3: There is no significant relationship between organizational culture traits of mission, consistency, involvement, and adaptability and employee retention performance in a merged Nigerian bank.

Ha3: There is a significant relationship between organizational culture traits of mission, consistency, involvement, and adaptability and employee retention performance in a merged Nigerian bank.

Chapter 4 presents the data and the results of the statistical analysis. The analysis provided the demographic information of the sample and other characteristics such as means and standard deviations for the three research questions. The study also presented a matrix of multiple regression and correlation results to test the hypothesis. Chapter 4 has three sections: (a) data collection, (b) findings, and (c) chapter summary.

4.3 DATA COLLECTION

Ten bank branches, including the head office in Abuja, participated in the study. The sample of 220 employees was drawn from the population of the merged bank, which includes ten branches and head office, due to the time constraints for the study. The selection process among the 10 merged bank branches, and head office in Abuja used the employee roaster to apply a stratified selection method. A total of 220 employees participated in the study, composed of employees (n=200), managers (n=10), and directors (n=10). The employees were asked in person and by electronic e-mail for their voluntary participation in the study. The potential participants were informed of the study purpose, voluntary nature of participation, and confidentiality of the participants. The current study applied a quantitative correlational and regression design to examine the data related to a merged bank in Nigeria and identify if a significant relationship in organizational performance could be detected based on the difference in organizational culture.

The study examined the differences between organizational culture (independent variable) and organizational performance (dependent variable). The organizational culture aspect of the survey was represented in the 60 closed-ended questions using the Likert-type scale ranging from 1 *(strongly disagree*) to 5 (*strongly agree*). The performance aspect of the survey was represented in three questions using the Likert-type scale ranging from 1 (*negligible*) to 7 (*extremely high*). The demographic element was represented in six questions used to classify the participants for the study.

Data collected during the study were checked for accuracy and manually entered onto a Microsoft Excel spreadsheet. Coded data in the spreadsheet were checked to ensure that no cells were missing data. Data were coded for analysis purposes. Culture survey questions were coded from 1 (strongly *disagree*) to 5 (*strongly agree*), and 8 of the 60 items were reverse coded to ensure coding in the same direction. The reverse coded questions were Q15, Q24, Q29, Q34, Q39, Q43, Q50, and Q58. Performance survey questions were coded from 1 (*negligible*) to 7 (*extremely high*). Male participants were coded with a 1; female participants were coded with a 2. Age categories were coded as a 1 for the 20–30 age group, 2 for the 31–40 age group, 3 for the 41–50 age group, 4 for the 51–60 age group, and 5 for the more than 61+ age group.

The study included four involvement scales, consistency, adaptability, and mission. Each scale had 15 items on the survey, bringing the number of survey questions to 60. Each item on the scale was summed up and divided by the number of questions. For example, the involvement scale was developed by adding Q1 through Q15 and dividing that sum by 15 (the number of questions). Developing the composite traits by summing each item on the scale and dividing by the number of questions enabled the use of the 5-point rating scale for agreement of SD, D, N, A, SA to 1, 2, 3, 4, and 5.

4.4 DEMOGRAPHIC STATISTICS

The DOCP survey instrument collected demographic data on gender, age, marital status, education, employment status, and years of service with the merged Nigerian bank. Demographic information provided the means to classify participants who agreed to the informed consent and responded to the survey ($n = 220$). A Microsoft Excel statistical add-in application program and SPSS statistical software were used to generate descriptive statistics such as mean, mode, and standard deviation. Tables and charts were constructed to depict the results. The demographic characteristics of the merged bank employees showed the features of the participants. Examination of demographic factors offered possible explanations for differences in extraneous variables such as gender, age, marital status, education, employment status, and years of service of the applicants.

The Demographic Characteristics of Participant Sample: Employment

Presents the frequency data for participant employment. All 220 employees received surveys through a hand delivery system. Of that number, 173 were full-time employees and 47 part-time employees. The majority of the participants are full-time employees.

Demographic Characteristics of Participant Sample: Education

Presents the frequency data for participant education. Of the 220 surveys distributed, 32 (15%) were filled out by high school educational level employees, 125 (57%) by college degree employees, 55 (25%) by master degree employees, and 8 (4%) by doctorate employees. The majority of the participants had a college degree.

Of the 220 participants, 150 (68%) were male, and 70 (32%) were female. The male gender represented 68% of the responses, indicating that more male employees participated in the survey.

Demographic Characteristics of Participant Sample: Age

Presents the frequency data for participant age. Of the 220 participants, 80 (36%) were of the age group 20–30, 78 (36%) were of the age group 31–40, 46 (21%) were of the age group 41–50, 14 (6%) were of the age group 51–60, and 2 (1%) were of the age group over 61. Majority of the participants in the age bracket of 20 to 30 represented 36% of the responses, indicating that more young employees participated in the study.

Demographic Characteristics of Participant Sample: Marital Status

Presents the frequency data for participant marital status. Of the 220 participants, 115 (52%) were married, 85 (37%) were single, 13 (6%) were divorced, and 7 (3%) were widowed. The majority of the participants are married employees.

Demographic Characteristics of Participant Sample: Years Employed

Presents the frequency data for participants years of experience in the merged bank under study. Of the 220 participants, 122 (56%) had tenure of service with the merged Nigerian bank of 1–5 years, 58 (26%) had tenure of 6–10 years, 24 (11%) had tenure of 11–15 years, 11 (5%) had tenure 16–20, and 5 (2%) had tenure above 21 years. The majority of the participants had 1–5 years of experience in the merged bank environment.

4.5 MEASURES AND RELIABILITY ANALYSIS OF CULTURE TRAIT SCORES

Organizational Culture Traits: Cronbach's alpha

Presents the Cronbach's alpha values of the analysis performed from data collected for the study. Cronbach's alpha is a tool for measuring the reliability of the research instrument. The Cronbach's alpha helps to measure internal reliability in a research study. The computations of Cronbach's Alpha are appropriate because the current study used summative scales for many interrelated questions intended to measure the same constructs (Vogt, 2007).[1] The study's computed Cronbach's alpha ranged between 0.74 and 0.84, thus validating Denison's organizational culture model. Desired Cronbach's alpha results should measure at least 0.70 to be reliable (Simon, 2006).[2]

The study's Cronbach alpha range is very acceptable and validates the internal reliability of the (DOCP) survey instrument. The model generalizes well with the organizational cultures of the studied merged bank. The higher values represent a more reliable measurement of a variable set of test items. The current study's high Cronbach's alpha range of 0.74 and 0.84 indicates that participants have similar responses to the study elements. In contrast, low Cronbach's alpha indicates variations in participants' reactions to the study elements. The values shown in organizational culture traits of Cronbach's alpha reflect highly consistent study elements. The constant study elements show that duplicating the study to the same sample would theoretically conclude similar results.

4.6 RESEARCH FINDINGS

The research findings are discussed in four sections comprising:

(a) descriptive statistics,

(b) associational and inferential statistics for Research Question 1 and hypothesis test 1,

(c) associational and inferential statistics for Research Question 2 and hypothesis test 2, and

(d) associational and inferential statistics for Research Question 3 and hypothesis test 3.

Descriptive Statistics

The descriptive statistics presents the descriptive statistics for the criterion variables from the 220 study participants. The descriptive statistics show the mean, standard deviation, median, mode, and range of the variables used for the study. For example, the mean of 4.38 for commitment shows that responses are more in agreement with the cultural traits survey questions under a scale of 1 (*strongly disagree*) to 5 (*strongly agree*). The higher score of the mean shows more agreement, while the lower mean score shows disagreement.

Descriptive Statistics: Frequency Percentage of Employee Retention Performance

The descriptive statistics for predictor variables present the descriptive statistics for the predictor variables from the 220 study participants. The descriptive statistics show the mean, standard deviation, median, mode, and range of the variables used for the study. For example, the mean of 3.63 for mission shows that responses are more in agreement with the mission cultural traits survey questions under a scale of 1 (*strongly disagree*) to 5 (*strongly agree*). The higher mean score shows more agreement, while the lower score of the mean shows disagreement—frequency percentages of the descriptive statistics on organizational culture traits 60 survey questions. The central tendency percentages were used. The frequency, rate of responses, a good percentage, and cumulative percentage summarizes the response to each question in the DOCP survey instrument. Organizational performance questions 61 through 63 provide frequency responses on a performance criterion. Most of the responses reflect as follows: employee commitment has the highest frequency of 93 (42%) under moderate performance, job satisfaction has the highest frequency of 70 (32%) under moderate performance, and employee retention has the highest frequency of 58 (26%) under moderate performance.

The highest frequency of 93 (42%) from the frequency percentage on employee retention performance shows that most of the responses to the survey questions are in agreement that the merged bank has a moderate performance rating for employee commitment to organizational performance. The lower frequencies of 2 (0.9%) show that common responses agree that the merged bank has insignificant performance with relationship to employee commitment.

The highest frequency of 70 (32%) shows that most of the responses to the survey questions are in agreement that the merged bank has a moderate performance rating for job satisfaction organizational performance. The lower frequencies of 6 (2.7%) show that inadequate responses agree that the merged bank has insignificant performance related to job performance.

The highest frequency of 58 (26%) shows that most of the responses to the survey questions are in agreement that the merged bank has a moderate performance rating for employee retention organizational performance. The lower frequencies of 17 (7.7%) show that low responses agree that the merged bank has insignificant performance in relation to employee retention.

Associational and Inferential Statistics for RQ 1 and Related Hypotheses

The first research question inquired if a relationship existed between organizational culture traits of mission, comprising consistency, involvement, and adaptability, and employee commitment performance in a merged Nigerian bank. Research Question 1 generated a null hypothesis: there is no significant relationship. The alternative hypothesis was the following: There is a significant relationship for testing organizational cultural traits of mission, comprising consistency, involvement, adaptability, and employee commitment performance. The Pearson r correlation statistic presented a statistically significant evaluation of the linear associations. A Pearson r correlation table was generated to show any correlation between the variables. The Pearson

Table 4.1. Association Statistics

Predictor Variables	*Involvement*	*Consistency*	*Adaptability*	*Mission*
Involvement	1.00	.76*	.73*	.60*
Consistency	.76*	1.00	.73*	.60*
Adaptability	.73*	.71*	1.00	.63*
Mission	.60*	.63*	.63*	1.00

Note: The $^{*}p < 0.05$ indicates the significance of the difference Pearson Product Moment Correlation Matrix for Predictors Variables.

product-moment correlations among the organizational cultural traits are strong and range from .60 to .76 (see Table 4.1). According to Salkind (2006), correlations between .0 and .20 are said to be very weak, correlations between .20 and .40 are said to be weak, .40 to .60 are moderate, .60 to .80 are strong, and .80 to 1.0 are very strong depending on the significance test conducted.

Association Statistics: Pearson Product Moment Correlation Matrix for Criterion Variables (N=220)

The Pearson r correlation was generated between the criterion variables. The Pearson product-moment correlations among the organizational performance are moderate and range from .24 to .55. The strong Pearson product-moment correlations of .60 and .76 among the organizational cultural traits indicate that one variable will allow the prediction of the other variables. The stronger the correlation, the closer the data scores will fall to the regression line toward an accurate forecast.

The standard multiple regression method was used to calculate the numerous correlational coefficients R for the study. The method is also called the simultaneous method or direct method. The direct method is the most widely used statistical method for multiple regression procedures. When the standard method is used, all predictors are entered into the equation in a single stage in the analysis. The standard method provides a complete model solution in that all predictors are part of it (Meyers, Gamst, & Gauarino, 2006)[3]. Variables are entered in a single step. The resulting equation is the outcome of all predictors entered simultaneously. The study's four predictors were the four scale scores on the measurement tool, involvement, consistency, adaptability, and mission. These were joined at once into the multiple regression equation for the three criterion measures and regression procedures.

The R^2, degree of freedom (df), and p-value are represented. R^2 represents the amount of variance in the dependent variable explained by the set of independent variables. R^2can be expressed as a percentage value from 0–100% or decimal from 0–1. The R^2 for the current study was expressed in a percentage representing the variability of the dependent variables explained by the regression model for the set of combined cultural traits. Degrees of freedom (df) are associated with the sources of variance. The regression degrees of freedom correspond to the number of coefficients estimated minus 1. The p-value, also known as the sig F Change, shows the probability level for rejecting the hypothesis. The p-value was compared to the selected confidence level (.05) for the study to test the null hypothesis.

Multiple Regression Model for Criterion Variables

A multiple regression analysis was conducted to evaluate how well the organizational culture traits measured employee commitment in a merged Nigerian bank. The predictors were four organizational culture trait variables: mission, consistency, involvement, and adaptability, whereas the criterion variable for the first regression procedure was employee commitment. The results reflected that the linear combination of the predictor organizational variables was significantly related to employee commitment: $F(4,215) = 21.84$, $p < .05$

Inferential Statistics: Multiple Correlational Coefficients for Employee Commitment

The sample multiple correlational coefficient R was .54, indicating that approximately ($R^2 = .289$) or 29% of the variance in employee commitment was explained. R^2 percentage represents the variability of the dependent variable explained by the regression equation. The correlation zero-order column represents the correlations between combined predictors and employee commitment. The partial zero-order correlation represents the correlation between each predictor and employee commitment while controlling all predictors. Only the partial correlation between employee commitment and mission was significant at .40. The bivariate correlations between the organizational cultural traits and employee commitment were positive. Bivariate correlations showed the data set that involved the paired values of the variables. All were statistically significant at the $p < .05$ level.

Scatter plots, correlation coefficients, and linear regression coefficients are interrelated. A scatter plot shows the typical graphical representation of the bivariate data set. The correlation coefficient measures the linear association between the variables. The regression coefficient describes the linear association through a number that gives the expected change in the response per unit change in the predictor. The scatter plots graph illustrates the differences between the individual predictors and the observed dependent variable. The scatter plot allows for the visual evaluation of the goodness of fit of the selected model. The partial regression plot portrays the involvement dependent variable and performance variable employee commitment. The regression plot depicts a graphical representation of the individual data set for the study. The negative correlation of -.08 predicts no significant relationship between the cultural trait of involvement and the performance variable employee commitment.

Partial Regression Plot for Involvement and the Dependent Variable: Employee Commitment

The partial regression plot for consistency dependent variable and performance variable employee commitment depicts a graphical representation of the individual data set for the study. The negative correlation of -.03 predicts no significant relationship between consistency's cultural trait and employee commitment's performance variable.

Partial Regression Plot for Consistency and the Dependent Variable: Employee Commitment

The partial regression plot for adaptability dependent variable and performance variable employee commitment. The regression plot depicts a graphical representation of the individual data set for the study. The correlation of .13 predicts no significant relationship between the cultural trait of adaptability and the performance variable employee commitment.

Partial Regression Plot for Adaptability and the Dependent Variable: Employee Commitment.

The partial regression plot for the mission-dependent variable and performance variable employee commitment depicts a graphical representation of the individual data set for the study. The positive correlation of .40 predicts a significant relationship between the cultural trait of mission and the performance variable employee commitment.

Based on the statistical analysis, one can conclude that mission probably accounted for 16% of the variance in employee commitment, and the other predictors accounted for 13% (29%–16%). The bivariate correlations between organizational cultural traits and employee commitment were positive. All were statistically significant at the $p < .05$ level. The predictors are highly inter-correlated, so the conclusion is speculative.

Partial Regression Plot for Mission and the Dependent Variable: Employee Commitment.

Correlational and regression analyses do not allow the interpretation of cause-and-effect relationships. Instead, correlation indicates the strength of relationships, and regression reveals dependence between variables. The analysis results indicate the null hypothesis should be rejected because a significant relationship exists between the combination of the predictor variables and employee commitment performance.

Associational and Inferential Statistics for RQ 2 and Related Hypotheses

The second research question inquired if a relationship existed between organizational culture traits of mission, comprising consistency, involvement, and adaptability, and on-the-job satisfaction performance in a merged Nigerian bank. Research Question 2 generated a null hypothesis: that there is no significant relation, and an alternative hypothesis: that there is an important relationship for testing organizational culture traits of mission, comprising consistency, involvement, adaptability, and on-the-job satisfaction performance.

A multiple regression analysis was conducted to evaluate how well the organizational culture traits measured job satisfaction in the studied merged bank. The predictors were four organizational culture trait variables: mission, consistency, involvement, and adaptability, whereas the criterion variable for the second regression procedure was job satisfaction. The sample multiple correlational coefficient R was .29, indicating that approximately ($R^2 = 0.85$) or 9% of the variance in job satisfaction was explained. The results reflected that the linear combination of the predictor organizational variables was significantly related to job satisfaction: $F(4,215) = 5.01$, $p < .05$

Inferential Statistics: Multiple Correlational Coefficients for Job Satisfaction

The multiple correlational coefficients for job satisfaction show the individual predictors' relative strength. The correlation zero-order column represents the correlations between combined predictors and job satisfaction. The partial zero-order correlation means the correlation between each predictor and employee commitment while controlling all predictors. The bivariate correlations between the organizational cultural traits and job satisfaction were positive. All were statistically significant at the $p < 0.05$ level.

Partial regression plot for involvement and the dependent variable: Job satisfaction.

The partial regression plot for involvement and the dependent variable for job satisfaction shows the partial regression plot for involvement cultural trait and performance variable job satisfaction. The regression plot depicts a graphical representation of the individual data set for the study. The correlation of 0.04 predicts no significant relationship between the cultural trait of involvement and the performance variable job satisfaction. The partial regression plot for consistency cultural trait and performance variable job satisfaction depicts a graphical representation of the individual data set for the study.

The negative correlation of -0.02 predicts no significant relationship between the cultural trait of consistency and the performance variable job satisfaction.

Partial Regression Pot for Adaptability Dependent Variable: Job Satisfaction

The partial regression plot for adaptability, cultural trait, and performance variable job satisfaction depicts a graphical representation of the individual data set for the study. The correlation of .06 predicts no significant relationship between the cultural trait of adaptability and the performance variable job satisfaction.

Partial Regression Plot for Mission Dependent Variable: Job Satisfaction

The partial regression plot for mission cultural trait and performance variable job satisfaction depicts a graphical representation of the individual data set for the study. The positive correlation of .15 predicts a significant relationship between the cultural trait of mission and the performance variable job satisfaction. The statistical analysis showed only the partial correlation between job satisfaction and mission was significant. One can conclude that mission accounted for 2% of the variance in job satisfaction and the other predictors accounted for 7% (9%–2%). The bivariate correlations between organizational cultural traits and job satisfaction were positive. All were statistically significant at the $p < 0.05$ level. The predictors are highly intercorrelated, so the results are speculative.

Partial Regression Plot for Mission Dependent Variable: Job Satisfaction

Using the correlational and regression analyses, the partial regression plot for mission dependent variable for job satisfaction does not allow interpretation of cause-and-effect relationships. Instead, correlation indicates the strength of relationships, and regression reveals dependence between variables. The analysis results indicate the null hypothesis should be rejected because a significant relationship exists between a combination of the predictor variables and job satisfaction performance.

Associational and Inferential Statistics for RQ 3 and Related Hypotheses

The third research question inquired if a relationship existed between organizational culture traits of mission, comprising consistency, involvement, adaptability, and employee retention performance. Research Question 3 generated a null hypothesis: that there is no significant relationship and an alternative hypothesis: that there is an essential relationship for testing organizational culture traits of mission comprising consistency, involvement, adaptability, and employee retention performance. A multiple regression analysis was conducted to evaluate how well the organizational culture traits measured employee retention in a merged Nigerian bank.

The predictors were four organizational culture trait variables: mission, consistency, involvement, and adaptability, while the criterion variable for the third regression procedure was employee retention. The results reflected that the linear combination of the predictor organizational variables was significantly related to employee retention: $F\ (4,215) = 3.95$, $p < 0.05$. The sample multiple correlational coefficient R was 0.26, indicating that approximately ($R^2 = 0.068$) or 7% of the variance in employee retention was explained.

Inferential Statistics: Multiple Correlational Coefficients for Employee Retention

The relative strength of the individual predictors and the correlation zero-order column represents the correlations between combined predictors and employee retention. The partial correlation zero-order represents the correlation between each predictor and employee commitment while controlling all predictors. The predictors are highly intercorrelated, so the results are speculative. Correlational and regression analyses do not allow the interpretation of cause-and-effect relationships. Instead, correlation indicates the strength of relationships, and regression reveals dependence between variables. The analysis results indicate the null hypothesis should be rejected because a significant relationship exists between the combination of the predictor variables and employee retention performance.

Partial Regression Plot for Involvement Dependent Variable: Employee Retention

The partial regression plot for involvement dependent variable and performance variable employee retention. The regression plot depicts a graphical representation of the individual data set for the study. The correlation of 0.01

predicts no significant relationship between the cultural trait of involvement and the performance variable employee retention.

Partial Regression Plot for Consistency Dependent Variable: Employee Retention

The partial regression plot for consistency dependent variable and performance variable employee retention. The regression plot depicts a graphical representation of the individual data set for the study. The negative correlation of -0.05 predicts no significant relationship between the cultural trait of consistency and the performance variable employee retention

Partial Regression Plot for Adaptability Dependent Variable: Employee Retention

The partial regression plot for adaptability dependent variable and performance variable employee retention. The regression plot depicts a graphical representation of the individual data set. The correlation of 0.13 predicts no significant relationship between the cultural trait of adaptability and the performance variable employee retention.

Partial Regression Plot for Mission Dependent Variable: Employee Retention

The partial regression plot for mission dependent variable and performance variable employee retention. The regression plot depicts a graphical representation of the individual data set for the study. The correlation of .12 predicts no significant relationship between the cultural trait of mission and the performance variable employee retention.

Based on the statistical analysis, none of the partial correlations between organizational cultural traits and employee retention was significant. The bivariate correlations between organizational cultural traits and employee retention were positive. All were statistically significant at the $p < 0.05$ level.

4.6 SUMMARY

The focus of the research study was to examine if there is a significant relationship between organizational culture traits of (mission, consistency, involvement, and adaptability) and organizational performance of (employee commitment, job satisfaction, and employee retention) in a merged Nigerian bank. The use of quantitative correlational and regression analyses supported the statistical goals of the study by identifying a significant positive relationship between a combination of cultural traits and organizational performance. The regression model only predicted a variance of 29% in employee commitment, 9% in job satisfaction, 7% in employee retention, and only mission is a significant predictor. The bivariate correlations between the combination of the organizational cultural traits and each performance criterion were positive. All were statistically significant at the $p < 0.05$ level.

The strong Pearson product-moment correlations among the organizational cultural traits ranged from 0.60 to 0.76. Based on the statistical analysis, the three null hypotheses for the study were rejected because a significant relationship exists between a combination of the predictor variables and each performance criteria. Overall, the data analysis results indicated that the considerable difference between the predictor cultural traits was related to enhanced or weakened organizational performance. Organizational performance was higher for integrated cultural traits, while execution was lower for the individual cultural traits. Chapter 5 includes discussions of business architecture and the challenges of post-merger integration.

4.7 CHAPTER 4 STUDY QUIZ QUESTIONS

Question 1. ________________ is the process of gathering and measuring information on variables of interest in an established systematic approach that enables one to answer stated research questions, test hypotheses, and evaluate outcomes.

A. Data analysis
B. Data collection
C. Data storage
D. Data cleaning

Question 2. The data collection component of research is common to all fields of study, including physical and social sciences, humanities, business, etc.

A. True
B. False

Question 3. Which of the following are methods of data collection?

A. Interviews
B. Surveys and questionnaires.

C. Observations.
D. All of the above

Question 4. ________________ is the process of collecting and analyzing numerical data.

A. Qualitative research
B. Quantitative research
C. Deductive study
D. All of the above

Question 5. ________________are used to find patterns and averages, make predictions, test causal relationships, and generalize results to wider populations.

A. Quantitative research
B. Qualitative research
C. Deductive study
D. All of the above

Question 6. __________________ relies on data obtained by the researcher from first-hand observation, interviews, questionnaires, recordings made in natural settings, documents, case studies, and artifacts.

A. Qualitative research
B. Quantitative research
C. Deductive study
D. All of the above

Question 7. Which of the following best describes a cultural trait?

A. A characteristic of human skills transmitted at a workplace.
B. A characteristic of human skills transmitted only via communication
C. a characteristic of human action that is not acquired socially and not transmitted via modes of communication.
D. A characteristic of human activity that's developed by people socially and sent via various methods of communication.

Question 8. Cultural traits allow for a part of one culture to be transmitted to another.

A. True
B. False

4.8 CHAPTER 4 STUDY QUIZ SOLUTIONS

1. B
2. A
3. D
4. B
5. A
6. A
7. D
8. A

4.9 CHAPTER 4 EXERCISES

1. What is correlation analysis?
2. What is regression analysis?
3. What is a statistics measurement?
4. What is a research problem?
5. What is the primary purpose of the Results Section in a research study?
6. What are the types of data collection processes?
7. Why is a demographic statistic important in a research study?
8. List and explain the two critical variables in the regression analysis?
9. Explain the contents of the Research Results
10. Why should Organization use regression analysis?

NOTES

1. Vogt, W. P. (2007). *Quantitative research methods for professionals*. Boston: Allyn & Bacon.
2. Simon, M. K. (2005). *Dissertation & scholarly research: A practical guide to start & complete your dissertation, thesis, or formal research project*. Dubuque, IA: Kendall/Hunt.
3. Meyers, L. S., Gamst, G., & Guarino, A. J. (2006). *Applied multivariate research*. Thousand Oaks, CA: Sage.

Chapter 5

Discussion

5.1 ENTERPRISES ARCHITECTURE INVOLVEMENT IN MERGER AND ACQUISITION STAGES

Enterprise Architecture in Mergers and Acquisitions

Business architecture offers a connection between an enterprise business model and strategy. The business functionality of a company enables the system to execute a mapped methodology. People who create and maintain business architecture are known as business architects. Figure 5.1 shows LeanIX surveyed in a global customer base showing enterprise architects' role in M&A activities. A vital part of merger and acquisition for an enterprise architect portrays more impact of 89% is in post-merger integration (PMI). The survey outcomes show that enterprise architects contribute to the business and IT integrations, especially during merger integrations.

5.2 MERGER AND ACQUISITION AS A CHANGE MANAGEMENT AGENT

Change management using the variables of the plan, improve, team, execute, and engage is drawing a plan for the changes coming within the organization, preparing how to train employees for the changes, and addressing all stakeholders affected by these changes. Many business leaders seek to overcome obstacles by establishing a change management program. Change program needs to involve the organization's leaders as sponsors of change and the project team members as change agents and the employees who will be affected by the alterations to the work environment" (Rothermel & LaMarsh, 2012).[1] The first things that change management is working on are how they will

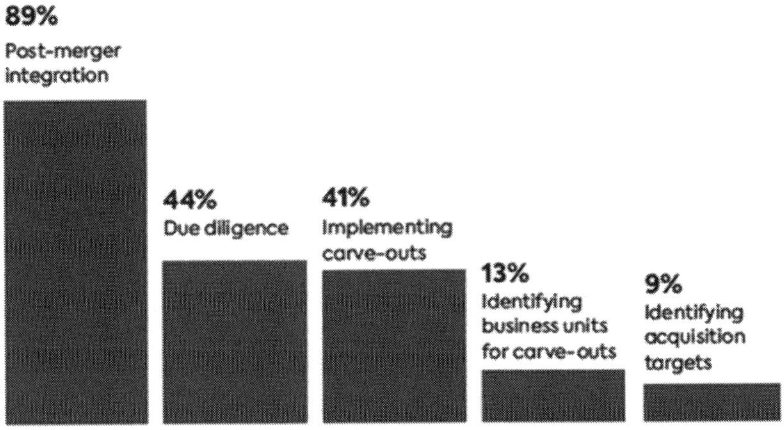

Figure 5.1. M&A Process: Enterprise Architecture Involvement Stages
Source: LeanIX Mergers & Acquisitions Survey, January 2021.

break the news and prepare employees for change. People are usually reluctant to change as they are comfortable with everyday activities. Many people become disrupted and fear change because they believe this can impact their job status, level of success, etc. Unfreezing is the first step that change management will conduct throughout the organization. Change management will support the plan to prepare workers and ensure they are ready for the change. Managers need to create a sense that there needs to be a change within the organization for these processes to be effective and for them to be more open to change. When workers see the positive results from the changes made, workers are more open to accepting change in the organization. The change plan helps prepare managers to conduct a mandatory meeting where all workers within a branch or their respective departments will attend to learn about the change process and the reason behind the change, and how these will help our organization and help them in the long run (Yurcan, 2012).[2]

The change process occurs after the freezing part. At that point, employees have learned about the changes being made in the organization and how the changes will help the organization. During this part, the company should teach employees how to deal with customer backlash, keep customers happy, and make sure they understand the changes and how they can help their relationship with us. Because of this, we are working on designing products that will be changed to keep us profitable and reward customers for doing business with us. We need to train employees to deliver this message to our customers and new customers to sell them on the idea that these changes are necessary. Still, even though changes can be daunting, these can be very effective and good for them. We are working on the refreezing part, which helps workers carry out these processes and continue to help through the aftermath of the changes. We will design a team that will help them answer any questions they may have about any of the changes made in the organization. Ensuring that we have a team that can continue to help workers through transition is essential and is something that we cannot look over. Therefore, we will have this team available for everyone for the next year to ensure that our transition and changes are smooth and that all questions can be answered by employees and customers.

Change Management for Improved Effectiveness

To make sure that the company reinforces throughout the workforce because changes are necessary and how they will help everyone across the organization. Change requires a system that will keep co-workers updated and upbeat about this change. Some improved effectiveness of change includes:

- To assist in career development and cater to more customers.
- To help in productivity because the new processes will streamline various tasks
- The change will help cut printing and paper costs and steer us toward becoming a "greener organization."
- The change will help career development.
- The change will help to attract more customers.

As the company continues to grow, the change process will keep employees updated on the results of the changes. These include having side-by-side comparisons of their productivity before and after the change. We will continue to send out notifications once a week that will contain updates on how our numbers have improved. These will keep employees up to date on how what we have been teaching them since the beginning of the change was not just word of mouth but rather something that has turned out to be what we had been predicting. These will also help employees' predisposition to change and help with any future changes the organization needs to make. These changes will attract customers, including an increase in production and customer base.

Change management with timely and effective implementation of business-required changes results to risk management and minimization of the negative impact of changes to the business. Adequate performance ensures that changes achieve desired business outcomes, and that governance and compliance expectations are met. Given the day and age of technology, it makes more sense for a company to adapt to change processes and move everything in that direction. These changes will impact employees because they will need to learn new techniques and products. Customers will also be affected by the changes. Overall, these changes will improve the organization and each employee.

5.2 CHALLENGES OF POST-MERGER INTEGRATION

Mergers and acquisition integration have many challenges, from technical integration to various business processes, strategic direction, people, and culture. To enable merger success, organizations need to develop a plan on ways to handle these challenges.

1. *Technical Challenges*—When organizations merge, technology is interlinked throughout the merger transformation process. The most critical challenge of combining two organizations is synchronizing different technology environments. Integrating information technology and legal entity alignment poses more hurdles in managing an M&A deal. The complexity of modern technology settings could lead to more IT challenges, including:
   - Lack of visibility in the technical assets and related to business capabilities.
   - Lack of compliance with cybersecurity standards and regulatory bodies during international mergers.
   - Insufficient resources from the merging companies
2. *Business Challenges*—Merger and acquisition integration faces technical challenges related to workforce management after the merger deal. Mergers and acquisition integrations could make top management apprehensive about the future of the newly established organization. They need to incorporate proactive leadership to retain skilled workers and successfully integrate post-merger.
3. *Lack of Strategic Direction*—During post-merger integration, the organization needs strategic direction to allow both organizations to remain operational while establishing the best solutions to support the new entity's business capabilities. If there is no clear direction, this merged company faces misinformation and workforce disconnection challenges.
4. *Change Management Challenges*—After a merger deal, the new company faces change management challenges. This challenge is lateral to the technical issues in any post-merger integration. The inability to communicate the value behind changes could cause negative impact

employee turnover. Lack of effective leadership from the combined organization could cause challenges in developing a robust technical environment, resulting in a weak future IT environment. Some examples of business challenges in post-merger integration include:

5. *Merger Process Integration*—Post-merger integration aims to plan and implement the integration of two businesses. Each business has many processes to be integrated with another company. This creates more challenges in combining both methods.
6. *Merger Cultural Integration*—Cultural integration during merger and acquisition is often overlooked until conflict emerges.
7. *Stakeholder Merger Alignment*—The process of stakeholders' merger integration focuses on the goals and tasks set at the merger process. In terms of growth of business efficiency, businesses could develop other forms of business integration which could pose challenges
8. *Merger Integration Performance*—Pre-merger and post-merger planning is critical as companies face pressure to deliver synergies as soon as possible. The factors that affect post-merger integration success, such as the culture of the companies, need to be assessed and spun into the merger synergy value.
9. *Clarity of Mission in the Merger Process*—Mergers and acquisitions need clarity of mission to be successful. The primary due diligence before a merger is defining a shared mission. Leaders at this level face challenges in integrating the task of both companies. For example, the merger of AT&T and DirecTV creates synergy and market disruption by merging distribution channels for entertainment and communication. Hence, starting with purpose and mission is vital in a merger to ensure the merger's success.
10. *Leadership Alignment in the Merger Process*—During the merger, the acquired company's management team faced challenges with expectations of buyer alignment. Mergers success requires executive alignment on the goals for value and performance as an approach to mitigating integration risks, culture, and ways of working. De-stabilization in the core leadership of an organization could inflict turmoil on growth and integration plans.
11. *Collaboration of Us Versus Them*—The acquired company could feel they were being swallowed. Humans are tribal. They might think that their best skills and qualities will be wiped away.
12. *Entrepreneur Versus Corporate in the Merger Process*—There are differences between private and public companies. These differences could conflict with the essential people-centered aspects of a business. Leadership accessibility could develop confusion as people try to navigate their differences.

5.3 POST-MERGER INTEGRATION CHECKLIST

Merger and acquisition integration is bringing two or more firms together to maximize synergies to ensure that the deal meets the target objective and its expected value. The exact process is sometimes referred to as post-acquisition integration. The importance of this post-acquisition integration includes the following:

1. *Relationship between Business and Technology*—Digital assets are the pillar for developing and maintaining customer relationships—the business and technology help automate processes and operations by saving costs and reducing overhead.
2. *The Digital Age*—The digital age is when people value meaningful relationships, feel connected to other people, and have opportunities to connect, learn, and share with others. Merger in the digital age contributes to the driving forces behind business activities' growth. Previously, companies entered M&A deals to realize economies of scale, such as to capture a more extensive customer base and increase their negotiating power. Recently, companies joined mergers and acquisitions for more factors and synergies using digital interconnectivity and market diversification techniques.
3. *Hiring Processes for Short- and Long-Term Needs*—The post-merger process includes hiring for short-term and long-term, redundancies, turnover, employee retention, M&A IT integration, technology, systems migrations, and tracking employee performance. The post-merger integration checklist includes the following: Source: DealRoom (n.d).

   A. Hiring Process
      - Short-term needs
      - Long -term needs
      - Process
      - Benefits/compensation

   B. Overlap and Redundancies
      - Secure top employees
      - Layoffs and severance forms

   C. Technology
      - New org chart
      - Merge systems

   D. Employee Performance
      - Training plans
      - Employee review documents and procedures
      - HR systems

5.4 IT STRATEGY CHALLENGES IN MERGER AND ACQUISITION DEAL

The IT challenges encountered during a merger could be divided into eight major factors:

1. IT Integration Strategy Challenge

An efficient IT Integration strategy should be adopted at the early stages of a merger once the deal is approved. Nevertheless, the need for technical compatibility is vital as a due diligence measure in the merger phase to standardize the IT applications, systems, and databases used in their business operations. Both merging companies should be clear and concise on their IT integration to decide on what to keep, discard or migrate, and align on the best practices.

2. IT Transparency Strategy Challenge

Lack of IT transparency causes mergers to fail. Enabling IT transparency is a requirement when integrating two or more separate organizations. There could be obsolete applications in the newly integrated IT design, resulting in unnecessary expenditures and increased IT risks.

3. IT Collaboration Strategy Challenge

IT collaboration among IT teams is vital when sharing current and relevant information during mergers. Thus, the collaboration strategy opens doors for clear visibility of the newly integrated IT environment. The main factor in ensuring visibility across both organizations' landscapes is business capabilities. IT best practices help to show that the post-merger integration process provides the right concept level for mapping applications. Once full transparency for all applications for the business capability is achieved, decisions could be made about what to keep or discard.

4. IT Compliance and Security Challenge

Two merging companies do not have the same compliance process. Thus, they could pose a technology risk in the M&A. IT encounters several challenges with data management, such as support for different cybersecurity standards. Certifying that all information is safe and secure is a crucial task for any organization during an M&A. If one organization is faster than the other, confidential information shared in one place could become vulnerable to hackers and different unwanted audiences.

5. Systems and Process Strategy Challenge

The acquired company's business processes and supporting IT systems must be migrated onto the acquirer's system to maintain and absorb merger integration. The challenge this creates relates to end-user training, which could be overlooked. For efficient integration, an assessment needs to be done to identify the strengths and weaknesses of each company and determine the component to be selected for the new company. However, this migration often requires additional application interfaces, third-party application interfaces, or a suitable middleware.

6. Data Integration Strategy Challenge

Merging firms need to create data interfaces between the systems of the acquirer and the acquired companies to support a consolidated outcome of business performance. Hence, there might be a potential risk of a data breach or unauthorized access. For example, a data breach disclosure by Yahoo in 2017 which showed a $350 million reduction in company sales price during a merger and acquisition by Verizon. Another example was the Starwood-Marriott merger deal that established a security breach shortly after the merger announcement that led to a 5.6% decrease in Marriott's share price (DealRoom, n.d).[3]

7. Asset Management Strategy Challenge

When the acquired company stops to exist legally post-merger, the transfer of related software licenses, services, and maintenance contracts could be challenging due to the "change of ownership" contract clauses and other associated rules and regulations.

8. Workforce Challenge Strategy Challenge

Among the most vital asset in any company is the workforce with their talents. The challenge of recruiting and retaining the high in a best-of-breed or absorption-style integration comes to play during integration. Uncertainty about future jobs and roles is increased during the pre-merger and post-merger phases. Hence, there is a risk of decreased productivity and losing high-performing employees during the merger integration.

5.5 ORGANIZATIONAL CULTURE CHALLENGES IN MERGER AND ACQUISITION

The M&A process is demanding and takes plenty of communication and patience to get a successful deal. Business activities are dynamic, and things frequently change, affecting a transition plan that keeps multiple systems running. This impacts IT in the business environment. As organizations think about the strategic and tactical responsibilities for a smooth transition, they also need to carry on with all the daily activities that keep the original company running. During the merger and acquisition planning, the top-level executives need to understand some common cultural challenges in the merger process, such as:

1. *Balancing Conflicting Priorities:*

The merger and acquisition process requires IT to focus on balancing conflicting responsibilities. Good communication and technology allow IT support to manage tasks and address concerns that may arise during the merger process.

2. *Inefficiency for Inability to Access Data:*

The inability to access data from the target company causes challenges. The IT might not see the details and affected components. This impedes technology's ability to take swift action on aligning technology and discovering synergies.

3. *Confusion from Inaccurate Data:*

The existence of the wrong data could cause the M&A process to fail. Only correct and verified data must be transferred with IT system integration.

4. *Inability to Keep a Schedule for Projects and Operations on*

IT must "keep the lights on" and ensure that the business operations are run as usual. The IT resources are at full capacity with people working on merger-related tasks, regular operations like accounts payable and accounts receivable need to keep running smoothly.

5. *Failure to Meet Business Goals*

The merger and acquisition are long-term projects. The IT support desk needs to be business-focused to help the organization understand the strategic goals of the deal.

Different situation faces different challenges; thus, it is essential to identify these issues as early as possible. Once the risk is identified, the team shall collaborate to address the issue. The organization needs to team up to reprioritize the routine tasks and duties. Mergers add some uncertainty to the process, which requires flexibility so the organization can handle new projects and issues as they transpire.

5.6 REASONS WHY MERGER FAILS

As merger and acquisition benefits organizations, some of the reason why merger fails to include the following nine factors:

1. *Lack of Good Motive for the Merger and Acquisition*

Merger and acquisition that lacks good motive fail. An excellent way to avoid more significant failure is to spend more time on practical strategic planning.

2. *Targeting the Wrong Company for the Merger and Acquisition*

When companies target the wrong company for merger and acquisition, the deal tends to fail. Doing research and analysis helps identify a suitable target company before conducting mergers or acquisitions. This involves avoiding bias at the heart of M&A. Thus, the success in M&A is acquiring the right firm.

3. *Overestimating Synergies for the Merger and Acquisition*

The overestimating synergies occur when inflated plans are made. This could generate increased revenue or cost savings due to the transaction. The overestimated merger issue could not be recovered throughout the lifecycle of the merger deal. To avoid overestimating synergies, conservatism is the best approach. For example, dividing the profit into two is conservative when the plan shows more profit.

4. *Overpaying for the Merger and Acquisition*

The most common issue in mergers or acquisitions is overpaying for acquiring companies. The mergers and acquisition challenges mostly devastate the company value, making an overpayment unavoidable. An efficient way of preventing overpayment is by using a suitable value for the acquiring company.

5. *Exogenous Risks for the Merger and Acquisition*

Industry, economic, and technological shifts could cause mergers to fail. It is an excellent plan to build conditions into the merger transaction to protect the firms against downside risks such as customer base numbers, termination of essential contracts, and dropping sales.

6. *Lack of Stakeholders' Trust in the Merger and Acquisition*

Human capital is a significant part of modern businesses, yet many mergers and acquisitions pay less attention to it, which leads to more M&A challenges. The non-buy-in of the stakeholders contributes to the merger and acquisition failure.

7. *Inadequate Due Diligence in the Merger and Acquisition*

Lack of due diligence contributes to merger failure. Everyone in M&A should adopt due diligence, but shortcuts are very common. Thus, following shortcuts causes the most common problems faced in mergers and acquisitions. Efficiency disallows cutting corners, and there is no excuse for not conducting thorough due diligence.

8. *Failing to Pull out of a Merger when all Evidence is Unfavorable*

If the due diligence analysis shows an unfavorable status during a merger and acquisition, it portrays a sign of merger failure. Failing to back out from the merger deal could lead to merger failure. In addition, there is always a temptation to go ahead with an agreement after a certain point has been reached. For example, if a good rapport with the owner of the target company deal is a guaranteed winner.

9. *Failed Merger and Acquisition Integration*

Merger integration occurs after a merger deal. Merger challenges during Integration include culture and change management, which could develop an inefficient work environment. Merger integration is part of the required due diligence to straighten the merger process. The organization should plan the integration in detail to ensure adequate implementation to avoid a failed integration.

5.7 MERGER BIBLIOGRAPHIES: BEST PRACTICES

Organizational restructuring such as mergers and acquisitions has become a worldwide trend for enterprises to achieve their strategic objectives. In a dynamic technology business environment, mergers and acquisitions have become one of the fastest paths for firms to operate in modern markets and integrate new resources. Thus, the value of M&A transactions rose from $200 billion in 1992 to about $4.74 trillion by 2017 (Kumar, 2019, pp. 1).[4] The following are some best practices of recent mergers and acquisitions:

Culjak (2021). Analysis of Acquisition Success in Soft Beverage Industry of the Republic of Croatia.

The Croatian food and beverage industry is essential since it has the largest share of Croatia's gross domestic product and total employment (Culjak, 2021).[5] The sector witnessed consistent growth, and the opportunities for geographic expansion of product portfolio are one of the main drivers of mergers and acquisitions transactions in the food and beverage industry. Culjak (2021) concluded that the food and beverage industry is appropriate for long-term investors looking to diversify their business holdings by entering a low-risk environment and thus creating multiple uncorrelated cash-flow streams. As consumer preferences evolve over time, the offering by soft beverage companies needs to keep up with this trend of growing consumer preferences. Culjak (2021) stated that the organizations that will be successful in consumer preferences provide the highest return for their owners and position themselves as the industry leaders.

Bor & Shargel (2020). The merger of Baltimore Hebrew University with Towson University: three leadership models converge

Baltimore Hebrew Institute (BHI), formerly Baltimore Hebrew University at Towson University, is committed to supporting the education of Jewish educators, communal professionals, and Judaic studies scholars who wish to excel in their chosen fields. The findings from the merger of Baltimore Hebrew University (BHU) with Towson University (TU) integrated the three leadership approaches that facilitated the successful merger to BHI. Bor & Shargel (2020) explored the confluence of leadership approaches, the mutual benefits for both universities, and resistance on both sides. They provided the implications to help inform other universities seeking to merge. The union of the three leadership approaches yielded a successful merger. The visionary leaders negotiated a "merger deal" to integrate BHU into Towson. The visionary leaders were at the top of each hierarchy and visualized the integration of a private nonprofit into a large public university. Furthermore, the leaders entrusted legal and financial advisors who helped them figure out logistical details outside of the academic decisions made by deans, chairs, and faculty members Bor & Shargel (2020).

Visionary leaders left the process and transmitted the mandate to merge with transformational leaders. The latter figured out how to evaluate the programs to find the correct placement for faculty and staff. In addition, the transformational leaders created the BHI so that BHU could retain part of its name and still be a known entity in the Jewish community. By creating BHI, the leaders made a place for a smaller community within Towson, which was essential as such a small university could quickly disappear into the larger milieu. Hence, transformational leaders worked closely in conjunction with servant leaders, who figured out how to obtain permissions from accreditors and coordinate the logistics of absorbing student records, new offices, and programs. Servant leaders cared for each student's needs. They made sure transfer students at all levels could continue their studies at Towson Bor & Shargel (2020).

Strategic Mergers in Higher Education by Ricardo Azziz, Guilbert C. Hentschke, Lloyd A. Jacobs, and Bonita C. Jacobs Johns Hopkins University Press Baltimore, MD 2019 288 Pages ISBN 9781421432601

Colleges and universities operate in an uncertain environment. Decreasing numbers of high school graduates, an international competition for students, the rise of different training programs, and the cost of maintaining technology and organizational change put many higher institutions in the challenging position of facing extreme measures to persist. The mergers of higher education institutions (HEIs) occurred in the mid-nineteenth century. Since the beginning of the current century, over 100 HEI mergers have happened in the United States (Hinton, 2020). Mergers of international HEIs occur at nearly the same rate, and the pace of mergers worldwide appears to be accelerating. Mergers are not commonplace, and people who have the experience needed to execute a merger successfully are relatively few. To heighten the challenges, the success of the process relies on factors unique to the specific institutions involved. This shows that the experience gained in one merger may not be applicable in another.

Bhattarai, K., Prasuna, A., & Kumar, S. N. V. S. (2021). Economic and institutional determinants of mergers & acquisitions in BRICS, G7, and G20 economies. The Journal of Applied Business and Economics, 23(7), 8–20.

Factors influencing the increase in the number of mergers and acquisitions (M &A) among corporations and the volume of business and sales of these firms are assessed empirically based on the static and dynamic panel data models for BRICS, G7, and G20 countries.

- BRICS is an acronym for Brazil, Russia, India, China, and South Africa. Goldman Sachs economist Jim O'Neill coined the term BRIC (without South Africa) in 2001, claiming that by 2050 the four BRIC economies would come to dominate the global economy by 2050. South Africa was added to the list in 2010.
- The G20 is the Group of Twenty of an intergovernmental forum comprising 19 countries and the European Union (EU). It focuses on addressing major issues related to the global economy, such as international financial stability, climate change mitigation, and sustainable development.
- The Group of Seven (G7) is an inter-governmental political forum consisting of Canada, France, Germany, Italy, Japan, the United Kingdom, and the United States. Its members are the world's largest International Monetary Fund (IMF) advanced economies and the wealthiest liberal democracies.

While the higher rates of economic growth and foreign direct investment (FDI) contribute positively to M &A activities, these effects are even more pronounced with greater productivity in government institutions on qualities of regulation, voice accountability, and control of corruption. Hence, higher inflation and corporation tax rates reduce the numbers but the volumes of the M & A activities. Size of the business matters; medium or large corporations merge to exploit scale economies, benefit from larger markets, and retain market power by operating across the globe.

According to Bhattarai, Prasuna, & Kumar (2021).

Economic and institutional determinants of mergers & acquisitions in BRICS, G7, and G20 economies quantile panel regressions using the value of mergers as the dependent variable, showed that the Foreign Direct Investment Inflows (FDIIN), Foreign Direct Investment Outflows (FDIOUT), corporate tax and six Institutional governance variables namely, government effectiveness (GE), control of corruption (CC), political stability (PS), Rule of Law (RL), regulatory quality (RQ), and voice accountability (VA) and the level of Gross Domestic Product (GDP) and institutional factors play highly significant roles in determining either the number or the value of the M&A deals among firms in BRICS, G7 and G20 countries with slight differences in magnitudes of these results. Significant findings of the study are that while the economic growth and FDI contribute positively to the occurrence of M&A activities, these effects are even more prominent with efficiency in a government institution, qualities of regulation, voice accountability, and control of corruption. However, higher inflation and corporation tax reduce the M&A activities. Medium or large companies merge to exploit scale economies, gain from larger markets, and retain market power by operating across the globe. These results are based on the static and dynamic panel data models for BRICS, G7, and G20 countries.

Williams, Henry E, M.B.A., PhD., Roberts, C., PhD., & Shires, J., Ph.D. (2019). Merger, acquisition, hostile takeover: Unification of two colleges. Organization Development Journal, 37(3), 31–44.

Strategic mergers are the proper unification of two or more organizations, including higher education institutions, to gain competitive advantages. In higher education, mergers and acquisitions serve as the rescue to more colleges or universities. Mergers have become the tool of boards of trustees and governmental agencies to address institutional problems such as declines in enrollment, demands for effectiveness, cost savings, and expanding the service area (Harman and Harman, 2008). Since mergers involve significant change for individuals in the organization, it becomes necessary to consider the impact of mergers on stakeholders as the focus of the study. The progress of the OneU institutional merger was extraordinarily rapid on many fronts-from, from the determination of a name and identity to the strategic plan, structure, operational infrastructure, computing, and academic programming. Thus, one will be a more substantial presence in the region if the enrollment does not continue to decline.

The growth and deployment of multiple task forces representing a variety of stakeholders create an effective mechanism for building relationships and achieving significant work in a limited time. Relationships have been growing more robust, and collaborative work between both campuses is increasing. It was an excellent opportunity for many to be involved in the campus more deeply than ever before. There have been more learning, research, and engagement opportunities presented for students and faculty. The stress levels related to uncertainty have been lowered as clarity about roles, structure, and personnel emerged after the merger and acquisition process.

5.8 PERSPECTIVES ON SUCCESSFUL MERGERS AND ACQUISITIONS

Different organizations entering mergers and acquisitions had separate functions and expectations until now. Those specialty functions post-merger exist under the same umbrella as the acquired company. They will connect as part of a team and as part of a new culture. There can be no more challenges as they collaborate and integrate both cultures and expectations. Where this challenging attitude surfaces, the merger will likely result in a weak organizational culture with little teamwork, low motivation, and inconsistent performance. Thus, instead of resulting in a cohesive responsibility that is prepared to take on the challenges of the daily activities, below are about ten steps that could help ensure a successful merger.

Step 1: Single New Entity Perspective

The single new entity perspective necessitates everyone to commit to the merger expectations and understand that a merger will transform two or more organizations into a new, single entity. The single new entity will have an organizational culture distinct from either company, whether it is a union of equals or an acquiring company and an acquired company. They should exhibit a unique culture designed from the previously independent organizations. Most mergers do not take advantage of this "single new entity perspective" with a "new culture" as a prospect to step forward and create a long-term valuable and successful organization.

Step 2: New Vision Perspective

The new organization needs to adopt a new vision entity perspective after the merger. It is a forward thinking view that the organization needs before it sets out to reach its objectives. The unique vision concept helps the new company deliver to its customers, employees, and shareholders. The new vision perspective will have new roles and define how the functions fit into this new vision and strategies to accomplish the new goals. The leaders face challenges of new norms and efforts to ensure the vision is on target.

Step 3: Define the Vision Perspective

The new vision of the organization needs to be clear and concise. The company needs to create a culture that can deliver the then-new vision—uncovering the optimal culture by involving all acquired and acquiring employees to ensure commitment. A survey could be used to brainstorm ideas, such as using the Organizational Culture Inventory (OCI), to create a vision of the culture that the new organization should strive to maximize for a long-term value. The use of the OCI Surveys could ask employees to identify behaviors expected to maximize the company's long-term effectiveness. The employees could discover the culture of affiliation with a high priority on interpersonal relationships. Thus, if the new leadership strives to have a constructive culture and puts steps in motion to ensure success, the result will be increased motivation, more cooperation, merger integration success, improved shared values, and quality.

Step 4: Leadership Characteristics Perspective

Effective leadership incorporates the vision at all levels and strives to develop an ideal culture. The leaders need to convey the perfect culture to the organization during the pre-merger and post-merger phases. The leaders need to be concise in explaining the direction they want to follow in the new organization. Using due diligence in selecting leaders and top-level executive management helps to set actions in motion, such as the architectures, structures, systems, technology, and training to attain the vision and ideal culture. However, these leaders and managers could be revitalized to function more efficiently with effective team building and training. Though some leaders may act awkwardly, this is part of leadership's challenge in forming a new entity that leads to a new vision (Boglarsky, 2005).

Step 5: Success Measure Perspective

Success Measures is an outcome evaluation resource for organizations' performance. Measuring success helps employees and stakeholders to feel confident that the merger and acquisition are working as expected and that the leadership is on board to make the new company achieve the set targets. Using a survey helps to measure the climate in an organization to reveal the adopted culture and produce the desired goals for employees, stakeholders, and the organization. Surveys help to expose the organization's weaknesses and strengths in various targeted areas. The strengths promote a positive culture, while the weaknesses hinder a positive culture by promoting either a defensive or aggressive culture (Boglarsky, 2005).

In organizations, defensive or aggressive cultures are produced from beliefs that protecting someone's status and security necessary to succeed or survive. In contrast, constructure or achievement cultures are based on assumptions that intrinsic satisfaction, self-respect, and working toward fulfilling one's potential. During post-merger, the ability to sustain a constructure or achievement culture helps attain merger success. So, leaders should avoid defensive or aggressive cultures to mitigate merger failures.

Step 6: Collaboration Perspective

Collaborating on an integration strategy Culture of Engagement framework helps measure the merger's success. Collaboration involves a dialogue before it is a decision. The collaboration process requires engagement with thought and intent, understanding the risks, and developing trust toward more formal partnerships and beyond to merger. The ten steps to enhance collaboration in an organizational environment include:

- Involvement and Engagement of the future
- New Identity formulation
- *Shared Vision:* Expanding the vision from mine to ours and giving it life
- *Analysis*: Evaluation of current reality in line with the strategy
- *Action:* Cascading the process by creating ownership in the process
- *Implementation*: Building and building momentum
- *Maintenance*: Focusing on direction and energy of corporate New Identity
- *Renewal*: Re-evaluation and re-creation
- Integration of the new organization
- Building the new vision and future together

Step 6: Leadership Role Perspective

The role of leadership in merger and acquisition integration has been largely neglected in M&A research. Sitkin and Pablo (2005) contended that while very notions of the importance of leadership are vital in the M&A literature, there is an incomplete understanding of what M&A leadership is and how M&A leadership influences M&A outcomes. However, because most M&As restructure organizations and intensely affect the employees of the merging organizations, understanding the role of effective leadership. Avoiding conflicted leadership is highly necessary. Establishing a unified and strong leadership team is an excellent strategic plan from start to finish. Despite that senior leadership teams are gathered to represent both entities and conduct due diligence, the primary decision-makers may be chosen to engage leaders from both organizations in the merger process, thus causing conflicting visions for the future, fostering differences in underlying norms and a lack of clarity about future direction. Part of the leadership due diligence means that potential acquisitions must fit a few rationales that the business has found to be part of successful transactions. Some of the rationales include:

Improvement of Company Performance—the performance improvement rationales aim at acquisitions that will help a company reduce costs, improve margins, and operate more effectively to achieve a combination of the three.

Reduce Competition—reducing the competition to allow the business to do better in the marketplace with fewer competitors; especially those that are being pressured by up-and-coming businesses

Increase Visibility and Customer Access—creating an increased visibility environment in the new vision business by cultivating new products, ideas, and customer access to deliver more quality and values, and as such, partnering with or being bought by a larger company may increase a small company's bandwidth and market share at the same time.

While leaders may think that a potential acquisition would achieve one, or a few of these goals, it is practical to have a professional legal opinion on how the merger deal will work, given the responsibilities and burdens each company must deal with. This is because what may make sense, in theory, might not make sense in actual practice.

Step 7: Communication Focus Perspective

Efficient communication should happen on two levels. Efficient communication comprises finding the best way to communicate about change with the target stakeholders. Sharing frequently with those impacted by a company merger and acquisition might be done. Still, if the communication is not getting a responsive handshake, the communication lacks focus and will not matter. In addition, communicating efficiently involves sharing information with key stakeholders in a timely fashion. This prevents speculation while helping to maintain trust during times of organizational change. When two or more companies merge, there are many uncertainties surrounding the deal, but successful communication could help dispel the challenges and successfully conduct the merger.

To ensure a successful merger and acquisition, it is essential to focus on communication. For example, the overestimation of synergies, a lack of strategic plans, overpayment, and inaccurate data contribute to the M&A failure. The teams neglecting to develop a post-merger integration and focusing on the financial gain causes more harm. Thus, the lack of awareness results in the failure of M&A within short periods. A clear vision and guiding principles are necessary and should be consistently communicated. Early development of mission and vision statements made the centerpiece of the unification rather than the periphery. Ineffective communication contributes to the absence of information, leading to inadequate information dissemination. Communication through many channels is essential, which is a central point to building trust and commitment. Communication is critical when working through a significant change such as a merger. It can also reduce conflict by assuaging uncertainty.

Step 8: Transparency and Trust Perspective

Transparency goes hand in hand with honesty. All communication during a merger and acquisition should be honest and straightforward. Both organizations involved in the change should feel well informed and maintain high trust in the organization and those enabling the change. Dishonest communication during organizational change breeds distrust and resentment, factors that could inspire bad morale, suspicion, and significant failure issues. Avoiding a lack of transparency helps to achieve merger success. Facilitating organizational change requires trust and transparency to be shared among each party. It is advisable to involve representatives from critical stakeholders in messaging, information transmission, and dialogue before announcing unification.

Step 9: Disregard Culture and Input Perspective

Culture goes beyond the mission and objectives of an organization. Cultural factors and organizational alignment are crucial to successful mergers. Lack of culture integration creates an oversight that leads to poor results. About 95 percent of top-level executives describe that cultural fit is critical to successful integration. They are disregarding culture and need to be eliminated. Closer attention must be paid to each institution's culture from pre- to post-merger. A cultural audit should take place to expose obstacles early to be proactively addressed. Facilitated dialogue that explores differences, assumptions, and beliefs should be used to pave the way to clarity, understanding, and possible acceptance. More involvement and consideration of stakeholders need to occur through inputs and brainstorming of ideas. They identify how the merger will affect the internal and external stakeholders concerning employment conditions and perceptions of fairness between employees and their employer. In addition, empowerment, delegation, and the creation of community within the new organization are vital to those affected by the merger. While the senior leadership had the right to act or not act based on recommendations, there needs to be a clear explanation of how and why decisions were made.

Step 10: Disproportionate Focus on Long Term Goals Perspective

The correct merger plan focuses on long-term value, a mix of combined efficiencies, and new competencies that exceed what both companies had before the merger or acquisition. For example, one oilfield firm increased revenues and margin by more than 40% in the two years following their merger and acquisition. Therefore, a disproportionate focus on both short-term and long-term goals is necessary. More emphasis is required on short-term goals. However, focusing only on the long-term might be complicated tasks, such as curriculum alignment and accreditation. It would be hard to celebrate the merger's success, build, and maintain morale with no immediate initial achievements. Thus, it might be more difficult for stakeholders to remain involved in the process with no clear end in sight.

5.9 TOP-LEVEL EXECUTIVES' PERSPECTIVES FOR MERGER SUCCESS

Although IR resources are essential in various business functions, not sufficient top-level executives are involved in the early stages of the merger deal. About 40% of total synergies require an IT framework. Consequently, applying IT from the pre-merger to the evaluation stage is necessary to ensure the smooth functioning of activities. The perspectives that top-level executives could use to facilitate merger success include

- Participate in the M & M&A Table:

The top-level executives would come with different questions that could potentially impact the final merger deal price. Questions could revolve around expiration, license, a maintenance fee of enterprise software, etc.

- *Assessing the Resources at Hand*:

Top-level executives are familiar with their organizations' existing processes, people, and standards. So, it is necessary to find out what is working and what is not. The ideas would help in taking various basis for other M&A activities.

- Prepare Systems Ready from the Initial Stage:

As IT plays a transversal role in an organization, the top-level executives must take steps to safeguard business continuity from the initial stage. Some of these steps include

- Executing quarantine measures plan to ensure systems security and confidentiality of data
- Retiring the redundant applications
- Resolving sourcing agreements for the interest of the acquiring and acquired companies' conditions.
- Limit the Loss of IT Talent:

Identifying talented IT workers is one way to limit loss in their activities. People with a wealth of IT knowledge and how it works within the enterprise also alleviate their fears about their future in the company. Such fears and concerns need to be addressed

- Maintaining Service Levels and Performance:

Though the companies in the merger are under transformation, the companies' customers expect a better performance from the merged entity. Therefore, the top-level executives should identify and plan for effective communication to allow normal business operations while the merger is ongoing.

5.10 REAL-WORLD PERSPECTIVES OF ORGANIZATIONAL CULTURE AND MERGERS

Digital Transformation Trend

The digital transformation of the business setting is challenging organizations with more expectations for the future. The future creates opportunities for activities to move faster, adapt more quickly, learn rapidly, and embrace dynamic culture change and new demands. According to Rahnema and Durme (2017). High-performance companies operate in an empowered network, collaborative culture, information systems, and talent mobility. Companies focus on restructuring the organization and developing new models. Many organizations are building this new organization through mergers and acquisitions to create an ecosystem while replacing organizational hierarchies and the traditional systems.

- About 88 percent of this year's survey respondents believe that building the organization of the future is an essential or critical issue (Rahnema and Durme, 2017).
- More than three in five (59 percent) say the issue is critical a 3 percent increase from last year.
- Yet challenges remain: Only 11 percent of survey respondents believe they understand how to build a future organization.

Future of Digital Transformation to Organizational Culture and Merger

The future of digital transformation relates to:

- 3D and VR visualization, as more companies need to train their employees and create virtual tours in their stores and factories.
- Data and sensors are more sophisticated yet functional software to gather, process, and analyze for business decisions
- Applications and software created to support retrofitting in consulting and scaling companies
- Robotics are embedded into the company's DNA to replace people when necessary, aiding automated work and risky situations.
- Artificial intelligence-based solutions to analyze data, drive internal changes in organizational culture and management
- Quantum computing from lead companies such as Microsoft, Google, and IBM
- IoT solutions working as a catalyst for the economic revival
- New revenue streams to enhance organizational productivity

Organizational Design Trend in the Global Human Capital

High-performing organizations radically operate these days differently from how they used about ten years ago. Some organizations continue to work according to industrial-age models that are 100 years older, which count down by legacy practices, systems, and behaviors that must be discarded before actual change or merger could take place (Rahnema and Durme, 2017).

As organizations become more digital, they face several challenges to redesign themselves to meet market demands, adapt more quickly, facilitate rapid learning, and embrace the emotional skills needs and business integrations such as mergers and acquisitions. Organizational design and change are complex. Many corporates restructure because they focus only on cutting costs and omit other cultural-related traits. Others face resistance from company leadership and top-level executives.

Constructing a future organization is difficult, as it could face trial and error. The organization design is a continuous and dynamic process. Yet, organizations that handle the challenge get an immense payoff in productivity, financial performance, employee commitment, and other benefits.

Organizing for Speed, Agility, and Adaptability

Most organizations worked towards efficiency and effectiveness in the previous era, leading to complex organizations. Hence, the results focus on predictable commercial patterns, which is not suitable for the current age of disruption and unpredictability. This goes beyond efficiency, as successful organizations work on speed, agility, and adaptability to facilitate competition in the global business environment.

The Power of Networks of Teams

Designing adaptability is vital for a network of teams shifting from hierarchical organizational structures toward models that adopt team collaboration. Instead, leading companies are pushing toward a more flexible, team-centric model. As organizations make this transition to a team-centric model, they found that reduced teams are a natural way to attain human work efficiency, promoting a network of teams in organizations.

Most successful companies are built around models that promote teams, transparently share information, and integrate groups depending on the issue to be addressed. Various networks can have different specialties, such as innovation, but the principle remains the same. Therefore, a company could maintain agile system development while sustaining team building. High-performing companies create digital customer experience groups to create new products in a specified time. Subsequently, the team diffuses as team members step on to new projects. Moving teams without risk is a critical attribute of today's high-performing companies.

Business Process Lifecycle

The business process lifecycle is a continuous cycle of improvement. The cycle involves identifying a new or existing business capability and its functionality at a high level. The vital information captured at this stage is the event sequence, dependencies, and broad ownership of the events, such as organizational groups, external partners, and others. With the process defined, it is possible to test some scenarios and see what can be done. It is also necessary to verify and see what has been done and even simulate use cases and see how it works. The steps are defining goals, planning, assigning stakeholders, testing the process, implementing the strategy, monitoring, and repeating when needed.

Step 1: Define Goals

This involves defining the purpose of the process and why the process was created—evaluating to ensure that the process is successful.

Step 2: Plan and Map the Process

This process maps the strategies that are needed to achieve the goals. This stage is broad and provides a roadmap for the procedure.

Step 3: Set Actions and Assign Stakeholders

This process requires identifying the individual tasks for the teams and the resources needed to execute the plan.

Step 4: Test the Process

Run and test the process to see how it performs. Observe variances or gaps and adjust as required.

Step 5: Implement the Process

Start running the process in a live environment. Properly communicate and train all stakeholders.

Step 6: Monitor the Results

Review the process and analyze its designs and document the process history.

Step 7: Repeat

If the process is to achieve the goals set for the project, replicate it for future operations and include it in process improvement.

The next step in the business process lifecycle is to focus on executing the process.

It is essential to test the plan with the end-users, who interact with this process daily. It is possible to detect challenges and improvement points in all the phases, so the process should be more efficient. The execution is a significant step in the business process lifecycle, and it is crucial to do it correctly.

5.11 INFORMATION GOVERNANCE ON MERGERS

Information governance (IG), Information Technology (IT) governance, Corporate Governance, and Data Governance are necessary factors that contribute to helping organizational performance in a merger environment. Emerging information technology governance structures in organizations have always been challenging. Corporate expansions through mergers and acquisitions face such challenges. Depending on the organizational location in different regions, the factors affecting merger integration and the choice of information governance structures vary. The study found that the corporate culture of top management, government regulation, competition, market stability, and IT competence are predispositions toward a specific business strategy and governance structure that can intensely influence the choice of information governance in organizations (Okoro, 2010). Hence, information governance addresses the designand development of effective organizations through IT, structures, and processes. In addition, information governance is affected by the corporate governance structure, stressing the integration of IT with the organization. The study findings emphasized the importance of integrating the organizational culture variables into the overall organizational information governance to provide strategic advantage, achieve business objectives, and optimize the value received from information technology. Hence, post-merger integration with centralized control of IT helps with board oversight, consistent strategic approach, and economies of scale.

Information Governance (IG)

Information governances the overall strategy for information at an organization. Information governance balances the risk that a report presents with the data's value. Information governance helps with legal compliance, operational transparency, and reducing expenditures associated with legal discovery. An organization can establish a consistent and logical framework. Hence, information governance is a fundamental part of good corporate Governance. Its mission is to maximize the value of information while minimizing the costs and risks of holding it. Information governance relates to the specification of decision rights and an accountability framework to ensure appropriate behavior in the valuation, creation, storage, use, archiving, and deletion of information. It includes the processes, roles, policies, standards, and metrics that ensure the effective and efficient use of information in enabling an organization to achieve its goals. Information governance focuses not on detailed IT or data capture and quality processes but on controlling the information generated by IT and office systems, especially during pre-merger and post-merger processes.

Corporate Governance (CG)

Corporate Governance refers to the top management process that manages andfacilitates value creation and transference among various organizations in a context that simultaneously ensures accountability and growth sustainability. Several critical aspects of the definition are worth noting. Corporate Governance is a process rather than an outcome. Governance is explicitly in the top management realm. Corporate governance practices define the role of the boards and officers of the corporation. Corporate Governance is the ultimate level of Governance of an organization. It includes the articles of incorporation, bylaws, shareholder agreements, policies, and procedures for managing the organization's relationship with its stakeholders. Hence, information governance is a crucial aspect of Corporate Governance.

Information Technology (IT) Governance

Information technology governance is the collaborative tools, processes, and methodologies that enable an organization to align business strategy and goals with IT services, infrastructure, or the environment. This plays a major during pre-merger and post-merger acquisition for organizations. IT Governance uses manages and optimizes IT in such a way that it supports, complements, or enables an organization to achieve its goals and objectives to improve performance. The information technology governance programs aim to elevate IT performance and deliver optimum business value while meeting regulatory compliance demands.

Data Governance (DG)

Data governance is part of information technology governance and information governance program. Data governance involves processes and controls to ensure that information at the data levels is true, accurate, and non-redundant. It requires data cleansing to strip out corrupted, inaccurate, or extraneous data and de-duplication to eliminate redundant occurrences of data. Merger organizations could use master data management (MDM) tools and techniques to clean their data and leverage business rules that can prevent inaccurate data from being entered into the database. MDM standardizes the data and ensures one single version within the system. MDM is a quality-control tool and set of processes used to provide control and consistency of data over time. Data governance is the most fundamental level at which to implement information governance. Data governance seeks to ensure that formal management controls, systems, processes, and accountable employees govern critical data assets to improve data quality and avoid adverse downstream effects of insufficient data. Hence, data governance helps to facilitate organizational performance after the merger and acquisition process.

5.12 THE ORGANIZATION OF THE FUTURE

Build the Organization of the Future

Top companies integrate systems that inspire teams to collaborate, share information, and work together depending on the task to complete. Different organizations use different specialties to change in innovation or mergers and acquisitions (Rahnema & Durme, 2017). For an organization to stay agile, team formation is necessary. High-performing organizations build a "digital customer experience" group, identify team skills, and assign tasks accordingly, such as making a new product or service within a set timeframe. Subsequently, the team dissolves and moves to new projects. Moving between groups without risk is a critical attribute of today's high-performing companies (Rahnema & Durme, 2017).

A leading North American bank recently embarked on an initiative to design a new way of working for faster deployments while competing with similar companies based on history, digital interfaces, and product delivery. The proposed operating model embeds agile practices and networked cross-functional teams, developers, analysts, and user design experts on a specific product outcome. Once the task is complete, teams redistribute and move to other projects.

According to Rahnema & Durme (2017). Top-performing organizations operate radically differently from how they worked ten years ago. Yet, some organizations continue to use legacy systems like industrial-age models that are 100 years old or more. Thus, the restructuring of legacy practices, procedures, and behavior needs adoption to allow change implementation. As organizations become more digital, they look into redesigning their systems to move faster, adapt to change, and facilitate rapid learning to embrace the dynamic career demands of their employees and stakeholders. Hence, many organizational businesses fail because they emphasize cutting costs. Others face resistance from company leadership. However, many consulting firms report that up to 70 percent of reorganizations fall short because of "creative disobedience" from the executive team (Rahnema & Durme, 2017).

Structuring for Speed, Agility, and Adaptability

Most organizations adopted systems to achieve efficiency and effectiveness in the past, leading to complex organizations. With the advancement of business innovation, instead of mere efficiency, successful organizations need to strive for speed, agility, and adaptability to help them to compete and excel in today's global business environment. Collaboration is vital and a stimulator for successful team building and organizational performance. Planning the team's work environment helps empower employees to enhance their work towards organizational performance.

Organizations need a people-focused strategy to aid team building and increase organizational performance, especially during post-the merger and acquisition phase. A collaborative approach serves as a fundamental to problem-solving.

People-Focused Strategy

Every successful business focuses on building its valuable assets, which are people. Leading with a people-first mindset is essential to success. It involves not just hiring people to provide a service for pay but acquiring the right talent with the knowledge that supports, recognizes, and invests in people's growth for running a successful business. When people-focused strategies are done right, employees feel heard, and they get committed to enhancing organizational performance. Recognizing people's hard work, celebrating successes, and making every employee feel like part of the business and a vital component of the team's success are essential to ensuring employees feel valued. Having people-focused strategies enables a team dedicated to the company's more tremendous success. More refined products are the output of a committed team, which enhances performance and tickles profits. Therefore, prioritizing people, products, and profit supports the greatest return on investment as an organization.

The Four Types of Organizational Agility

Organizational agility involves our mutually enforcing elements that include: agility-leadership, culture, architecture, and careers

1. *Agility leadership*

Agility leadership is leading and making tough decisions in complex, fast-changing environments. Agility leadership looks to the future rather than the past while thinking and changing strategies with new information. Agility leaders do not fear failure in business, but they quickly adapt and recover after a setback. Companies need to thrive in today's fast-moving and digital world to achieve organizational agility. People and culture become more paramount in designing a new structure or modifying an existing system. As managers adopt new agility levels, they develop new leadership capabilities and retain the capacities and skills acquired at previous levels.

2. *Agility Culture*

An agile culture fosters collaboration and cooperation and minimizes autocracy, control, and bureaucracy. Agile culture ignites decision-making down the organization to enable teams to take ownership of business outcomes and holds them to account. Adopting an agile culture framework requires more than adding a new project methodology and developing a new culture alongside it. Agile culture support:

- Changing requirements
- Trust and empowerment of teams
- Low barriers to communication
- Low bureaucracy
- Technical excellence
- Self-organizing teams
- Frequent delivery
- Continuous improvement

3. *Agility Architecture*

Agile architecture relates to how company architects, system architects, and software architects apply the architectural practice in agile company or application development.

Agile architecture refers to design practices that support the principles and values of agile, which enable the continuous delivery of valuable software. Agile architecture manages and redesigns efforts with principles of agile methods for faster development times.

4. *Agility* Careers

Career agility relates to the ability to keep pace with the demands of the modern business environment. Employees who are agile in skills and mindset are considered to have a more extraordinary ability to adapt to new roles, changing work environments, and business demands, especially in the case of mergers and acquisitions. Employees who excel at career agility move into new positions where their skills change from one role to another. Employees need to be career agile because it helps them respond to and ultimately succeed in changing business environments and models, evolving roles, and industry demands. Employees with agile careers complete the following functions:

- Translate existing skills into multiple roles
- Move effectively from one to another
- Adapt to changes in business and industry models
- Thrive in unique situations for processes and tools

5.13 SUMMARY

However, the challenges of successfully executing a merger and acquisition have grown significantly in the modern era. Integrating organizations among the complexity of the current IT environment is a problem that counts heavily on enterprise architects. Following the recommended post-merger integration is crucial to gaining leaders' visibility and avoiding merger failures. The steps of unifying entities help create a joint facility based on the corporate strategy. Unifying entities lay the foundation for all future actions and help to speed up the realization of synergies between the underlying technology environments. The process of M&A will always face issues. However, adequate planning, knowledge, and practical lessons from experienced practitioners help avoid some major problems. The chapter explained the business architecture in merger and acquisition, post-merger integration challenges, significant reasons why mergers fail, and ways to mitigate the challenges.

Mergers help to improve operational and financial performance, which serves as the drivers of a great deal of change and managing complexity. Organizational mergers could significantly impact many employees and stakeholders of the organizations, leading to resistance, lack of commitment, conflict, and ultimately withdrawal from the institution. Mergers and acquisitions are also becoming more commonplace in higher education institutions, a sector that has been typically considered as slow to change and keepers of tradition. No merger is easy. Each finds different variables: employees, products, culture, history, etc. Planning, including the ten steps outlined above, will help the mergers and acquisitions to go smoothly and ensure a successful merger while making employees have job satisfaction and be part of the new organization. Training on specialized activities and various large-scale interventions across all functions at different merger stages helps to smoothen the process. In addition, competency gaps, unique identity simulations, and team workshops to develop integration process skills are other areas to stimulate and catalyst the merger success. Chapter 5 further highlighted the real-world perspectives of organizational culture on mergers. Chapter 6 includes implications of the results, recommendations, and conclusion.

5.14 CHAPTER 5 STUDY QUIZ QUESTIONS

Question 1. ________________ serves as a conceptual plan for organizational analysis, planning, design, and implementation through an extensive program to achieve profitable growth and strategy execution consistently.

A. Enterprise leadership (EL)
B. Leadership architecture (LA)
C. Enterprise architecture (EA)
D. Enterprise vision (EV)

Question 2. ____________________in post-merger integration and the role of the change manager to manage the people during merger integration to achieve the declared goals.

A. leadership management
B. Change management
C. Change vision
D. Change mission

Question 3. The ____________________ is a critical aspect of merger and acquisition which is a complex process of combining businesses with the aim to maximize potential efficiencies and synergies.

A. post-merger sale
B. post-merger cost
C. post-merger skills
D. post-merger integration

Question 4. Which of the following are correct for the Post-Merger Integration Checklist?

A. The pre-merger questionnaire, hiring process, overlap/redundancies, technology integration, and employee performance.
B. The pre-merger questionnaire, overlap/redundancies, technology integration, and employee performance.

C. Post-merger questionnaire, hiring process, technology integration, and employee performance.
D. Post-merger questionnaire, hiring process, overlap/redundancies, technology integration, and employee performance.

Question 5. Which of the following are among the reasons why a Merger Fails?

A. Lack of good motive for the merger and acquisition
B. Targeting the wrong company for the merger and acquisition
C. Overestimating synergies for the merger and acquisition
D. All of the above

Question 6. Overpaying for the merger and acquisition is part of the reason why a merger fails?

A. True
B. False

Question 7. A lack of stakeholders' trust in the merger and acquisition contributes to a merger failure.

A. True
B. False

Question 8. Failing to pull out of a merger when all evidence is unfavorable helps make the merger successful?

A. True
B. False

5.15 CHAPTER 5 STUDY QUIZ SOLUTIONS

1. C
2. B
3. D
4. D
5. D
6. A
7. A
8. B

5.16 CHAPTER 5 STUDY EXERCISES

1. What is enterprise architecture?
2. What is change management?
3. How can Change Management improve effectiveness?
4. What are the challenges of post-merger integration during the merger process?
5. How can organizations mitigate technical challenges in the merger process?
6. What is the post-merger integration checklist?
7. What are the cultural challenges in the merger process?
8. What are the differences between information governance, corporate governance, information technology governance, and data governance?
9. What are the reasons why Merger fails?
10. What is the top-level executive's perspective on merger success?
11. What is a Collaboration perspective in a merger process?

NOTES

1. Rothermel, R., & LaMarsh, J. (2012, January). Managing change through employee empowerment. *Global Business and Organizational Excellence*, 31(2), 17. Retrieved from ABI/INFORM Global. (Document ID: 2543274101).

2. Yurcan, B. (2012, February). Bank fees, along with value-added services, on the rise. Bank Systems + Technology—Online. Retrieved March 3, 2012, from ABI/INFORM Global. (Document ID: 2598790381).

3. DealRoom (n.d). The Ultimate Guide to Post Merger (M&A) Integration Process. Retrieved from https://dealroom.net/faq/post-merger-and-acquisition-m-a-integration-process

4. Kumar, B. R. (2019). *Wealth Creation in World's Largest Mergers and Acquisitions: Integrated Case Studies*. Cham, Switzerland: Springer.

5. Culjak, N. B. (2021). Analysis of Acquisition Success in Soft Beverage Industry of the Republic of Croatia. Varazdin Development and Entrepreneurship Agency (VADEA).

Chapter 6

Conclusions and Recommendations

6.1 CONCLUSIONS

The current research study provided quantitative data within a merged Nigerian bank in Abuja that examined the relationship between organizational culture and performance variables (employee commitment, job satisfaction, and employee retention). Two hundred and 20 employees voluntarily participated in the study. The participants answered 69 survey questions distributed by a hand delivery system. Chapter 4 presented the results, which supported alternative Hypotheses 1, 2, and 3. Chapter 5 provides discussions on enterprise architecture in mergers and acquisitions, change management, and building the organization of the future. Chapter 6 provides conclusions, interpretations, and implications of the findings with specific recommendations.

6.2 INTERPRETATION OF FINDINGS

Interpretation of Findings: Hypothesis 1

The null hypothesis (H_o1) predicted no significant relationship between organizational cultural traits of mission, consistency, involvement, adaptability, and employee commitment performance in a merged Nigerian bank. Alternative hypothesis (H_a1) predicted a significant relationship between organizational cultural traits of mission, consistency, involvement, adaptability, and employee commitment performance in a merged Nigerian bank. Hypothesis 1 intersected organizational culture, employee commitment, transformational leadership theory, and equity theory.

Organizational culture relates to the shared pattern, assumptions, values, and norms within a group (Schein, 1992).[1] Employee commitment embodies an employee's emotional attachment and level of dependence on an organization (Tay, 2009).[2] Transformational leadership theory relates to values, emotions, and leadership that encourage creativity in employees (Garcia-Morales, Matias-Reche, & Hurtado-Torres, 2008).[3] Equity theory relates to treating employees within a fair and equitable structure to receive similar roles and responsibilities (Adams, 1965).[4]

Bambacas and Patrickson (2008) and Tay (2005) noted that the feeling of responsibility of employees within the organizational goals and values relates to their commitment. Previous studies suggested that organizational commitment links to organizational culture (Chang & Huang, 2005; Cooper-Hakim & Viswesvaran, 2005; Tay, 2009).

Cultural integration may help to enhance organizational commitment to align employee commitment with organizational goals (Yao & Wang, 2008).[5] Transformational leadership theory supports the need for organizational leaders to integrate culture into a business environment (Xenikou & Simosi, 2006). The employees' perceptions of fairness relate to organizational outcomes and employee commitment (Anderson & Patterson, 2008).

The regression model only predicted approximately 29% of the variation in the employee commitment variable, and only mission was a significant predictor. The model shows that only the partial correlation between employee commitment and mission was substantial. In contrast, the bivariate correlations between organizational cultural traits and employee commitment were positive. The variance is not much because there may have been other variables that could explain employee commitment performance that was not measured in the current study but will require further research to identify. Based on the findings, the null hypothesis was rejected. The alternative hypothesis was accepted because hypothesis 1 confirmed a positive and significant relationship between the combination of the cultural traits and employee commitment. The findings support Yao and Wang (2008) and Camerer and Weber's (2003) contention that cultural integration helps to enhance organizational commitment to align employee commitment with organizational goals.

Interpretation of Findings: Hypothesis 2

Null Hypothesis (H_o2) predicted no significant relationship between organizational cultural traits of mission, consistency, involvement, adaptability, and job satisfaction performance in a merged Nigerian bank. Alternative hypothesis (H_a2) predicted a significant relationship between organizational cultural traits of mission, consistency, involvement, adaptability, and on-the-job satisfaction performance in a merged Nigerian bank. Hypothesis 2 linked organizational culture, job satisfaction, transformational leadership theory, and equity theory. Organizational culture has a positive relationship with job satisfaction (Denison & Mishra, 1995; Ghazzawi, 2008). Job satisfaction refers to employees' positive emotional state regarding experiences and perceptions (Anderson & Patterson, 2008; Greenberg & Baron, 2008; Warr, 2007). Luna-Arocas and Camps (2008) confirmed that job satisfaction might be enhanced when employees are equitably rewarded. Transformational leadership theory relates to values, emotions, and leadership that encourage creativity in employees (Garcia-Morales, Matias-Reche, & Hurtado-Torres, 2008) and culture integration (Xenikou & Simosi, 2006). The application of equity theory enhances fairness and equitable structure for employees to receive similar roles and responsibilities (Adams, 1965) and improves job satisfaction (Anderson & Patterson, 2008; Carr, 2007).

The regression model only predicted approximately 9% of the variation in the job satisfaction variable, and only mission was a significant predictor. The model shows that only the partial correlation between job satisfaction and mission was substantial, whereas the bivariate correlations between the combination of organizational cultural traits and job satisfaction were positive. The variance was not much because there may have been other variables that could explain job satisfaction performance that was not measured in the current study but will require further research to identify. Based on the findings, the null hypothesis was rejected. The alternative hypothesis was accepted because Hypothesis 2 confirmed a positive and significant relationship between the combination of cultural traits and job satisfaction. The finding is consistent with the research findings of Denison and Mishra (1995) and Ghazzawi (2008) that organizational culture has a positive relationship with job satisfaction. Denison and Mishra (1995) established a correlation between organizational performance and culture integration and the four cultural traits used in the current study. Measures of the four cultural traits used in the present study had significant relationships with job satisfaction. The research findings are consistent with the correlations found by Denison and Mishra (1995). The findings also were based on Denison's cultural model because the predictor variables maintained their correlation to performance even when a measure of multiple cultural traits was applied.

Interpretation of Findings: Hypothesis 3

The null hypothesis (H_o3) predicted no significant relationship between organizational cultural traits of mission, consistency, involvement, adaptability, and employee retention performance in a merged Nigerian bank. The alternative hypothesis (H_a3) predicted a significant relationship between organizational cultural traits of mission, consistency, involvement, adaptability, and employee retention performance in a merged Nigerian bank. Hypothesis 3 intersected organizational culture, employee retention, transformational leadership theory, and equity theory.

Organizational culture involves internally and externally designed programs to increase employee development by maintaining the skills and knowledge necessary to realize the organization's goals and improve performance (Weinzimmer, Franczak, & Michel, 2008). Employee retention denotes the turnover rate that an organization retains. Inadequate cultural integration and inappropriate employees fit in organizations may increase the employees' rate of turnover (Benson, 2006). Transformational leaders encourage followers to improve productivity, team values, and growth by responding to job challenges (Burns, 1978; Kest, 2006). Leaders acting as advisors in a merged group may allow the opportunity to build trust and reduce employee turnover. Equity theory relates to treating employees within a fair and equitable structure to receive similar roles and responsibilities (Adams, 1965).

The employee retention criterion variable regression model and the combination of predictor variables were significant. The relationship between cultural traits and employee retention may represent a strong association rather than causation. Alternatively, the reported relationships might be indicative and imply that the combination of the four cultural traits (mission, comprising consistency, involvement, and adaptability) represents leading indicators that can predict employee retention. The regression model only predicted approximately 7% of the variation in the employee retention variable, and none of the predictors were significant factors. The model shows that none of the partial correlations between employee retention and all the predictor variables was significant, whereas the bivariate correlations between the combination of organizational cultural traits and employee retention were positive. The regression model variance was not much because there may have been other variables that can explain employee retention performance that was not measured in the current study but will require further research to identify. Based on the findings, the null hypothesis was rejected. The alternative hypothesis was accepted because hypothesis 3 confirmed a positive and significant relationship between the combination of cultural traits and employee retention.

Findings for Hypothesis 3 are in accord with a transformational leadership theory. A transformational leadership theory approach emphasizes an integrative view of organizational issues (Bass & Avolio, 1994; Kirkbride, 2006; Walumbwa et al., 2005). Given turnover intention issues, a management focus on multiple independent variables rather than on one variable represents a transformational leadership orientation. The integrative approach to leadership is helpful to merged organizations, especially in the banking and telecommunication industries. Leaders in these organizations can view turnover intention as a construct with multiple antecedents.

6.3 IMPLICATIONS

Research implications show the conclusions drawn from research results and are used to explain how the findings may be necessary for policy, practice, or theory. The current study expands organizational culture, leadership, and organizational performance of employee commitment, job satisfaction, and employee retention research by confirming the positive relationship between an employee's perception of cultural traits integration and resultant organizational performance. The study findings support the significant positive relationship between the four cultural characteristics and the performance of each of the research criteria. The research findings were specific to one merged Nigerian bank in the FCT, Abuja. The primary study implication is that organizational cultural differences hinder organizational performance. The implication section includes an interpretation of the findings, the implication to organizational leadership, and its contribution to leadership scholars.

6.4 IMPLICATIONS TO ORGANIZATIONAL LEADERSHIP

Organizational Leadership Implications

Despite all the investment in recent mergers, most organizational leaders still face challenges in maintaining high performance (Atkinson, 2005; Garver, 2006; Terranova, 2007). Some of the consequences of merger failure relate to high employee turnover, decreased job satisfaction, and low performance (Badrtalei & Bates, 2007). Organizational culture and organizational performance are well-studied conceptualizations, although the relationship between organizational culture and organizational performance is understudied in the environment of developing countries. The growth of global mergers and acquisitions keeps increasing with technological advancement. The continuing merger increase in technical industries supports the need to identify ways to meet expectations and achieve merger success. The most significant number of M&As in 2008 amounted to $65 billion. These mergers involved information technology services. The current study introduced the integration of four cultural traits into the merger environment, confirming expected correlations between the combination of cultural traits and organizational performance.

Given the correlational design, the inference in any of the bivariate relationships depicted in the study is speculative. This notwithstanding, the results indicate that in the participation of the merged Nigerian bank employees, the combination of the four organizational cultural traits is positively related to each of the performance variables (employee commitment, job satisfaction, and employee retention), given the positive consequences of organizational culture and organizational performance from prior studies (Rose et al., 2008; Weinzimmer et al., 2008; Xenikou & Simosi (2006), the current study findings validate previous research in a new research environment.

Visual inspection of the relationship between individual cultural traits and each of the performance variables indicates a weaker correlation when compared to the relationship between combinations of cultural traits. The weaker relationship between individual cultural traits and organizational performance may indicate that merely being aware of one of the cultural traits (mission, consistency, involvement, and adaptability) in an organization provides insufficient motivation for employee commitment, job satisfaction, and employee retention.

Alternatively, the findings may indicate that mission responses take precedence over consistency, involvement, and adaptability. Further research is required. The cultural traits of involvement and consistency appear to be less impacting and less relevant to employee retention in the merged Nigerian bank environment.

Organizational performance is systems-oriented and integrates interrelated factors, including organizational culture (Behery & Paton, 2008). Organizational culture relates to cognitive components, such as values, beliefs, and assumptions (Schein, 1992). Culture in an organization shows how employees are managed while considering why individuals act in a certain way in the work environment (Rosenberg, 2005; Zhang & Tansuhaj, 2007). The current study provided insights into the organizational culture in a merged Nigerian bank as measured by employee commitment, job satisfaction, and employee retention. Like organizational culture, organizational performance is well studied.

Organizational performance enables organizations to measure productivity in employees' commitment, job satisfaction, turnover rate, shareholders' returns, and organizational growth (Behery & Paton, 2008; Weinzimmer, Franczak, & Michel, 2008). Kotter and Heskett (1992) indicated that lower performance in organizations could be attributed to an inability to maintain culture integration within the business environment. Organizational leaders may help to improve organizational performance through cultural adaptation and integration (Shimoni, 2008). Despite the research and the plethora of study findings, employee commitment, job satisfaction, and employee retention research in a merged Nigerian bank are scarce.

6.5 IMPLICATIONS FOR LEADERSHIP SCHOLARS

Leadership Scholars Implications

As mergers and acquisitions continue to fail, stockholders' equity declines with the corresponding cost to the taxpayers in trillions of dollars (Brock, 2005). The cost to taxpayers results from poorly managed cultures in the merged environment (Dyer et al., 2004; Kanter, 2004; Pultz, 2005). Organizational mergers are rapidly increasing in today's business and global environments to increase efficiencies and achieve strategic objectives. Yet, many mergers are taking place with positive rhetoric from the leaders and shareholders about how much value a merger will add to an organization, even though most mergers fail (Mitleton-Kelly, 2006). The implications of overlooking the actual challenges of a merger are too expensive.

A merger could involve disparate cultures, and the current study findings conclude that such a condition is a precursor to low-performing organizations. The correlation of the organizational cultural traits with the performance criteria of employee commitment, job satisfaction, and employee retention in the merged Nigerian bank extends the current knowledge domain. The current study extends the organizational culture, leadership, and organizational performance academic discourse and expands the research domain to include a merged Nigerian bank in a developing country.

6.6 STUDY LIMITATIONS

Study Limitations

Several limitations relating to implementation and design existed for the study. A research limitation is essential, given the extent to which the study findings can be generalized (Creswell, 2005). The first limitation related to the study's generalizability. The population incorporated all employees from the merged Nigerian bank. With the selected population size, the generalizability of the results beyond the specific merged bank studied to the general Nigerian bank employees' population was questionable. Generalizability provides the link between the knowledge obtained from a study and the ability to transfer that knowledge beyond the research goal (Creswell, 2005). The merged Nigerian bank orientation limits the generalizability of the study findings.

A second study limitation involved the voluntary nature of participation. Employee participation was strictly voluntary, and a sample of 220 employees voluntarily participated. The findings represent the perspectives of the sample drawn from the population. Survey participants represented the employees who experienced the merger. Nonresponse degrades a survey's validity and impedes generalizability, affecting the degree of conclusions attributed to the target population (Cooper & Schindler, 2008). Nonresponse bias occurs when the participant and nonparticipant differences affect variable representation (Cooper & Schindler, 2008). Thus, the volunteer nature of participation may have unintentionally influenced the study results.

A third limitation resulted from the limits of correlational design. The design included measuring and relating organizational cultural traits and organizational performance of employee commitment, job satisfaction, and employee retention based on participant answers to DOCP scaled survey items. The correlations measured degrees of variable association. Variable manipulation does not occur in a correlational design (Vogt, 2007). The non-manipulation of variables in correlational research makes causation supposition difficult (Vogt, 2007)

Correlational research creates correlation coefficients that signify degrees of relationship between two variables (Cooper & Schindler, 2008), although the correlations do not present evidence that *x* leads to *y* (Cooper & Schindler, 2008). In correlations, multiple explanations exist regarding variable influencing direction. The use of correlations cannot infer how *x* and *y* variables influence one another in a mutually reciprocal manner (Cooper & Schindler, 2008). The study did not investigate causal relationships between any of the study variables.

A fourth limitation involved determining participants' emotional state during the survey. The study's cross-sectional survey design was limiting. Cross-sectional surveying is single-point-of-time oriented and provides a survey design to collect data about current attitudes, opinions, or beliefs (Creswell, 2005). Participants completed an assessment to exemplify a behavior which emanate from beliefs and feelings (Cooper & Schindler, 2008). Participants' survey replies may have changed at different times, depending on the participants' current thoughts and feelings. Determining a participant's emotional mood when completing a survey is problematic. Individuals with a negative mood may be biased more negatively than others with a positive mood (Cooper & Schindler, 2008).

In contrast to a cross-section survey design, a longitudinal survey allows assessments at different time points (Creswell, 2005). A longitudinal study may not completely alleviate the effects of a negative mood bias. The longitudinal approach would measure mood-based survey responses using the multiple time orientations created in longitudinal research.

6.7 RECOMMENDATIONS

The current study reported strong correlations among the organizational cultural traits ranging from .60 to .76. The data indicated a significant, positive relationship between a combination of the predictors and each criterion variable: employee commitment, job satisfaction, and employee retention. The study results also confirmed the results of past research, indicating a strong positive relationship exists between organizational culture and organizational performance. The results indicated the organizational virtue of cultural traits integration, implementation, and organizational performance. The following section provides recommendations for organizational leadership, tech industry leaders, banking industry leaders, merger organizations, and recommendations for future research.

6.8 RECOMMENDATIONS FOR ORGANIZATIONAL LEADERSHIP

Recommendations for Organizational Leadership

The first recommendation entails the criticality of organizations proactively integrating cultural traits into the organizational leadership development system. The process of developing leaders has organizational implications. A leader's behavior demonstrably affects the work culture (Bass & Avolio, 1994). The work culture affects the financial results (Sharma, 2005), employee commitment (Tay, 2009), job satisfaction (Ghazzawi, 2008), and employee retention (Benson, 2006). The study's results, which indicate a positive and statistically significant relationship exists between a combination of predictor cultural traits and employee commitment, supported prior studies by Denison (2006), Rose et al. (2008), and Weinzimmer et al. (2008) that showed that organizational culture positively affects performance. Given the values and behavioral orientation, the cultural traits provide a framework to support transformational leadership development and organizational performance. The 60-item DOC survey questions incorporate 60 discrete behaviors that integrate the four cultural traits (Denison & Neale, 1998). Integrating organizational culture requires aligning vision and shared assumptions such as values and norms (Bass & Avolio, 1994).

The first recommendation incorporates implementing a transformational leadership model that integrates the four cultural traits elements during the merger and acquisition process. The aspects of the transformational leadership model include values, emotions, and leadership that encourage creativity in employees (Garcia-Morales, Matias-Reche, & Hurtado-Torres, 2008).

Improving creativity in employees supports collective decision-making, employee empowerment, and higher performance (Avey, Hughes, Norman, & Luthans, 2008).

The first recommendation offers a holistic transformational development strategy that allows leadership practices to maximize higher performance during the pre-merger and post-merger change process. The transformational leadership approach recognizes that leadership has moved from an internal leadership style to a broader focus to accommodate external factors (Walumbwa, Avolio, & Zhu, 2008). The 60-item Likert-type scale-based instrument measuring cultural traits provided insights because evaluation enhances leaders' self-awareness concerning employees' perceptions of the organizational culture and leaders' behaviors (Xenikou & Simosi, 2006). The instrument evaluated values and behaviors associated with the four cultural traits identified by Denison & Neale (1998).

The first recommendation recognized the interconnectivity of value actions and organizational procedures. The recommendation built on transformational leadership concepts supports the belief that cultural integration and organizational change are systems in which interrelationships and interconnections manifest. Fairness perceptions using the equity theory (Adams, 1965) may help to build interrelationships among managers and employees to enhance job satisfaction, commitment, and performance (Anderson & Patterson, 2008).

6.9 RECOMMENDATIONS FOR TECH INDUSTRY LEADERSHIP

Recommendation for Tech Industry Leadership

Speculations about failed mergers in the tech industry and a decrease in organizational performance have a common area of interest for scholars and technology leaders. Tech industry leaders are responsible for improving employees' collaboration and cooperation. Organizational culture relies not only on the members' contribution but also on the vision, leadership, and support of their superiors (Schein, 1999). With frequent mergers and acquisitions in the tech industry (Network World, 2008), leadership challenges exist to ensure that cultural integration takes place while organizational performance is maintained. Such challenges are more vital when an organization is embarking on an international merger that involves two or more distinct cultures.

Involvement of distinct cultures raises the risks of mergers and acquisitions because participants' commitment could be at stake, depending on the fairness perception and merger outcome. Tech industry leaders should approach a merger with caution and acknowledge the challenges of making a merger a reality. These leaders need to recognize the magnitude of the transformation paradigm and mission strategy and how the changes affect organizational performance. A key recommendation to tech industry leaders is to: (a) assess and evaluate cultural studies ahead of a merger to enable effective culture integration and (b) define clear and concise mission objectives to employees.

Findings in the current study show that the survey instrument developed by Denison (2006) generalizes well. The study's Cronbach's alpha ranged between 0.74 and 0.84, thus validating Denison's organizational culture model. These cultural assessments focus on the target areas of cultural traits (involvement, consistency, adaptability, and mission) that will enable tech industry leaders to perform effective evaluations. By knowing that culture conflicts exist during pre-and post-merger, tech industry leaders may develop strategies to target the focus areas to avoid significant organizational disruptions. Adequate communication of mission strategy to involved participants will help measure a combination of cultural traits towards employee commitment and job satisfaction as identified in the current study: that mission trait is a significant factor in performance outcomes.

6.10 RECOMMENDATIONS FOR BANKING INDUSTRY LEADERSHIP

Recommendations for Banking Industry Leadership

In the United States and developing countries, banking industry leaders are dealing with many changes and challenges because of technological advancements and rapid innovations. The countries that experienced a high wave of bank mergers include the U.S. banks (Rodriguez, 2008), German banks (Koetter, 2008), Taiwan (Lin, 2005), Austrian banks (Herbst, 2008), Malaysian banks (Radam et al., 2009), Nigerian banks (Aburime & Uche, 2008), and Indian banks (Jayadev & Sensarma, 2007). Leadership plays an essential role in steering these organizations through unstable situations. A key finding from the study is that most participants from the merged Nigerian bank agree that the organization has moderate performance after the merger. Most of the responses from the descriptive statistics frequency table reflect moderate performance. The findings of moderate performance show the need to increase the performance rating in the studied merged bank to the next level.

The research findings support the following effective merger strategies for organizational leaders to manage culture integration and maintain a high level of organizational performance. Leaders understand the value of leadership styles to empower employees and improve communication appear to work for different people. Knowing when to integrate culture and apply suitable leadership styles is essential for leading. Banking industry leaders should initiate ways to learn culture integration and improve the leaders in the industry. The global pressure of worldwide competition is growing enormously. The perceptions in the Nigerian banking system in terms of cultural integration and organizational performance may be different from those of other developing countries. Organizational culture and leadership style can make a difference in the success or failure of any organization. Based on the research findings, the partial correlation between employee commitment and mission was significant. The partial correlation between job satisfaction and mission was also significant.

Thus, lack of employee commitment and job satisfaction are inhibitors of workers' productivity that link to organizational goals and mission. Banking industry leaders should analyze the organizational cultures and leadership styles. Employees should be trained to understand the components of the transformational leadership model (Bass & Avolio, 1994). Leaders and managers should be aware of the organizational culture in conjunction with employees' involvement and creativity. Understanding the relationship between leadership styles and cultural values will help leaders and workers reduce cultural conflicts in the workplace, resulting in more productivity and increased organizational performance.

6.11 RECOMMENDATIONS FOR MERGER ORGANIZATIONS

Recommendations for Merger Organizations

To improve merger performance, De Mattos, Salciuviene, and Lewis (2007) suggested two important merger implications during the M&A process. The first is that organizations should perform a cultural assessment with the companies intending to merge before implementing the merger process. The second is that banks should use social controls to manage the integration process to eliminate the cultural effects between the merger companies. Badrtalei and Bates (2007) and Cartwright and Cooper (1993) suggested that organizations should integrate soft and complex issues of organizational cultures and economic information to mitigate merger failures. "Soft" issues represent the people in the organization, and "hard" data represent the financial and strategic fit of the merger. The distinction between "hard" data and "soft" issues creates a complex problem in a merged environment. The study findings of a significant positive relationship between the combination of cultural traits and each of the organizational performance (employee commitment, job satisfaction, and employee retention) in the studied merged bank supported Badrtalei and Bates and Cartwright and Cooper's integration of soft and hard cultural issues in a merger environment.

De Mattos et al. (2007) also specified that cultural assessment includes the fit between the merging companies, while the social controls include the strategy to coordinate the transition teams of participants from both merging companies during the merger implementation. Similarly, Iyer and Miller (2008) noted that merger strategies need to include factors that motivate participants to implement significant changes in the organizational activities. The merger organizations performing a cultural assessment before implementing the merger process and using social controls to manage the integration process of "hard" data and "soft" issues will increase organizational performance during the pre-merger and post-merger transformation processes.

6.12 RECOMMENDATIONS FOR FUTURE RESEARCH

Recommendations for Future Research

The current research results indicate the statistical significance of various bivariate relationships relating to organizational cultural traits and organizational performance. While stating that the relationship between variable pairs based on employees' perspectives from a merged Nigerian bank adds to the knowledge base, future research can extend the study's findings. The following section outlines five areas for future research.

The first area for future research involves extending the explanatory criteria variables relationships: employee commitment, job satisfaction, and employee retention, as categories of employee behavior through work team, collaboration, and training (Rose et al., 2008; Schein, 1992). The organizational performance in the paradigm presented by Denison (2006), Gillespie et al. (2008), and Weinzimmer et al. (2008) could be decoupled into other variables. Extending the study in a merged bank environment by reconceptualizing organizational performance into additional variables may enhance distinct performance insights. Determining the relationship between the cultural traits and return on assets, sales growth, customer satisfaction, and organizational commitment in the reconceptualized organizational performance paradigm represent an area for future research.

Another area for future research involves knowing how the results will change over time in a merged organization. The study examined an organization three years after it had merged with other banks. The findings indicated that the merger process had not met all the goals of the top management of the bank. The performance rating primarily scored moderate performers for all study performance indicators (employee commitment, job satisfaction, and employee retention). Interest exists in knowing how the results change over time. Researchers should examine the same organization periodically, indicating if organizations retain the integration of cultural traits when higher performance and successful mergers are achieved.

The third area for future research concerns incorporating premerger and post-merger data for comparison. The current study could not determine causality but could only make predictions based on correlations. A variation of the present study would be to create a form of intervention for other merged banks in different developed and developing countries. Researchers could apply an intervention strategy to integrate other cultural traits amongst banking and telecommunication industries and follow up with another survey using the methodology employed in the current study.

Further research could investigate the lack of culture integration and apply an intervention using non-merged and merged organizations in the banking and telecommunication industries.

The current study only considered a merged Nigerian bank population as participants. In terms of generalizing, using a broader audience of participants, interest exists in considering how the study replicates other industries in developed and developing countries. Even with the study's contribution, much remains to discover regarding the relationship between the four cultural traits and other organizational performance variables that have not been considered in the current research. A fifth area involves extending the present study's quantitative design into a mixed-methods study. Correlational designs measure degrees of association between variables (Creswell, 2005). In correlational research, attributing causality is difficult (Vogt, 2007). The combination of qualitative and quantitative design methodologies, delineators of mixed-methods research, helps researchers understand a research problem (Creswell, 2005). Creswell noted that a mixed-method (quantitative and qualitative) design can illuminate and clarify the initial quantitative findings.

6.13 CURRENT ORGANIZATIONAL CHANGE TRENDS

To enhance merger performance, the need to embrace organizational change is imperative. Several factors contribute to the future trends, such as workflow, artificial intelligent impact, new information, engaging employees, shared experiences, continuous improvement, change implementation, and digitalization. These trends could offer a catalyst in helping organizations sustain mergers and improve performance.

Workflow Enhancement

Every organization's growth focuses on quickly learning the workflow and task expectations. Learning is a vital part of the work in every business division. After the merger, the need to retrain employees becomes necessary. Focusing on learning instead of efficiency, organizations could improve their team resilience to drive growth and navigate uncertainty.

Artificial Intelligent (AI) Impact

The use of machine learning is growing with advancements in technology. Thus, practical applications of machine learning and AI are penetrating the business arena. Merger organizations need to incorporate intense learning to go with change processes. Helping employees to connect with topics and stronger teams is based on their needs and interests. Hence, artificial intelligent knowledge becomes necessary for everyone within the organization. The development of most projects requires enormous amounts of qualitative data that could overwhelm the teams. Relying on personal judgment is more tasking with massive data. Hence AI helps to alleviate the analysis without bias.

Engaging Teams for Company Purposes

A purpose-driven company could be built with participatory ways of working. It is challenging to communicate purpose with traditional one-way messages. The entire team of employees needs to participate in the dialogue where the objective is discussed. With the advancement in technology, social media plays a vast role internal and external environment. This is evident in transparency and the culture of continuous communication and sharing, which is key to building trust. Open collaboration and transparency help prevent disconnects based on wrong interpretations and assumptions. Thus, the need to demand increased transparency from companies. A transparent work culture creates structures for reporting fewer complex data and information. Transparency helps to replace traditional management approaches with coordination and connection. Organizational cultures and systems become barriers to working efficiently to adapt people's ability to work together in a self-guided manner.

Continuous Process Development (CPD)

Continuous process development is identifying and acting on identified development needs such as skills learning and process restructuring. Organizations instead of having a static ready-made plan for change, companies want genuine changes where the general direction is known and dynamic to give room for future improvements. Transformation is not about having a set goal; instead, the result is created and shaped through learning.

Facilitating Organizational Change

Organizational change is when organizations aim to develop and deal with new situations or markets. To enable organizational change and learning, sense-making, and engagement, the mindset and facilitation skills are becoming highly appreciated. Thus, facilitation is a way of co-creating transformation. Effective facilitators strive to inspire people in processes and how to handle the process. Essentially, facilitators motivate people and develop favorable conditions to aid commitment and higher performance.

Digitalization and Transformation

Digitalization allows companies to transform, especially during the merger and acquisition process. The transformation process comes in stages, and when organizations are unable to change, they face the risk of going out of business. Hence, digital ways of work allow people to participate and make collective efforts that enable real-time processes. Digitalization is rapidly growing with change opportunities. Thus, digitalization helps communities to build on real-time technologies and adopt new types of communication practices.

6.14 SUMMARY

The study's findings show a significant relationship between the combination of cultural traits of involvement, consistency, adaptability, and mission and each of the performance criteria (employee commitment, job satisfaction, and employee retention). The more two or more cultures differ in their values, norms, perceptions, beliefs, and assumptions, the lower the organizational performance. Cultures integration and similarity in values improve organizational performance. The study supported the acceptance of the alternative hypotheses H_a1, H_a2, and H_a3 and rejected the null hypotheses H_o1, H_o2, and H_o3. Integration of cultural traits acts as a mediator effect on organizational performance. Although the study answered the research questions by testing three hypotheses, the quantitative correlational and regression research also provides a reference point for applying the study findings and additional research.

The study recommendation suggests that organizational leaders should proactively integrate cultural traits into the leadership development system. With the increase in failed mergers in the tech industry and a decrease in organizational performance, tech industry leaders should approach a merger cautiously and acknowledge the challenges of making a merger a reality. Organizations performing a cultural assessment before implementing the merger process and using social controls to manage the integration process of cultural issues will increase organizational performance during the pre-merger and post-merger transformation processes.

The findings of moderate performance show the need to increase performance rating in the studied merged bank. Banking industry leaders should be aware of the organizational culture and employees' commitment, involvement, and creativity. Understanding the relationship between leadership styles and cultural values will help leaders and workers reduce cultural conflicts in the workplace, resulting in more productivity and increased organizational performance. The current study advances the organizational culture, leadership, and organizational performance body of knowledge. The present study incorporated transformational leadership theory, equity theory, and Denison organizational culture model sourced to DOCP instruments to respond to three research questions. The analysis contextualizes organizational culture, leadership practices, and organizational performance in the studied merged bank.

6.15 CHAPTER 6 STUDY QUIZ QUESTIONS

Question 1. The main objective of the finding section in a research study is to display or showcase the study's outcome.

A. True
B. False

Question 2. Research findings aim to provide a holistic view of the latest research findings in related areas.

A. True
B. False

Question 3. ________________________ are the constraints placed on the ability to generalize from the results, to further describe applications to practice.

A. Study delimitations
B. Study guidance
C. Study limitations
D. Study result

Question 4. What is the best reason to acquire a company?

A. Track Record of Success.
B. Strong Brand.
C. Training Programs and operational support
D. All of the Above

Question 5. What is a merger?

A. When there is no difference.
B. A merger is when one firm separates to become two.
C. A merger is when two firms combine and form a new legal entity.
D. A merger is when a firm changes its title.

Question 6. There are many reasons to acquire a company. Most deals fall under which the following common causes:

A. Top-Line Growth
B. Expanding customer base
C. Leverage Technologies
D. All of the above

Question 7. ____________________ is the purchasing of a direct competitor to provide economies of scale and cost reduction but may not change your overall strategic position.

A. Merger
B. Acquisition
C. Consolidation
D. None of the above

Question 8. Expanding talent is among the reasons to acquire a company and can be attractive because of the people it brings with it, such as technology innovators, an exceptional sales team, or seasoned executives

A. True
B. False

6.16 CHAPTER 6 STUDY QUIZ SOLUTIONS

1. A
2. A
3. C
4. D
5. C
6. D
7. C
8. A

6.17 CHAPTER 6 EXERCISES

1. What are the research implications?
2. What is a research interpretation of findings?
3. What is a study limitation?
4. What are the recommendations in a research study?
5. Explain study recommendations for organizational leadership?
6. Explain study recommendations for Tech Industry leadership?
7. Explain study recommendations for Banking Industry leadership?
8. Explain study recommendations for Merger Organizations?
9. Explain study recommendations for future research?
10. Explain current organizational change trends?

NOTES

1. Schein, E. H. (1992). *Organizational culture and leadership* (2nd ed.). San Francisco: Jossey-Bass.

2. Tay, A. (2009). Developments in research on employee commitment. *International Journal of Management and Innovation*, 1(1), 57–66. Retrieved from Entrepreneurship database.

3. Garcia-Morales, V. J., Matias-Reche, F., & Hurtado-Torres, N. (2008). Influence of transformational leadership on organizational innovation and performance depending on the level of organizational learning in the pharmaceutical sector. *Journal of Organizational Change Management*, 21(2), 188–212. Retrieved from ABI/INFORM Global database.

4. Adams, J. S. (1965). Inequity in social exchange. In Berkowitz, L. (Ed.), *Advances in Experimental Social Psychology*, 2, (pp. 267–299). New York: Academic Press.

5. Yao, X., & Wang, L. (2008). Socially oriented values and reciprocity norms predict organizational commitment. *Asian Journal of Social Psychology*, 11, 247–252.

References

Aburime, U., & Uche, C. (2008). Impact of share capitalization on bank profitability in Nigeria. *European Journal of Scientific Research, 19*(3), 438–452. Retrieved from Academic Search Complete database.

Accenture (2020). COVID-19 Rebalance for resilience with M&A. Retrieved from https://www.accenture.com/_acnmedia/PDF-122/Accenture-COVID-19-Rebalance-for-Resilience-Mergers-and-Acquisitions.pdf

Adams, J. S. (1963). Toward an understanding of inequity. *Journal of Abnormal and Social Psychology, 67,* 422–436.

Adams, J. S. (1965). Inequity in social exchange. In Berkowitz, L. (Ed.), *Advances in experimental social psychology, 2* (pp. 267–299). New York: Academic Press.

Afzal, H., Butt, B., Rehman, K., & Safwan, N. (2009). An investigation of intragroup conflict and its impact on employee performance in the Pakistani banking sector. *South Asian Journal of Management, 16*(1), 92–101. Retrieved August 20, 2009, from ABI/INFORM Global database.

Agboola, A., & Salawu, R. (2008). Optimizing the use of information and communication technology (ICT) in Nigerian banks. *Journal of Internet Banking and Commerce, 13*(1), 1–15. Retrieved from ABI/INFORM Global database.

Alaranta, M., & Henningsson, S. (2008). An approach to analyzing and planning post-merger IS integration: Insights from two field studies. *Information Systems Frontiers, 10*(3), 307–320.

Alas, R., Tafel, K., & Tuulik, K. (2007). Leadership style during transition in society: Case of Estonia. *Problems and Perspectives in Management, 5*(1), 50–60, 147. Retrieved from ABI/INFORM Global database.

Alavi, M., Kayworth, T., & Leidner, D. (2006). An empirical examination of the influence of organizational culture on knowledge management practices. *Journal of Management Information Systems, 22*(3), 191–224. Retrieved from EBSCOhost database.

Ali, A. B., Tang, N., Rolf, V. D., & Mir, U. R. (2019). Authoritarian leadership, organizational citizenship behavior, and organizational deviance: Curvilinear relationships. *Leadership & Organization Development Journal, 40*(5), 583–599. http://dx.doi.org/10.1108/LODJ-08-2018-0313

Allen, R. S., Takeda, M., & White, C. S. (2005). Cross-cultural equity sensitivity: A test of differences between the United States and Japan. *Journal of Managerial Psychology, 20*(8), 641–662. Retrieved from ABI/INFORM Global database.

Allert, J., & Innes-Brown, M. (2005). Building trust, communication, and leadership for new globalization. *Journal of Asia Pacific Marketing, 4*(1), 41–51. Retrieved from ABI/INFORM Global database.

Allred, B. B., Boal, K. B., & Holstein, W. K. (2005). Corporations as stepfamilies: A new metaphor for explaining the fate of merged and acquired companies. *Academy of Management Executive, 19*(3), 23–37. Retrieved from General OneFile database.

Alston, F., & Tippett, D. (2009). Does a technology-driven organization's culture influence the trust employees have in their managers? *Engineering Management Journal, 21*(2), 3–10. Retrieved from ABI/INFORM Global database.

Anderson, J., & Billou, N. (2007). Serving the world's poor: Innovation at the base of the economic pyramid. *The Journal of Business Strategy, 28*(2), 14–21. Retrieved from ABI/INFORM Global database.

Anderson, W., & Patterson, M. (2008). Effects of social value orientations on fairness judgments. *The Journal of Social Psychology, 148*(2), 223–45. Retrieved from ABI/INFORM Global database.

Andreadis, N. (2009). Learning and organizational effectiveness: A systems perspective. *Performance Improvement, 48*(1), 5–11. Retrieved from ABI/INFORM Global database.

Antila, E. M., & Kakkonen, A. (2008). Factors affecting the role of HR managers in international mergers and acquisitions: A multiple case study. *Personnel Review, 37*(3), 280–299. Retrieved from ABI/INFORM Global database.

Appelbaum, S. H., Lefrancois, F., Tonna, R., & Shapiro, B. T. (2007). Mergers 101 (Part 1): Training managers for communications and leadership challenges. *Industrial and Commercial Training, 39*(3), 128. Retrieved from ABI/INFORM Global database.

Appelbaum, S. H., Gandell, J., Yortis, H., Proper, S., & Jobin, F. (2000). Anatomy of a merger: Behavior of organizational factors and processes throughout the pre-during-post stages (Part 1). *Management Decision, 38*(9), 649–661.

Atkins, J. R., & Turner, D. S. (2006). Upgrade stakeholder service by changing your agency's organizational culture. *Institute of Transportation Engineers, 76*(12), 30. Retrieved from EBSCOhost database.

Atkinson, P. (2005). Managing resistance to change. *Management Services, 49*(1), 14–19. Retrieved from EBSCOhost database.

Avey, J. B., Hughes, L. W., Norman, S. M., & Luthans, K. W. (2008). Using positivity, transformational leadership and empowerment to combat employee negativity. *Leadership & Organization Development Journal, 29*(2), 110–126. Retrieved from ABI/INFORM Global database.

Azofra, S., Olalla, M., & Olmo, B. (2008). Size, target performance and European bank mergers and acquisitions. *American Journal of Business, 23*(1), 53–63. Retrieved from ABI/INFORM Global database.

Badrtalei, J., & Bates, D. (2007). Effect of organizational cultures on mergers and acquisitions: The case of Daimler Chrysler. *International Journal of Management, 24*(2), 303–317. Retrieved from Business Source Complete database.

Balthazard, P. A., Cooke, R. A., & Potter, R. E. (2006). Dysfunctional culture, dysfunctional organization: Capturing the behavioral norms that form organizational culture and drive performance. *Journal of Managerial Psychology, 21*(8), 709. Retrieved from ABI/INFORM Global database.

Bambacas, M., & Patrickson, M. (2008). Interpersonal communication skills that enhance organisational commitment. *Journal of Communication Management, 12*(1), 51–72. Retrieved from ABI/INFORM Global database.

Baranes, E., & Flochel, L. (2008). Competition in telecommunication networks with call externalities. *Journal of Regulatory Economics*, *34*(1), 53–75. Retrieved from ProQuest database.

Bass, B. M., & Avolio, B. J. (1994). Transformational leadership and organizational culture. *International Journal of Public Administration, 17*(3–4), 541–554. Retrieved from General OneFile database.

Baughn, M., & Finzel, P. (2009). A clash of cultures in a merger of two acquisition project offices. *Engineering Management Journal*, *21*(2), 11–17. Retrieved from ABI/INFORM Global database.

Bayer, S., & Gann, D. (2006). Balancing work: Bidding strategies and workload dynamics in a project-based professional service organization. *System Dynamics Review*, *22*(3), 185–211, Retrieved from EBSCOhost database.

Beard, D. R. (2007). A cross-sectional analysis of earn-out contracting in acquisitions. *The Business Review, Cambridge, 7*(2), 8–14. Retrieved from ABI/INFORM Global database.

Becher, D. A., & Campbell, T. L. (2005). Interstate banking deregulation and the changing nature of bank mergers. *The Journal of Financial Research*, *28*(1), 1–20.

Behery, M. H., & Paton, R. A. (2008). Performance appraisal-culture fit and organizational outcomes within the U.A.E. *Journal of American Academy of Business, Cambridge, 13*(1), 166–176. Retrieved from ABI/INFORM Global database.

Benson, G. S. (2006). Employee development, commitment, and intention to turnover: A test of employability policies in action. *Human Resource Management Journal, 16*, 173–192. Retrieved from EBSCOhost database.

Berkovitch, E., & Narayanan, M. P. (1993). Motives for takeovers: An empirical investigation. *Journal of Financial and Quantitative Analysis, 28*(3), 347. Retrieved from ABI/INFORM Global database.

Berman, D. (2006, October 2). Stock market quarterly review: Merger activity sets stage for record year. *The Wall Street Journal*, New York, p. C11. Retrieved from ProQuest database.

Bhattarai, K., Prasuna, A., & Kumar, S. N. V. S. (2021). Economic and institutional determinants of mergers & acquisitions in BRICS, G7 and G20 economies. *The Journal of Applied Business and Economics*, 23(7), 8–20. https://coloradotech.idm.oclc.org/login?url=https://www.proquest.com/scholarly-journals/economic-institutional-determinants-mergers-amp/docview/2617204320/se-2?accountid=144789

Bor, H., & Shargel, R. (2020). The merger of Baltimore Hebrew University with Towson University: Three leadership models converge. *The International Journal of Educational Management, 34*(10), 1595–1613. http://dx.doi.org/10.1108/IJEM-12-2018-0397

Boglarsky, C. A. (2005). 5 Steps to Successful Mergers and Acquisitions. Workspan, 48(2), 50–52. Retrieved from https://coloradotech.idm.oclc.org/login?url=https://www.proquest.com/trade-journals/5-steps-successful-mergers-acquisitions/docview/194716661/se-2?accountid=144789

Brahy, S. (2006). Six solution pillars for successful culture integration of international M&As. *Journal of Organizational Excellence*, *25*(4), 53–63. Retrieved from Business Source Complete database.

Brock, J. (2005). Merger mania and its discontents. *Multinational Monitor*, *26*(7/8), 10–14. Retrieved from EBSCOhost database.

Brouwer, M. T. (2008). Horizontal mergers and efficiencies; Theory and anti-trust practice. *European Journal of Law and Economics*, *26*(1), 11–27. Retrieved from Academic OneFile database.

Brown, S. P., Jones, E., & Leigh, T. W. (2005). The attenuating effect of role overload on relationships linking self-efficacy and goal level to work performance. *Journal of Applied Psychology*, *90*(5), 972–979. Retrieved from General OneFile database.

Burns, J. M. (1978). *Leadership*. New York: Harper & Row.

Caligiuri, P. M., & Day, D. V. (2000). Effects of self-monitoring on technical, contextual, and assignment-specific performance. *Group & Organization Management*, *25*(2), 154–74. Retrieved from General OneFile database.

Cambra-Fierro, J., Polo-Redondo, Y., & Wilson, A. (2008). The influence of an organization's corporate values on employees' personal buying behavior. *Journal of Business Ethics*, *81*(1), 157–167.

Carr. C. L. (2007). The Fairserve Model: Consumer reactions to services based on a multidimensional evaluation of service fairness. *Decision Sciences*, *38*(1), 107–130. Retrieved from ABI/INFORM Global.

Cartwright, S., & Cooper, C. L. (1993). The roles of culture compatibility in successful organizational marriage. *Academy of Management Executive*, *7*(2), 57–70.

Cervantes, Y. (2008). "Fin rah!" A welcome change: Why the merger was necessary to preserve U.S. market integrity. *Fordham Journal of Corporate & Financial Law*, *13*(5), 829–862. Retrieved from General OneFile database.

Chang, W. (2009). Roadmap of co-branding positions and strategies. *Journal of American Academy of Business, 15*(1), 77–84. Retrieved from ABI/INFORM Global database.

Chang, W. J., & Huang, T. C. (2005). Relationship between strategic human resource management and firm performance: A contingency perspective. *International Journal of Manpower*, *26*(5), 434–452. Retrieved from General OneFile database.

Chen, S. (2008). The motives for international acquisitions: Capability procurements, strategic considerations, and the role of ownership structures. *Journal of International Business Studies, 39*(3), 454–471. Retrieved from ABI/INFORM Global database.

Chen, Y. (2008). Restructuring the organizational culture of medical institutions: A study on a community hospital in the I-Lan area. *Journal of Nursing Research, 16*(3), 211–218. Retrieved from CINAHL Plus with Full Text database.

Chew, I. K. H., & Sharma, B. (2005). The effects of culture and HRM practices on firm performance: Empirical evidence from Singapore. *International Journal of Manpower, 26*(6), 560–581, 604–605. Retrieved from ABI/INFORM Global database.

Chow, I. H., & Liu, S. S. (2007). Business strategy, organizational culture, and performance outcomes in China's technology industry. *HR. Human Resource Planning, 30*(2), 47–56. Retrieved ProQuest database.

Cigola, M., & Modesti, P. (2008). A note on mergers and acquisitions. *Managerial Finance, 34*(4), 221–238. Retrieved from ABI/INFORM Global.

Coffey, C., & Tombari, N. (2005). The bottom-line for work and life leadership: Linking diversity and organizational culture. *Ivey Business Journal Online*, 1–7. Retrieved from ProQuest database.

Collins, C. J., & Smith, K. G. (2006). Knowledge exchange and combination: The role of human resource practices in the performance of high-technology firms. *Academy of Management Journal, 49*(3), 544–560. Retrieved from General OneFile database.

Contiu, L.C., Gabor, M.R., Oltean, F.D., (2012). Employee's Motivation from a Cultural Perspective-A Key Element of the Hospitality Industry Competitiveness. Procedia Economics and Finance, 3: 981–986.

Cooke, R. A., & Rousseau, D. M. (1988). Behavioral norms and expectations: A quantitative approach to the assessment of organizational culture. *Group and Organizational studies, 13*(3), 245–273. Retrieved from General OneFile database.

Cooper, C., Densten, I., Gray, J., & Sarros, J. (2005). The organizational culture profile revisited and revised: An Australian perspective. *Australian Journal of Management, 30*(1), 159–183. Retrieved from General OneFile database.

Cooper-Hakim, A., & Viswesvaran, C. (2005). The construct of work commitment: Testing an integrative framework. *Psychological Bulletin, 131*(2), 241–258. Retrieved from General OneFile database.

Cooper, D. R., & Schindler, P. S. (2008). *Business research methods* (10th ed.). Boston: Irwin.

Coy, P., Thornton, E., Arndt, M., Grow, B., & Park, A. (2005, January 10). Shake, rattle, and merge. *Business Week*, pp. 32–36. Retrieved from General OneFile database.

Creswell, J. W. (2005). Educational research: Planning, conducting, and evaluating quantitative and qualitative research (2nd ed.). Columbus, OH: Merrill Prentice Hall.

Culjak, N. B. (2021). Analysis of acquisition success in soft beverage industry of the Republic of Croatia. Varazdin Development and Entrepreneurship Agency (VADEA).

Cuong, D. M., & Swierczek, F. W. (2008). Corporate culture, leadership competencies, job satisfaction, job commitment, and job performance: A comparison of companies in Vietnam and Thailand. *Journal of American Academy of Business, 13*(1), 159–166. Retrieved from ProQuest database.

DealRoom (n.d). The Ultimate Guide to Post Merger (M&A) Integration Process. Retrieved from https://dealroom.net/faq/post-merger-and-acquisition-m-a-integration-process

De Mattos, C., Salciuviene, L., & Lewis, L. (2007, August). Cultural compatibility in the implementation of mergers and acquisitions: The banking sector. *Economics & Management*, 338–345. Retrieved from Business Source Complete database.

De Hilal, A. V. G., Wetzel, U., & Ferreira, V. (2009). Organizational culture and performance: A Brazilian case. *Management Research News, 32*(2), 99–119. Retrieved from ABI/INFORM Global database.

Denison, D. (2005, April). Overview of the reliability and validity of the Denison organizational cultural survey. Ann Arbor, MI: Denison Consulting.

Denison, D. (2006). Linking organizational culture and business performance: A brief overview in assessment, evaluation, and improvement. Washington, DC: Denison Consulting.

Denison, D., Haaland, S., & Goelzer, P. (2004). Corporate culture and organizational effectiveness: Is Asia different from the rest of the world? *Organizational Dynamics, 33*(1), 98–109. Retrieved from General OneFile database.

Denison, D. R., Janovics, J., Young, J., & Cho, J. H. (2006). *Diagnosing organizational cultures: Validating a model and method.* Washington, DC: Denison Consulting.

Denison, D. R., & Mishra, A. (1995). Toward a theory of organizational culture and effectiveness. *Organizational Science, 6*, 204–223.

Denison, D. R., & Neale, W. S. (1998). *Denison organizational cultural model survey.* Ann Arbor, MI: Aviat.

Dewhurst, S. (2009). How to regain your motivation for work. *Strategic Communication Management, 13*(3), 14–15. Retrieved from ABI/INFORM Global database.

Diller, J., (2010). *Cultural Diversity: A Primer for the Human Services*, New York, NY: Cengage Learning

Dounis, N. (2008). The auditor's role in mergers and acquisitions. *Internal Auditor, 65*(3), 61–63. Retrieved September 7, 2009, from Business Source Complete database.

Duffy, J. (2007). The 10 largest U.S. telecom carrier mergers/acquisitions. *Network World.* Retrieved from http://www.networkworld.com/news/2008/121008-tech-industry-merger-acquisition.html

Dulewicz, V., & Higgs, M. (2005). Assessing leadership styles and organizational context. *Journal of Managerial Psychology, 20*, 105–124. Retrieved from ProQuest database.

Dunham, B. S., & Davis, T. L. (2008). Literature of acquisitions in review, 1996–2003. *Library Resources & Technical Services, 52*(4), 238–253. Retrieved from Research Library database.

Dutta, K., & Dutta, A. (2009). Customer expectations and perceptions across the banking industry and the resultant financial implications. *Journal of Services Research*, 9(1), 31–49. Retrieved from ABI/INFORM Global database.

Dyer, J., Kale, P., & Singh, H. (2004). When to ally and when to acquire. *Harvard Business Review*, *82*(7/8), 108–115. Retrieved from EBSCOhost database. The effects of organizational culture and market orientation on the effectiveness of strategic marketing alliances. (2002). *The Journal of Services Marketing*, *16*(3), 201–222. Retrieved from Business Source Complete database.

Elashmawi, F. (1998). Overcoming multicultural clashes in global joint ventures. *European Business Review*, *98*(4), 211–216. Retrieved from ABI/INFORM Global database.

Emery, C. R., & Barker, K. (2007). The effect of transactional and transformational leadership styles on the organizational commitment and job satisfaction of customer contact personnel. *Journal of Organizational Culture, Communication and Conflict*, *11*(1), 77–90. Retrieved from ProQuest database.

Epstein, M. J. (2004). The drivers of success in post-merger integration. *Organizational Dynamics*, *33*(2), 174–89. Retrieved from General OneFile database.

Erkutlu, H. (2008). The impact of transformational leadership on organizational and leadership effectiveness: The Turkish case. *The Journal of Management Development*, *27*(7), 708–726. Retrieved from ABI/INFORM Global database.

Ezeoha, A. E. (2005). Increasing incidence of poverty in Nigeria: An impact assessment of the government's economic reform programme. *Journal of Social Development in Africa* (Zimbabwe), *22*(2), 112–131.

Ezeoha, A. (2007). Structural effects of banking industry consolidation in Nigeria: A review. *Journal of Banking Regulation, 8*(2), 159. Retrieved from ABI/INFORM Global database.

Fadil, P. A., Williams, R. J., Limpaphayom, W., & Smart, C. (2005). Equity or equality? A conceptual examination of the influence of individualism/collectivism on the crosscultural application of equity theory. *Cross Cultural Management*, *12*, 17–35.

Farrell, M. A., Oczkowski, E., & Kharabsheh, R. (2008). Market orientation, learning orientation, and organizational performance in international joint ventures. *Asia Pacific Journal of Marketing and Logistics*, *20*(3), 289–308. Retrieved from ABI/INFORM Global database.

Fealy, L., & Kompare, D. (2003). When worlds collide: Culture clash. *Journal of Business Strategy*, *24*(4), 9–14. Retrieved from Business Source Complete database.

Feast, R. (1998). How Ford and GM manage their European acquisitions. *Automotive Industry*, *178*(4), 1–4. Retrieved from General OneFile database.

Feast, R. (2003). Automotive mergers rarely meet expectations. *Automotive News, 78*(6069), pp. 32f–32h. Retrieved from Business Source Complete database.

Fey, C., & Denison, D. R. (2003). Organizational culture and effectiveness: Can an American theory be applied in Russia? *Organization Science, 14*(6), 686–706. Retrieved from Business Source Complete database.

Ficery, K., Herd, T., & Pursche, B. (2007). Where has all the synergy gone? The M&A puzzle. *The Journal of Business Strategy, 28*(5), 29–35. Retrieved from ABI/INFORM Global database.

Field, J., & Peck, E. (2003). Mergers and acquisitions in the private sector: What are the lessons for health and social services? *Social Policy and Administration, 37*(7), 742–756. Retrieved from EBSCOhost database.

Freeland, C. (2005). Aiming towards true integration. *Precision Marketing, 17*(47), 12. Retrieved from EBSCOhost database.

Freund, A. (2005). Commitment and job satisfaction as predictors of turnover intentions among welfare workers. *Administration in Social Work, 29*(2), 5–22. Retrieved from Academic Search Complete database.

Gabriel, Y. (2009). Organizing words: a critical thesaurus for social and organization studies' London: Oxford University Press, 2009.

Garcia-Morales, V. J., Matias-Reche, F., & Hurtado-Torres, N. (2008). Influence of transformational leadership on organizational innovation and performance depending on the level of organizational learning in the pharmaceutical sector. *Journal of Organizational Change Management, 21*(2), 188–212. Retrieved from ABI/INFORM Global database.

Garver, R. (2006). *Merger right: Numbers don't drive deals, People do*. Retrieved from http://www.CFO.com

Gay K., (2003). *Cultural diversity: conflicts and challenges: the ultimate teen guide*. London: Scarecrow Press.

Gebler, D. (2009). The ten merger commandments. *Risk Management, 56*(5), 10–13. Retrieved from ABI/INFORM Global database.

Ghazzawi, I. (2008). Job satisfaction antecedents and consequences: A new conceptual framework and research agenda. *The Business Review, 11*(2), 1–10.

Gillespie, M. A., Denison, D. R., Haaland, S., Smerek, R., & Neale, W. S. (2008). Linking organizational culture and customer satisfaction: Business-unit results from two companies in different industries. *European Journal of Work and Organizational Psychology, 17*(1), 112–132. Retrieved from EBSCOhost database.

Gillespie, R. (2008). Manufacturing Knowledge: A History of the Hawthorne Experiments' London: Cambridge University Press.

Gordon, J. (2008). The human resources evolution. *Network Journal, 15*(10), 10–12. Retrieved from Ethnic News Watch (ENW) database.

Green, D. D. (2007). Leading a postmodern workforce. *Academy of Strategic Management Journal, 6*, 15–27. Retrieved from ProQuest database.

Greenberg, J., & Baron, R. A. (2008). *Behavior in organizations* (9th ed.). Upper Saddle River. NJ: Prentice Hall-Pearson.

Guillén, M., Ferrero, I. and Hoffman, W.M. (2015). "The neglected ethical and spiritual motivations in the workplace," Journal of Business Ethics, Vol. 128 No. 4, pp. 803–816.

Haag, S., Cummings, M., & McCubbrey, D. (2005). *Management information systems for the information age* (5th ed.). Boston: McGraw-Hill.

Hagendorff, J., Collins, M., & Keasey, K. (2007). Bank deregulation and acquisition activity: The cases of the U.S., Italy, and Germany. *Journal of Financial Regulation and Compliance, 15*(2), 199–209. Retrieved from ABI/INFORM Global database.

Hall, E. (1959). *The silent language*. Garden City, NY: Doubleday.

Hardy, L. (2010). *The fabric of this world: inquiries into calling, career choice, and the design of human work.* London: Wm. B. Eerdmans Publishing, 1990.

Harford, J. (2005). What drives merger waves? *Journal of Financial Economics, 77*(3), 529–560. Retrieved from Business Source Complete database.

Hennart, J. F., & Zeng, M. (2005). Structural determinants of joint venture performance. *European Management Review, 2*(2), 105.

Herbst, C. (2008, March). Austrian M&A activity at record levels in 2007. *International Financial Law Review, 27*, 10–11. Retrieved from Business Source Complete database.

Higgins, J. (2001). *The Raymond Williams reader*. Malden, MA: Blackwell Publishers.

Hon, C. M. (2002). *A quantitative analysis of organizational culture perception in a same industry merger*. Retrieved from ProQuest Dissertations and Theses database. (AAT No. 3068401)

Hopkins, H. (2008). Cross-border mergers and acquisitions: Do strategy or post-merger integration matter? *International Management Review, 4*(1), 5–7. Retrieved from ABI/INFORM Global database.

Horvath, M., & Andrews, S. B. (2007). The role of fairness perceptions and accountability attributions in predicting reactions to organizational events. *The Journal of Psychology, 141*(2), 203–223. Retrieved from ProQuest database.

Howell, J. M., Neufeld, D. J., & Avolio, B. J. (2005). Examining the relationship of leadership and physical distance with business unit performance. *The Leadership Quarterly, 16*(2), 273–285. Retrieved from Academic OneFile database.

Hubert, O. E., & Van, L. D. (2006). Are acquisitions worthwhile? An empirical study of the post-acquisition performance of privately held Belgian companies. *Small Business Economics, 27*(2–3), 223. Retrieved from ProQuest database.

Hunt, W. (2007). Business implications of divergences in multi-jurisdictional merger review by international competition enforcement agencies. *Northwestern Journal of International Law & Business, 28*(1), 147–170. Retrieved from ABI/INFORM Global.

Idea to Value (2021). The law of diffusion of innovation. Retrieved from https://www.ideatovalue.com/inno/nickskillicorn/2021/01/the-law-of-diffusion-of-innovation/

Indridason, T., & Wang, C. L. (2008). Commitment or contract: What drives performance in public private partnerships? *Business Strategy Series, 9*(2), 78–90. Retrieved from ABI/INFORM Global database.

Iyer, D., & Miller, K. (2008). Performance feedback, slack, and the timing of acquisitions. *Academy of Management Journal, 51*(4), 808–822. Retrieved from Business Source Complete database.

Jackson, S. E. (2007). Creating value through acquisitions. *The Journal of Business Strategy, 28*(6), 40–41. Retrieved from ABI/INFORM Global database.

Janjua, K., Noor, S., & Khan, S. (2008). A critical evaluation of telecommunication act 1996. *Journal of Service Science and Management, 1*(1), 83–90. Retrieved from ProQuest Computing database.

Jayadev, M., & Sensarma, R. (2007). Mergers in Indian banking: An analysis [dagger]. *South Asian Journal of Management, 14*(4), 20–49. Retrieved ABI/INFORM Global database.

Jehanzeb, K., & Mohanty, J. (2020). The mediating role of organizational commitment between organizational justice and organizational citizenship behavior: Power distance as moderator. *Personnel Review, 49*(2), 445–468. http://dx.doi.org/10.1108/PR-09-2018-0327

Jing, R., & Graham, J. (2008). Values versus regulations: How culture plays its role. *Journal of Business Ethics, 80*(4), 791–806. Retrieved from Business Source Complete database.

Johnson, C. A. (2007). The effects of culture on performance: Merging Air Force active duty and National Guard personnel. (Doctoral dissertation. University of Phoenix. United States—Arizona). Retrieved from ProQuest Dissertations and Theses database. (UMI No. 3279397)

Joiner, T. A. (2007). Total quality management and performance: The role of organization support and co-worker support. *The International Journal of Quality & Reliability Management, 24*(6), 617. Retrieved from ProQuest database.

Kahn, R. L. (1964). Organizational stress: Studies in role conflict and ambiguity. New York: Wiley.

Kanter, R. M., Raffaelli, R., & Raymond, D. (2004). *The making of Verizon.* Boston: Harvard Business School Publishing.

Katz, M., & Shelanski, H. (2007). Merger analysis and the treatment of uncertainty: Should we expect better? *Antitrust Law Journal, 74*(3), 537–574. Retrieved from ABI/INFORM Global database.

Kest, R. T. (2006). Principles of leadership: Leadership management. *Futurics, 30*(1/2), 52–71. Retrieved December 6, 2008, from Research Library database.

Kinicki, A., & Kreitner, R. (2009). *Organizational behavior: Key concepts, skills & best practices* (4th ed.). New York, NY: McGraw-Hill Irwin.

Kirkbride, P. (2006). Developing transformational leaders: The full range leadership model in action. *Industrial and Commercial Training, 38*(1), 23–33. Retrieved, from ProQuest database.

Kiymaz, H., & Baker, H. K. (2008). Short-term performance, industry effects, and motives: Evidence from large M&As. *Quarterly Journal of Finance and Accounting, 47*(2), 17–44. Retrieved from ABI/INFORM Global database.

Koetter, M. (2008). An assessment of bank merger success in Germany. *German Economic Review, 9*(2), 232–264. Retrieved from EBSCOhost database.

Kotter, J., & Heskett, J. (1992). *Corporate culture and performance.* New York: Free Press.

Konorti, E. (2008). The 3D transformational leadership model. *Journal of American Academy of Business, 14*(1), 10–20. Retrieved from ABI/INFORM Global database.

Kumar, B. R. (2019) Wealth Creation in World's Largest Mergers and Acquisitions: Integrated Case Studies. Cham, Switzerland: Springer.

LaHuis, D. M., & Avis, J. M. (2007). Using multilevel random coefficient modeling to investigate rater effects in performance ratings. *Organizational Research Methods, 10*(1), 97–107. from Business Source Complete database.

Lai, M., & Lee, G. (2007). Risk-avoiding cultures toward achievement of knowledge sharing. *Business Process Management Journal, 13*(4), 522. Retrieved from ProQuest database.

Lainema, T., & Lainema, K. (2007). Advancing acquisition of business know-how: Critical learning elements. *Journal of Research on Technology in Education, 40*(2), 183–198. Retrieved from Research Library database.

Lambrecht, B., & Myers, S. (2007). A theory of takeovers and disinvestment. *Journal of Finance, 62*(2), 809–845. Retrieved from Business Source Complete database.

Lajoux, A. R. (1998). The art of M&A integration: A guide to merging resources, processes, & responsibilities. New York: McGraw-Hill.

Lang, R. (2008). Culture strikes back! Some reasons for the persistence and increasing importance of local cultures in times of globalization. *Journal for East European Management Studies, 13*(3), 191–192. Retrieved from Business Source Complete database.

Laohavichien, T., Fredendall, L. D., & Cantrell, R. S. (2009). The effects of transformational and transactional leadership on quality improvement. T*he Quality Management Journal, 16*(2), 7–24. Retrieved from ABI/INFORM Global database.

Larsson, R., & Lubatkin, M. (2001). Achieving acculturation in mergers and acquisitions: An international case survey. *Human Relations, 54*(12), 1573–1605. Retrieved from ProQuest database.

Laudon, K. C., & Laudon, J. P. (2006). *Management information systems: Managing the digital firm* (9th ed.). Upper Saddle River. NJ: Prentice Hall-Pearson.

Lausberg, C., & Stahl, T. (2009, February). Motives and non-economic reasons for bank mergers and acquisitions. *ICFAI Journal of Bank Management*, *8*(1), 7–30. Retrieved from Business Source Complete database.

Lawler, E. J. (2001) Affect Theory of Social Exchange. The Academy Journal of Sociology, 107, 321–352. http://dx.doi.org/10.1086/324071

Leach M. (2006). *Cultural diversity and suicide: ethnic, religious, gender, and sexual orientation perspectives*, London: Routledge.

LeanIX Mergers & Acquisitions Survey (2021). Retrieved from https://www.leanix.net/en/wiki/ea/post-merger-integration

Leavy, B. (2005). A leader's guide to creating an innovation culture. *Strategy & Leadership*, 33(4), 38–45. Retrieved from ABI/INFORM Global.

Leedy, P. D., & Ormrod, J. E. (2005). *Practical research: Planning and design* (8th ed.). Upper Saddle River, NJ: Prentice Hall-Pearson Merrill.

Leland, H. (2007). Financial synergies and the optimal scope of the firm: Implications for mergers, spinoffs, and structured finance. *Journal of Finance*, *62*(2), 765–807. Retrieved from Business Source Complete database.

Limsila, K., & Ogunlana, S. O. (2008). Performance and leadership outcome correlates of leadership styles and subordinate commitment. *Engineering, Construction and Architectural Management, 15*(2), 164–184. Retrieved August 7, 2009, from ABI/INFORM Global database.

Lin, P. (2005). An empirical analysis of bank mergers and cost efficiency in Taiwan. *Small Business Economics, 25*(2), 197. Retrieved from ABI/INFORM Global database.

Lissitz, R., & Samuelsen, K. (2007). A suggested change in terminology and emphasis regarding validity and education. *Educational Researcher, 36*(8), 437–448. Retrieved from ProQuest Psychology Journals database.

Li, S., Liu, G. S., & Andros, G. (2021). Do more mergers and acquisitions create value for shareholders? Review of Quantitative Finance and Accounting, 56(2), 755–787. http://dx.doi.org/10.1007/s11156-020-00908-7

Liu, D., & Chen, S. (2008). The role of innovation capability in organizational change: The case of J&S bank. *The Business Review, Cambridge, 11*(1), 90–96. Retrieved from ABI/INFORM Global database.

Luna-Arocas, R., & Camps, J. (2008). A model of high-performance work practices and turnover intentions. *Personnel Review, 37*(1), 26. Retrieved from ABI/INFORM Global database.

Luo, Y. (2005). Do insiders learn from outsiders? Evidence from mergers and acquisitions. *Journal of Finance, 60*(4), 1951–1983. Retrieved from Business Source Complete database.

Luthans, F., & Youssef, C. M. (2007). Emerging positive organizational behavior. *Journal of Management, 33*(3), 321–349. Retrieved from Business Source Complete database.

Lytle, R. S., & Timmerman, J. E. (2006). Service orientation and performance: An organizational perspective. *The Journal of Services Marketing, 20*(2), 136. Retrieved from ProQuest database.

MacDonald, R. (2005). A template for shareholder value creation on M&As. *Strategic Direction, 21*(5), 3–10. Retrieved from ABI/INFORM Global database.

Mancheno-Smoak, L., Endres, G., Potak, R., & Athanasaw, Y. (2009). The individual cultural values and job satisfaction of the transformational leader. *Organization Development Journal, 27*(3), 9–21. Retrieved from ABI/INFORM Global database.

Mann, B., & Kohli, R. (2009). HDFC bank and CBoP merger: A quest for growth. *ICFAI Journal of Mergers & Acquisitions, 6*(1), 38–59. Retrieved from Business Source Complete database.

Mann, S. B., & Kohli, R. (2008). An empirical analysis of bank mergers in India: A study of market driven versus non-market driven mergers. *Decision (0304–0941), 35*(1), 47–73. Retrieved from Business Source Complete database.

Mateja, J. (2001, March). DaimlerChrysler talks shop. *Chicago Tribune*, 1–2.

McLaurin, J. R., Bushanain, M., & Amri, A. (2008). Developing an understanding of charismatic and transformational leadership. Allied Academies International Conference. *Academy of Organizational Culture, Communications and Conflict. Proceedings, 13*(2), 15–19. Retrieved from ABI/INFORM Global database.

McNurlin, B. C., & Sprague, R. H. (2006). *Information systems management in practice* (7th ed.). Upper Saddle River, NJ: Prentice Hall/Pearson.

Meyers, L. S., Gamst, G., & Guarino, A. J. (2006). *Applied multivariate research.* Thousand Oaks, CA: Sage.

Mezzich, J., Ruiperez, M., Yoon, G., Liu, J., & Zapata-Vega, M. (2009). Measuring cultural identity: Validation of a modified Cortes, Rogler, and Malgady Bicultural Scale in three ethnic groups in New York. *Culture, Medicine and Psychiatry, 33*(3), 451–72. Retrieved from Research Library database.

Michalakelis, C., Dede, G., Varoutas, D., & Sphicopoulos, T. (2008). Impact of cross-national diffusion process in telecommunications demand forecasting. *Telecommunication Systems*, *39*(1), 51–61. Retrieved from ProQuest database.

Mitleton-Kelly, E. (2006). Co-evolutionary integration: The co-creation of a new organizational form following a merger and acquisition. *Complexity & Organization*, *8*(2), 36–47. Retrieved from Business Source Complete database.

Moeller, S. B., Schlingemann, F. P., & Stulz, R. M. (2005). Wealth destruction on a massive scale? A study of acquiring firm returns in the recent merger wave. *Journal of Finance, 60*(2), 757–782. Retrieved from Business Source Complete database.

Morales-Sánchez, R., & Pasamar, S. (2020). How to improve organisational citizenship behaviour by combining ability, motivation, and opportunity: The moderator role of perceived organisational support. *Employee Relations, 42*(2), 398–416. http://dx.doi.org/10.1108/ER-04-2019-0169

Morellec, E., & Zhdanov, A. (2005). The dynamics of mergers and acquisitions. *Journal of Financial Economics*, *77*(3), 649–672. Retrieved from Business Source Complete database.

Morrison, N., & Szumilo, N. (2019). The drivers and implications of mega-mergers: Evidence from English not-for-profit housing organizations. *Journal of Housing and the Built Environment*, 34(3), 661–681. http://dx.doi.org/10.1007/s10901-019-09696-6

Mowday, R. T. (1991). Equity theory perceptions of behavior in organizations. In R. M. Steers & L. W. Porter (Eds.), *Motivation and work behavior* (pp. 111–131). New York: McGraw-Hill.

Nadolska, A., & Barkema, H. (2007). Learning to internationalize: The pace and success of foreign acquisitions. *Journal of International Business Studies*, *38*(7), 1170. Retrieved August 20, 2009, from ABI/INFORM Global database.

Nazir, N., & Lone, M. (2008). Validation of Denison's model of organizational cultural effectiveness in the Indian context. *Vision*, *12*(1), 49–58. Retrieved from Business Source Complete database.

Ness, R. (2005). The latest mergers: Why some will fly, and others won't. *Knowledge Wharton*, 1–5. Retrieved from the Knowledge Wharton database.

Network World. (2008). Tech industry's biggest M&A deals of 2008. Retrieved from http://www.networkworld.com/news

Ogba, I. (2008). Commitment in the workplace: The impact of income and age on employee commitment in Nigerian banking sector. *Management Research News*, *31*(11), 867–878. Retrieved from ABI/INFORM Global database.

Okoro, H. M. (2010). The relationship between organizational culture and performance: Merger in the Nigerian banking industry (Order No. 3424825). Available from ProQuest Dissertations & Theses Global. (756488303).

Olmstead L. (2022). The 11 Best Contract Lifecycle Management (CLM) Software. Retrieved from https://whatfix.com/blog/clm-software/

Olson, B. J., Parayitam, S., & Twigg, N. W. (2006). Mediating role of strategic choice between top management team diversity and firm performance: Upper echelons theory revisited. *Journal of Business and Management*, *12*(2), 111–127. Retrieved from ProQuest database.

Paliwal, R. (2007). Takeovers and agency problems: A reexamination of the pre-acquisition operating performance of targets. *The Business Review, 8*(2), 29–37. Retrieved from ABI/INFORM Global database.

Parish, J. T., Cadwallader, S., & Busch, P. (2008). Want to, need to, ought to: Employee commitment to organizational change. *Journal of Organizational Change Management, 21*(1), 32–52. Retrieved from ABI/INFORM Global database.

Parris, C., Hegtvedt, K., Watson, L., & Johnson, C. (2014). Justice for All? Factors Affecting Perceptions of Environmental and Ecological Injustice. Social Justice Research, 27(1), 67–98. doi:10.1007/s11211-013-0200–4

Peete, T. (2007). *Selecting the right merger relationship: A phenomenological case study*. (Doctoral dissertation. University of Phoenix. United States—Arizona). Retrieved from ProQuest Dissertations and Theses database. (UMI No. 3292693)

Peloza, J., & Papania, L. (2008). The missing link between corporate social responsibility and financial performance: Stakeholder salience and identification. *Corporate Reputation Review*, *11*(2), 169–181. Retrieved from Business Source Complete database.

Pickett, L. (2005). Optimizing human capital: Measuring what really matters. *Industrial and Commercial Training*, *37*(6), 299–304. Retrieved from ProQuest database.

Pike, C. (2006). Mergers and acquisitions: Managing culture and human resources. *Personnel Psychology*, *59*(2), 480–484. Retrieved from Business Source Complete database.

Pollitt, D. (2007). Telecom firm connects with culture change and improved performance. *Training & Management Development Methods, 21*(4), 351–358. Retrieved from ProQuest database.

Pooley, R. (2005). When cultures collide. *Management Services*, *49*(1), 28–31. Retrieved from EBSCOhost database.

Porath, D. (2006). Estimating probabilities of default for German savings banks and credit cooperatives. *Schmalenbach Business Review*, *58*(3), 214–233. Retrieved from Business Source Complete database.

Pultz, J. E. (2005). The AT&T and MCI acquisitions will shape the future of the U.S. network services market. *Gartne*, 1–3.

Quinlan, R. (2008). Ideal acquisitions need effective evaluation. *Financial Executive*, *24*(5), 17–17. Retrieved from Business Source Complete database.

Radam, A., Baharom, A., Dayang-Affizzah, A., & Ismail, F. (2009). Effect of mergers on efficiency and productivity: Some evidence for banks in Malaysia. *ICFAI Journal of Bank Management*, *8*(1), 31–46. Retrieved from Business Source Complete database.

Rahnema, A. & Durme, Y. V. (2017). The organization of the future: Arriving now 2017 Global Human Capital Trends. Retrieved from https://www2.deloitte.com/us/en/insights/focus/human-capital-trends/2017/organization-of-the-future.html

Ranft, A. L., & Marsh, S. J. (2008). Accessing knowledge through acquisitions and alliances: An empirical examination of new market entry. *Journal of Managerial Issues, 20*(1), 51–67. Retrieved from ABI/INFORM Global database.

Reigle, R. F. (2001). Measuring organic and mechanistic cultures. *Engineering Management Journal, 13*(4), 3–8. Retrieved from ProQuest database.

Reiskin, J. (2006, January). Big mergers dominated trucking as companies extended global reach. *Transport Topics, 36,* 10–12. Retrieved from ProQuest database.

Reynolds, C. R., Livingston, R. B., & Wilson, V. (2006). *Measurement and assessment in education.* Boston: Pearson.

Rhodes-Kropf, M., Robinson, D., & Viswanathan, S. (2005). Valuation waves and merger activity: The empirical evidence. *Journal of Financial Economics, 77,* 561–603. Retrieved from ProQuest database.

Risher, H. (2007). Fostering a performance-driven culture in the public sector. *Public Manager, 36*(3), 51–57. Retrieved from ProQuest database.

Rodriguez, A. (2008). Mergers and acquisitions in the banking industry: The human factor. *Organization Development Journal, 26*(2), 63–73. Retrieved from Business Source Complete database.

Romeo, C. J., & Dick, A. R. (2005). The effect of format changes and ownership consolidation on radio station outcomes. *Review of Industrial Organization, 27*(4), 351. Retrieved from ABI/INFORM Global database.

Rose, R. C., Kumar, N., Abdullah, H., & Ling, G. Y. (2008, March). Organizational culture as a root of performance improvement: Research and recommendations. *Contemporary Management Research, 4,* 43–56.

Rosen, R. J. (2006). Merger momentum and investor sentiment: The stock market reaction to merger announcements. *Journal of Business, 79*(2), 987–1017. Retrieved from Business Source Complete database.

Rosenberg, C. (2005). EMEA-US culture clash: Resolving diversity issues through reflective evaluated action learning. *Industrial and Commercial Training*, 37(6/7), 304–308. Retrieved from ABI/INFORM Global database.

Rothermel, R., & LaMarsh, J. (2012, January). Managing change through employee empowerment. Global Business and Organizational Excellence, 31(2), 17. Retrieved from ABI/INFORM Global. (Document ID: 2543274101).

Rothman, S. (2008). Job satisfaction, occupational stress, burnout and work engagement as components of work-related well-being. *South Africa Journal of Industrial Psychology, 34*(3), 11–16.

Salkind, N. J. (2006). *Exploring research.* (6th ed.). Upper Saddle River, NJ: Pearson Prentice Hall.

Schein, E. H. (1992). *Organizational culture and leadership* (2nd ed.). San Francisco: Jossey-Bass.

Schein, E. H. (1999). *The corporate culture survival guide.* San Francisco: Jossey-Bass.

Schraeder, M., & Simpson, J. (2006). How similarity and liking affect performance appraisals. *The Journal for Quality and Participation, 29*(1), 34–38. Retrieved from ProQuest database.

Shahrur, H. (2005). *Industry structure and horizontal takeovers: Analysis of wealth elects on rivals, suppliers, and corporate customers.* (Doctoral dissertation. Georgia State University. United States—Georgia). Retrieved from ProQuest Theses and Dissertations database. (AAT 3090716)

Shay, K. J. (2006, March). State's mergers are fewer, bigger. *Maryland Community Newspapers Online*. Retrieved from http://www.gazette.net /stories/031706/business185322_31941.shtml

Shimoni, B. (2008). Separation, emulation, and competition: Hybridization styles of management cultures in Thailand, Mexico, and Israel. *Journal of Organizational Change Management*, 21(1), 107–119. Retrieved from ABI/INFORM Global database.

Shivers-Blackwell, S. (2006). The influence of perceptions of organizational structure & culture on leadership role requirements: The moderating impacts of locus of control & self-monitoring. *Journal Leadership & Organizational Studies*, *12*(4), 27–50. Retrieved from ProQuest database.

Siapera, E., (2010). '*Cultural Diversity and Global Media: The Mediation of Difference,* London: John Wiley and Sons.

Sidener, J., & Kinsman, M. (2008). The wireless revolution. *Network Journal*, *15*(7), 30–31. Retrieved from ProQuest database.

Simon, M. K. (2005). Dissertation & scholarly research: A practical guide to start & complete your dissertation, thesis, or formal research project. Dubuque, IA: Kendall/Hunt.

Singh, K. (2008). Relationship between learning organization and transformational leadership: Banking organizations in India. *International Journal of Business and Management Sciences*, *1*(1), 97–111. Retrieved from ABI/INFORM Global database.

Sitkin & Pablo (2005) Sitkin, S. B., & Pablo, A. (2005). The neglected importance of leadership in mergers and acquisitions. In G. K. Stahl & M. E. Mendenhall (Eds.), Mergers and acquisitions: Managing culture and human resources (pp. 412–422). Stanford, CA: Stanford University Press.

Smith, A. (2008, January). Oracle, BEA systems in $8.5B deal. *CNN Money*. Retrieved January 9, 2009, from http://money.cnn.com/2008/01/16/news/companies/oracle

Smith, P. (2008). Culturally conscious organizations: A conceptual framework. *Portal, Libraries and the Academy*, *8*(2), 141–148, 150–155. Retrieved from Research Library.

Streeter, B. (2006). M&A: The deals just keep on coming. *American Bankers Association. ABA Banking Journal*, *98*(2), 50–54. Retrieved from ABI/INFORM Global database.

Sull, D. N. (2007). Closing the gap between strategy and execution. *MIT Sloan Management Review, 48*(4), 30–10. Retrieved from EBSCOhost database.

Sung, N., & Gort, M. (2006). Mergers, capital gains, and productivity: Evidence from U.S. telecommunications mergers. *Contemporary Economic Policy, 24*(3), 382–394. Retrieved from ABI/INFORM Global database.

Tabachnick, B. G., & Fidell, L. S. (2007). *Using multivariate statistics* (5th ed.). Boston: Allyn & Bacon.

Tanure, & Gonzalez-Duarte, R. (2007). Managing people in radical changes (M&As): The adoption of intrinsically consistent HRM strategies in Brazilian companies. *International Journal of Manpower*, *28*(5), 369–383. Retrieved from ABI/INFORM Global database.

Tay, A. (2009). Developments in research on employee commitment. *International Journal of Management and Innovation, 1*(1), 57–66. Retrieved from Entrepreneurship database.

Terranova, C. (2006). Assessing culture at Sun Microsystems. *Strategic HR Review, 5*(6), 24–27. Retrieved December 12, 2008, from Business Source Complete database.

Terranova, C. (2007). Assessing culture during an acquisition. *Organizational Development Journal, 25*(2), 43–49. Retrieved from ProQuest database.

Tierney, S., (2007). *Accommodating cultural diversity*, Washington, DC: Ashgate Publishing, Ltd.

Toby, A. (2006). Empirical study of the liquidity management practices of Nigerian banks. *Journal of Financial Management & Analysis, 19*(1), 57–70. Retrieved from Business Source Complete database.

Trim, P. R. J., & Lee, Y. (2008). A strategic approach to sustainable partnership development. *European Business Review, 20*(3), 222–239. Retrieved from ABI/INFORM Global database.

Tucker, S., Turner, N., Barling, B., Reid, E. M., & Elving, C. (2006). Apologies and transformational leadership. *Journal of Business Ethics, 63*(2), 195–207. Retrieved from ABI/INFORM Global database.

Tyler, K., Stanley, E., & Brady, A. (2006). Relationship development in a multinational utilities network. *The Journal of Services Marketing, 20*(5), 333–345. Retrieved from ABI/INFORM Global database.

Ungan, M. C. (2007). Manufacturing best practices: Implementation success factors and performance. *Journal of Manufacturing Technology Management, 18*(3), 333. Retrieved from ProQuest database.

Valant, L. B. (2008). Why do both marriages and business mergers have a 50% failure rate? *The CPA Journal, 78*(8), 15. Retrieved from ABI/INFORM Global database.

Vallejo, M. C. (2008). Is the culture of family firms really different? A value-based model for its survival through generations. *Journal of Business Ethics, 81*(2), 261–279. Retrieved from ABI/INFORM Global database.

Vandergriff, L. J. (2007). Complex venture acquisition: Going beyond the traditional systems engineering paradigm. *Vine, 37*(3), 262. Retrieved from ABI/INFORM Global database.

Vaughn, R. (2008). Navigating a successful merger. *Risk Management, 55*(1), 36–41. Retrieved from Business Source Complete database.

Vermeulen, E. (2005). How acquisition can revitalize companies. *MIT Sloan Management Review, 46*, 45–51.

Vlasic, B., & Stertz, B. (2000). *Taken for a ride: How Daimler-Benz drove off with Chrysler*. New York: William Morrow & Co.

Vogt, W. P. (2007). Quantitative research methods for professionals. Boston: Allyn & Bacon.

Xenikou, A., & Simosi, M. (2006). Organizational culture and transformational leadership as predictors of business unit performance. *Journal of Managerial Psychology, 21*(6), 566–579. Retrieved from ABI/INFORM Global database.

Walumbwa, F. O., Avolio, B. J., & Zhu, W. (2008). How transformational leadership weaves its influence on individual job performance: The role of identification and efficacy beliefs. *Personnel Psychology, 61*(4), 793–825. Retrieved from ABI/INFORM Global database.

Walumbwa, F. O., Lawler, J. J., Avolio, B. J., Wang, P., & Shi, K. (2005). Transformational leadership and work-related attitudes: The moderating effects of collective and self-efficacy across cultures. *Journal of Leadership & Organizational Studies, 11*(3), 2–16. Retrieved from ABI/INFORM Global database.

Warr, P. (2007). Searching for happiness at work. *The Psychologist, 20*(12), 726–729. Retrieved from EBSCOhost database.

Weber, R. A., & Camerer, C. F. (2003). Culture conflict and merger failure: An experimental approach. *Management Science, 49*(4), 400–415. Retrieved from ABI/INFORM Global database.

Weinzimmer, L., Franczak, J., & Michel, E. (2008). Culture-performance research: Challenges and future directions. *Journal of the Academy of Business & Economics, 8*(4), 152–162. Retrieved from Business Source Complete database.

Weston, J. F., Mitchell, M. L., & Mulherin, J. H. (2004). Takeovers, restructuring, and corporate governance (4th ed.). Upper Saddle River, NJ: Prentice Hall/Pearson.

Williams, Henry E, M.B.A., PhD., Roberts, C., PhD., & Shires, J., Ph.D. (2019). Merger, acquisition, hostile takeover: Unification of two colleges. Organization Development Journal, 37(3), 31–44. https://coloradotech.idm.oclc.org/login?url=https://www.proquest.com/scholarly-journals/merger-acquisition-hostile-takeover-unification/docview/2292032762/se-2?accountid=144789

Wriston, M. J. (2007). Creating a high-performance culture. *Organization Development Journal, 25*(1), 8–16. Retrieved from ABI/INFORM Global database.

Yao, X., & Wang, L. (2008). Socially oriented values and reciprocity norms predict organizational commitment. *Asian Journal of Social Psychology, 11*, 247–252.

Yang, Y., & Cipolla, J. (2007). Relationships between goal setting, innovation, project management, quality, speed to market, and new product success. *The Business Review, 9*(1), 1–8. Retrieved from ABI/INFORM Global database.

Yilmaz, C., & Ergun, E. (2008). Organizational culture and firm effectiveness: An examination of relative effects of culture traits and the balanced culture hypothesis in an emerging economy. *Journal of World Business, 43*(3), 290–306. Retrieved from EBSCOhost database.

Yurcan, B. (2012, February). Bank fees, along with value-added services, on the rise. *Bank Systems + Technology—Online*. Retrieved March 3, 2012, from ABI/INFORM Global. (Document ID: 2598790381).

Zhang, M., & Tansuhaj, P. (2007). Organizational culture, information technology capability, and performance: The case of born global firms. *Multinational Business Review, 15*(3), 43–78. Retrieved from ProQuest database.

Zhao, Y., & Chen, K. (2008). The influence of takeover protection on earnings management. *Journal of Business Finance & Accounting, 35*(3/4), 347–375. Retrieved from EBSCOhost database.

Zhu, Z., & Huang, H. (2007). The culture integration in the process of cross-border mergers and acquisitions. *International Management Review, 3*(2), 40–44. Retrieved from ABI/INFORM Global database.

Zollo, M., & Meier, D. (2008). What Is M&A performance? *Academy of Management Perspectives*, *22*(3), 55–77. Retrieved from Business Source Complete database.

Zou, H., & Ghauri, P. (2008). Learning through international acquisitions: The process of knowledge acquisition in China. *Management International Review*, *48*(2), 207–226. Retrieved from ABI/INFORM Global database.

Defining of Terms

The purpose of defining important terms is to help the reader understand the words used in the study. Words often assume operational meanings within the context of a research study. While many of the following terms may seem familiar, they have specific meanings within the intercultural environment.

Acquisition: is the process of transferring assets or stocks of organizations to be owned by another firm. An acquisition transaction involves one firm purchasing the assets and stocks of another firm, thus indicating ownership transfer (Lajoux, 1998, p. 4).

Competitive Advantage: involves providing a product that customers value more than other competitors in the same business (Haag, Cummings, & McCubbrey, 2005).

Merger: is the combination of one or more organizations directly or indirectly to control and manage the whole or part of the new business. In other words, a merger means integrating two or more firms to form a new one (Lajoux, 1998, p. 4).

Organizational Culture: Schein (1992) described culture as new beliefs, assumptions, and values expressed by groups. Organizational culture can relate to the products and services offered, how and where the products are made, and the target customers (Laudon & Laudon, 2006).

Organizational Performance: comprises outputs and results from organizations' set goals and objectives. The measurement of an organization's performance determines how well the company is doing. Organizational performance enables an organization to measure productivity regarding employees' commitment, job satisfaction, turnover rate, shareholders' returns, and organizational growth (Behery & Paton, 2008; Weinzimmer, Franczak, & Michel, 2008).

Transformational Leadership Theory refers to the theory whereby leaders try to understand the organizational culture and align the culture to a new vision of making a change in the organization (Bass & Avolio, 1994).

Motivational Theory: refers to the theory that influences peoples' behavior, whether for personal or professional reasons. Motivation is essential in business, as it helps commit employees and contribute to their productivity.

Equity Theory: refers to the theory that aims to balance an employee's input and output in a workplace. Once the employee finds the correct balance, that would lead to a more productive relationship with the management.

Synergies: is the cooperation or interaction of two or more organizations or agents to generate a combined effect more significant than the sum of their particular products.

Diversification is the act of expanding something or the fact of becoming more disparate.

Market Share is the portion of a market controlled by a particular company or product, such as a leading tech company with a 50 percent market share of another company.

Human Relations relate to managing human problems arising from organizational and interpersonal relations. It helps to develop better interpersonal and intergroup adjustments.

Quantitative Research: is a research approach that focuses on gathering, analyzing, and quantifying data. It is formed from a deductive approach, emphasizing testing theory, hypothesis, and rationalist values. The data are generally numerical.

Qualitative Research: involves gathering data from first-hand observation, interviews, and questionnaires made in natural settings, documents, case studies, and artifacts. The data are generally nonnumerical. Qualitative methods include ethnography, grounded theory, and discourse analysis.

Employee Retention is the organization's overall strategy to preserve its best employees and maintain a lower turnover. Employee retention rate could increase by adopting several employee retentions programs.

Employee Commitment: relates to the employees' bonding experience with their organization, which involves employee connection with their organization, feeling that they fit in and understand the organization's goals, be more determined in their work to be more productive and proactive.

Job Satisfaction: relates to a feeling of fulfillment that a person derives from their job.

Organizational Performance: involves evaluating and analyzing a company's performance against its objectives and goals. The organizational performance comprises actual outputs and results compared with intended outcomes.

Culture Clashes: relates to the behavior differences, such as mapping a people or social group differences that reflect and promote various assumptions.

Culture Traits are things that allow one part of a culture to be communicated to another.

Information Governance: is policy-based control of information to meet all legal, regulatory, risk, and business demands.

Corporate Governance: is a set of regulations, policies, and procedures that control the functioning of an organization, such as roles, composition, risk management strategies, control mechanisms, and action plans.

Information Technology Governance: is the collaborative tools, processes, and methodologies that enable an organization to align business strategy and goals with IT services in the business environment.

Data Governance: is establishing the technology and infrastructure to maintain the processes and policies and identifying the teams within an organization that have both the authority and responsibility for handling and safeguarding specific data types.

Index

About the Author

Dr. Henrietta M. Okoro is an adjunct professor of computer information systems and business studies at the Colorado Technical University, National University, and the University of the Cumberlands. She serves at the University of the Cumberlands as a dissertation committee member for doctoral students. She is a Certified Data Privacy Solutions Engineer (CDPSE). Over the last decade, Dr. Okoro has researched, taught, and published information technology, information governance, cybersecurity, data analytics, management, leadership, decision-making, and organizational culture. In these areas, Dr. Okoro applies research to promote insight and action in integrating theory and practice into cognitive learnings. She has over twenty-four years of professional experience as a lead software test engineer in the telecommunication industry—focusing on quality control and assurance of short messaging service center applications. Dr. Okoro received a Bachelor of Arts degree in Business Administration and a dual Master of Business Administration degree in Accounting and Management from Southeastern University, Washington, DC. She also received a Doctor of Management in Organizational Leadership with specialization in Information Systems and Technology from the University of Phoenix and an Executive Education Certificate in Leadership Decision Making from Harvard University, John Kennedy School of Government. She is the founder/CEO of two nonprofit organizations: the World Association for Academic Doctors (WAAD) and the International Association for Female Academic Doctors (IAFAD), which provide a platform for promoting professional developments, research, and publications for scholars, teachers, researchers, and multi-disciplinary professionals while igniting project initiatives and quality education across the nations.